GIANTS IN THE EARTH

GIANTS IN THE EARTH

THE CALIFORNIA REDWOODS

Edited with an Introduction by Peter Johnstone
Photo Editor, Peter E. Palmquist

HEYDAY BOOKS ◇ BERKELEY, CALIFORNIA

Library of Congress Cataloging-in-Publication Data:

Giants in the earth : the California redwoods / edited with an introduction by Peter Johnstone.
   p. cm.
  ISBN 1-890771-23-6 (pbk.)
  1. American literature--California. 2. Coast redwood--Literary collections. 3. California--Literary collections. 4. Trees--Literary collections. 5. Trees--California. 6. Coast redwood. I. Johnstone, Peter, 1959-
  PS571.C2 G53 2001
  810.8'0364--dc21

               2001003721

Cover Photograph: Courtesy of the Humboldt County Historical Society
Interior Design: Rebecca LeGates
Printing and Binding: Publishers Press, Salt Lake City, UT

The publishers wish to acknowledge the generosity and vision of the Candelaria Fund, whose assistance enabled us to produce a more ample and beautiful book than we might otherwise have done.

Orders, inquiries, and correspondence should be addressed to:
      Heyday Books
      P. O. Box 9145, Berkeley, CA 94709
      (510) 549-3564; fax (510) 549-1889
      www.heydaybooks.com

Printed in the United States of America

10 9 8 7 6 5 4 3 2 1

CONTENTS

THE COAST REDWOODS

THE LOGGING CAMPS

PORTFOLIO

FOLLOWING PAGE 208

INTO THE MYSTIC

SAVING THE REMNANT

DEDICATED TO GAIL AND NICHOLAS

Countless people have contributed to the making of this book; I wish to single out a few in particular for their special efforts. I would like to thank Malcolm Margolin for encouraging me to follow my vision for the book and for sticking with it (and me) in spite of the various roadblocks that we met in bringing it to life; Peter Palmquist for the original idea for the book, for his tremendous contributions, and for his help, advice, and encouragement; Josh Paddison for his constant moral support and encouragement, for his research assistance, and for listening to my ideas for the book all along the way; Jeannine Gendar, Carolyn West, Julianna Fleming, and Rina Margolin for skillful editing and research, patience, and encouragement; Andrew Nystrom for an initial bibliography and extensive research; Rebecca LeGates for her countless design contributions that make the book a thing of beauty; Simone Scott and Liz Madans for hard work and calm good humor; and all the Heyday staff for their many labors on the book's behalf.

Thanks also to Robert Hass for his friendly encouragement and suggestions for reading; to Glenn Keator for an education in conifers; to the entire Bancroft Library staff for their gracious help throughout more than two years of research; to Mary B. Castiglione for encouraging the folly of a life of books and for teaching me to research and edit until it hurts; to Beth and George Johnstone for fruitful discussions about editing; to Sharon Calandra for her constant faith in my efforts to embrace the literary life in spite of prevailing doubt; and to Gail Martin for the three years of profound and unflagging love and support, both material and emotional, without which I could not have done the work.

INTRODUCTION

An encounter with redwoods creates an unsettling paradox for a visitor. Whether at first or hundredth viewing, these creatures of strange beauty and stunning size seem immediately to require some verbal response from the awestruck observer; inevitably, some attempt to make the experience containable through analysis, imagination, metaphor, or metaphysics interposes itself. And yet, even for those to whom words usually come with little effort or reflection, speech may take flight, leaving the man or woman whose command of language remains the last bastion against mortality and stupidity utterly dumbstruck and perhaps vaguely shamed.

The history of writing about redwoods might thus be viewed as a quixotic effort, a noble and sometimes pathetic attempt to recover some sense of human proportion and meaning, which, along with the gift of speech, the godlike plant has stolen from mortals who dare to measure its breadth and significance. Even so, among the hundreds of works that treat redwoods as subject or setting, there are examples of this challenge well met; the decided success of the authors of the best selections in this anthology comes from their willingness to take on the difficult task of conveying the redwoods' power to move and transform the human subject.

The writings in *Giants in the Earth* represent a range of genres: diary, essay, fiction, poetry, journalism, history, and diatribe. The structure of the book follows the narrative of California history—and the history of human interaction with redwoods—closely, reflecting the changing sentiments and preoccupations of the state. The oldest stories in the book derive from the oral literature of native peoples, describing not only the practical uses of the trees but their cosmological role; while native peoples viewed redwoods with intimate practical regard for their usefulness, they also viewed them with reverence and delight, recognizing in their stunning proportion and unusual beauty an intrinsic mystery. The first European explorers, by contrast, saw the phenomenal size of the trees as their most important attribute; the trees were primarily a source of the timber that would be needed to build settlements. The Spanish soon began logging, an enterprise that continued beyond the mission period (1769 until the 1830s), and, as evidenced by French explorer Auguste Duhaut-Cilly's account (included in this collection), a thriving Russian effort existed as well.

The Gold Rush accelerated the sense of landscape as resource. The tone of writing on the subject of the giant sequoias of the Sierra Nevada after their "discovery" in the 1850s mirrors the extravagant descriptions of gold discoveries from the same period, replete with exaggeration and accompanied by dreams of the abundant wealth that would attend the exploitation of redwoods. A new boosterism made its appearance at this time. The attempt to promote giant redwood tourism as a vital industry, as evidenced by J. M. Hutchings' *Scenes of Wonder and Curiosity in California,* permeates the tone of gifted journalists like Bayard Taylor, and this hyperbolic flavor continues in the writing of several generations of otherwise sober observers.

The nature of those early accounts of *Sequoiadendron giganteum* (the giant sequoias of the Sierra Nevada) differs significantly from the early literature of the *Sequoia sempervirens* coast, an expanse of coastal redwoods that stretched uninterrupted from Big Sur to the Oregon border until the timber industry took hold in the second half of the nineteenth century. With the notable exception of L. K. Wood, who described the Humboldt County redwoods as a "dismal forest prison," settlers among coast redwoods emphasized not the exotic size of the trees, but the idyllic qualities of living among them. William Taylor's *California Life Illustrated* (1858) exemplifies the sweet, dreamy quality of life among the *sempervirens,* as do such later writings as Ninetta Eames' "Staging in the Mendocino Redwoods" (1892) and Jack London's *Valley of the Moon* (1911).

The next shift in writing on redwoods finds its primary exemplar in the most deservedly renowned and influential of natural history writers, John Muir. Reflecting Muir's considerable skills of observation and no doubt inspiring other naturalists such as François Leydet, Verna Johnston, and Elna Bakker, much of what Muir had to say could nonetheless be included under the rubric "redwood mysticism and aestheticism." The period poems of Edward Markham and George Sterling may appear pale next to Muir's ecstatic paeans to the redwood, but they contain a similarly genuine reverence mixed with introspection. This quality, so abundant in Muir's voice, elevates his prose to greater heights than most American poets of the same period ever reach. A writer like Mary Austin follows in this same vein, with perhaps a more inward looking gaze, in her communion with the Sierran landscape. Arthur Conan Doyle, Judy Van der Veer, Czeslaw Milosz, Tom Wolfe, and Lew Welch—all successors of Muir—evoke the mystic quality of the redwood forest, each acknowledging the timelessness of the trees in a voice representing the society of the moment.

Walt Whitman's view of a godlike redwood prophesying its own eventual demise and replacement by an almost Nietzschean superman will strike many modern readers as disturbingly prescient, and a particularly abhorrent vision for Whitman to celebrate—at the farthest remove from Muir, who preferred trees to men. Yet this anthropocentrism can be viewed as a parallel approach in an aesthetic mystic view of redwoods. Count Hermann Keyserling entertains a spiritualized view of nature and humanity, growing out of German Idealism, and finds the redwoods useful as symbolic matter with which to engender philosophical speculation. One encounters a similar metaphysical tendency in Kerouac's rambling dialogue with

Japhy (Gary Snyder) in *Dharma Bums,* where redwoods serve to inspire flights of fancy about the nature of being and becoming.

In a more tangible attempt to appropriate the symbolic power of the redwood in the pursuit of far-reaching human idealism, the utopian Kaweah Commonwealth located itself in the Sierra redwoods, proposing to log these largest trees in the world in order to provide a living for its members and bring international attention to their cause. Their principal leader, Burnette Haskell, tells the story of the community's demise.

Many of the writers represented here find inspiration in the redwood grove's cathedral-like spaciousness, dwelling at length upon its silent presence. In Ernest Peixotto's description of the early twentieth-century Bohemian Club's frolicking pageant we find aestheticism of the most refined, decadent sort, yet still related to the romantic sensibility that informs Muir's quest for transcendence. Nearly eighty years later, Armistead Maupin takes a more skeptical view of the Bohemian Grove proceedings.

Some of the pieces contained in these pages take another view of the redwoods, far removed from poetry or nature mysticism: that of the working men and women who labored among them for the California timber industry. An account from the 1880s by Ernest Ingersoll and one by Anna Lind from the 1920s provide descriptions of backbreaking and frequently dangerous work. A fictional selection from a long-out-of-print novel of the post–World War I timber industry, Vernon Patterson's *Wise As a Goose,* is included in this collection as well. It recounts the struggles of a Northern California company town in relatively unsentimental terms.

The distinctive perspective of twentieth-century redwood writings can perhaps best be summed up as a call for saving the remnant; much of it reflects some degree of unease, pessimism, or panic on the issue of the rapidly disappearing redwood forests. John Muir heralds this pervasive theme in his last written work, published posthumously by the Sierra Club and titled, simply, "Save The Redwoods." By influencing presidents and such philanthropic capitalists as Joseph D. Grant to enact laws and buy up forests for permanent preservation as national treasures, Muir created a new standard for viewing wilderness that would set the terms for all future discussions between industry, government, and the public, and color all writing on the subject of redwoods.

A kind of antihumanism pervades much of this new writing as the century progresses; mankind is seen primarily as a threat to nature and ultimately as a usurper whose eventual disappearance is guaranteed by greed. Such a vantage point appears central to the worldview of poet Robinson Jeffers. It intrudes subtly on Thurston Clarke's determinedly journalistic exploration of California and informs Joan Dunning's *From the Redwood Forest* as well as the poems by Jane Hirshfield and Jerry Martien reprinted here.

Julia Butterfly Hill best exemplifies the apocalyptic mood at the end of the century. Like Muir, her evangelical fervor has its origins in her familial roots. *The Legacy of Luna* recounts her effort to gain collective redemption from human excess and the resulting despair through an extraordinary act of personal theater. In "The High Embrace," William Everson, poet, Catholic monk, and literary disciple to Robinson Jeffers, attempts to transfigure Jeffers' antihumanist stance with one that includes the dark view of human nature yet embraces nature's power to extend human limitations.

Everson saw the Western landscape as the source of an intrinsically new Western writing. By immersion in the natural environment, a new and redemptive art might emerge, bringing with it the possibility of unifying nature and the human spirit. Similar attempts to overcome pervasive environmental pessimism through acts of vision mark the work of poets like Gary Snyder and Dana Gioia. Such visions as Julia Butterfly Hill and Snyder embody at the beginning of the twenty-first century may portend a more sanguine view of the human relationship to nature, one that finds itself reflected anew in redwoods of the imagination.

◇————————◇

Redwoods have been a defining figure in my own personal land-scape, which unfolded for the most part without a grounding in nature; music, books, and television made up most of the stuff that occupied my attention—and that of most children of my genera-tion in California—not rocks, streams, and trees. Yet I was raised in Visalia, a community that attempted to dignify its provincial status by calling itself the gateway to the sequoias. I attended Redwood High School and ate burgers at the drive-in across from the College of the Sequoias. My grandparents had a magically double-trunked giant sequoia growing in their front yard, under which my brothers and I would play. Our own backyard had a towering coastal red-wood that provided the only substantial shade in the blistering heat of Central Valley summers. Across the creek from our house was a Boy Scout cabin crafted Abe Lincoln–like with redwood logs by my grandfather and his scoutmaster cohorts. As children we visited the redwoods of Grant Grove and the Giant Forest of Sequoia National Park, situated little more than an hour's drive from our town.

As I took my Californian identity away from its origins into the wider world, I found that the redwood defined my geographic self in the eyes of others as well. When I was an exchange student in Skopje, Macedonia, my host family would always return to two images from the photo book on California that I had given them as a present upon my arrival. One image was of the Golden Gate Bridge in San Francisco; the other was of the Giant Forest. While I viewed the Macedonians as surrounded by an aura of rich and ancient history that gave them depth, they viewed me as part of a nation of people who possessed powerful, unlimited natural poten-tial, as embodied by my native giant trees.

This experience was reinforced when I later encountered the writing of philosopher George Santayana, whose 1911 address to the Philosophical Union of the University of California at Berkeley admonished educated Californians to look to their monumental landscape as a source of self-definition instead of imitating their more culturally seasoned East Coast countrymen or the Europeans. In so many ways, California industry and tourism had already shown this solution to California writers who yearned for a distinctive cultural identity. They touted the proportions and abundance of the redwood as evidence of a unique and predestined greatness for the young state; these gargantuan trees that thrust themselves into the starry heavens seemed to contain a promise of infinitude, a gateway to grandiose expectations. Earnest California artists and writers did indeed celebrate the redwoods, finding some sense of maturity and tradition, however vicarious, in the ancient forests.

Yet, knowing the sad history of the destruction of most of the original redwood coast in the twentieth century gives the literature of the redwoods a tragic underpinning; one cannot read it without a sense of pathos and irony. We have been moved by these trees, we have seen their power, and we have taken it upon ourselves to master and harness it. This effort to respond to a plant that leaves us in awe, even diminished and intimidated, has become our focal point for viewing them, even when we deplore the excess of their destruction. And so it seems that human activity, even reflective activity, obscures a clear and pure viewing of the trees on their own terms. In reading of redwoods at this point in our history, we have removed ourselves from a direct appreciation by so many leaps and bounds. The only antidote to this dilemma remains obvious. Go and be among the redwoods for a while. If possible, read these pieces under their shade, closing the cover every now and again to breathe in their fragrance, finger their bark, taste a leaf of sorrel growing at their foot. In returning to read again, let the unmediated moment you may have enjoyed serve to awaken some sense of the writer's original view of a real redwood, and of the all too human redwood that found its way to the page before you.

Peter Johnstone
June 2001

AN ANCIENT STOCK

DANA GIOIA

BECOMING A REDWOOD

Dana Gioia (b. 1950) decided as a graduate student that he would not thrive as a poet in academia and went to work as a manager for General Foods for some fifteen years, eventually becoming a vice president. His growing literary reputation, boosted by controversy and enthusiasm generated by his essay "Can Poetry Matter" (first published in Atlantic Monthly, *later the title of a collection of essays), led him to become a full-time writer. He has published nine books of poetry as well as translations, a libretto, and several works of literary criticism. His most recent book is* Interrogations at Noon. *"The task of a serious poet," Gioia said in a 1992* New York Times *interview, "is to master the craft without ever losing sight of the spiritual purpose."*

Stand in a field long enough, and the sounds
start up again. The crickets, the invisible
toad who claims that change is possible,

And all the other life too small to name.
First one, then another, until innumerable
they merge into the single voice of a summer hill.

Yes, it's hard to stand still, hour after hour,
fixed as a fencepost, hearing the steers
snort in the dark pasture, smelling the manure.

And paralyzed by the mystery of how a stone
can bear to be a stone, the pain
the grass endures breaking through the earth's crust.

Unimaginable the redwoods on the far hill,
rooted for centuries, the living wood grown tall
and thickened with a hundred thousand days of light.

The old windmill creaks in perfect time
to the wind shaking the miles of pasture grass,
and the last farmhouse light goes off.

Something moves nearby. Coyotes hunt
these hills and packs of feral dogs.
But standing here at night accepts all that.

You are your own pale shadow in the quarter moon,
moving more slowly than the crippled stars,
part of the moonlight as the moonlight falls,

Part of the grass that answers the wind,
part of the midnight's watchfulness that knows
there is no silence but when danger comes.

FRANÇOIS LEYDET

from THE LAST REDWOODS

Born in Neuilly-sur-Seine, France, François Leydet (1927–1997) first came to the United States in 1947 to attend Harvard, and later Johns Hopkins University. An enthusiastic outdoorsman, he belonged to a number of environmental organizations and authored and edited several Sierra Club books, including The Last Redwoods: Photographs and Story of a Vanishing Scenic Resource *(by Leydet and Phillip Hyde). This selection from the book, published in 1969, details the ancient presence of sequoias on earth.*

Standing at the foot of a giant redwood, craning your neck to look up the soaring trunk, you sense your puniness. This tree, you are told, is probably well over a thousand years old. You are impressed, but you do not fully grasp the meaning of the figure until you reduce it to human terms, until you calculate that this tree was alive when William conquered England; that while forty, perhaps fifty generations of humans lived and loved and fought and died, this tree always stood in this very place, aloof and mindless of human antics.

No such convenient scale exists to help us comprehend the age of the redwoods as a race. Long before the first prehumans lived, the redwoods were there. Before the first small mammal had evolved, the redwoods were there. Before the original primitive ancestors of most of today's plants had developed, the redwoods were there.

The first positively identified redwood fossils, represented by characteristic cones, date back to the Upper Jurassic period—some one hundred and thirty million years ago. Could a man be transported back to those times, there would be little around him that he would recognize. The continents had not yet taken their present forms. The stresses in the earth's crust that would thrust up our great mountain chains, the Alps, the Himalayas, the Rockies, the Andes, had yet to build up.

A strange fauna then inhabited the earth. Swarms of sharks and ganoid fishes, huge marine reptiles—serpent-like plesiosaurs, dolphinlike ichthyosaurs—prowled the seas. Flying reptiles, which in the next period, the Cretaceous, would reach wingspreads of fifteen to twenty feet, circled overhead. Dinosaurs of gigantic size and weird shapes were the lords of the land.

The flora was equally strange—great ferns, an enormous variety of cycads, and the many ancestors of that living fossil of today, the ginkgo or maidenhair tree. There were as yet no angiosperms, the flowering plants that dominate the vegetable kingdom today. But among all these bizarre and now long-vanished forms of life, the redwoods flourished.

Through sixty million years of the Cretaceous period, down into the Tertiary, they thrived and extended their sway, while the world's flora and fauna were being radically remade. Species after species of the dull-witted clumsy reptiles declined and became extinct. The age of mammals had begun. The little eohippus—the four-toed ancestor of the horse—primitive rhinoceroses, tapirs and camels, the forebears of the cat and dog tribes, inherited the earth. The plants, too, were changing. Broad-leaved conifers, juniper-like

The big tree (Sequoia gigantea) is Nature's forest master-
piece, and, so far as I know, the greatest of living things. It
belongs to an ancient stock, as its remains in old rocks show,
and has a strange air of other days about it, a thoroughbred
look inherited from the long ago...
                          JOHN MUIR, "HUNTING BIG REDWOODS"

evergreen, then, later, hardwood trees such as the oaks and maples, hickory and ash we know today, displaced the earlier dominants.

By the Miocene, which began twenty-five million years ago, a redwood empire stretched across the Northern Hemisphere—from western Canada to the Atlantic, from France to Japan. In the United States, fossil remains of redwoods have been found in Texas, Pennsylvania, Colorado, Wyoming, Oregon, Washington, and California. In Yellowstone National Park, whole forests have been changed to stone by the mineral waters or buried in showers of ashes from active volcanoes in the vicinity; sections of the trunks are six to ten feet in diameter, and the butts still stand just as they grew, often thirty feet or more in height. In the petrified forest of Sonoma County are giant logs that were buried and turned to stone.

The Arctic was then no land of snow and ice but rather a humid and temperate region, and redwood fossils have been found in Spitzbergen, in Greenland, on many of the arctic islands north of the continent of North America, in Alaska, and on St. Lawrence Island.

The redwoods in those times were as varied as they were far-flung. Paleobotanists have identified at least a dozen species. One, *Sequoia reichenbachi,* found in Cretaceous clays, had cones almost like those of the big trees *[Sequoiadendron giganteum]* of the Sierra. The most common, *Sequoia langsdorfi*, was almost indistinguishable from the modern *Sequoia sempervirens*. Still another, otherwise similar to the coast redwood, had the peculiarity that its twigs and cones had an opposite arrangement, whereas *Sequoia sempervirens* shows a spiral attachment of the twigs, needles, and cone scales; also its cones grew at the end of naked stalks instead of on needle-bearing twigs. To this fossil redwood was given the generic name *Metasequoia*, the dawn redwood, to distinguish it from the true sequoias.

With the close of the Miocene, the redwoods began to retreat from the north. Over millions of years the climate grew colder and drier. The arctic became chill, then frozen, and where dense forests had stood, only lichens, dwarf willows, and sphagnum moss clothed the ground above the permafrost. Great icecaps formed, and in time the glaciers advanced to the south, inexorably bulldozing everything in their way. In Europe, where they had formed forests in England, France, Germany, Bohemia, Austria, Switzerland, the redwoods withdrew before the glaciers until they were back up against the Mediterranean—a Dunkirk in slow motion. Only there was no evacuation for them, no way by which they could escape across to Africa. And so they perished.

In Asia, land of the dawn redwood, the story was the same— or so it was thought until 1944. In that year, a forester chanced across an immense tree in a remote village of Sichuan province in central China. He had never seen one like it, so he brought out with him samples of twigs and cones. To their amazement, experts found them to be identical with *Metasequoia* fossil specimens gathered in Manchuria and Japan. Here, indeed, was a spectacular discovery: a fossil come to life, a tree thought dead for twenty-five million years but still growing, as it turned out, by the hundred in an isolated region of Sichuan and neighboring Hubei provinces. In this one small area, where conditions of temperature and humidity were just right, this tree which once reigned from the Black Sea to Greenland had made its last stand.

In America, too, the redwood empire shrank. The southward march of the glaciers, great volcanic eruptions, and the upthrust of mountain ranges singly and collectively undid the work of one hundred million years. In eastern Oregon, for instance, there had stood a mixed forest of dawn redwoods and of the immediate ancestors of our modern coast redwoods. Then the Cascades reared up their fiery summits in the path of the ocean winds. Today, eastern Oregon is an arid land, with rainfall sufficient only for the growth of scattered juniper trees and sagebrush.

As the redwoods' domain shrank so did the number of their species. In time just two were left, and as it happened, California was where they both made their last bid for survival. The big tree, *Sequoia gigantea* [now called *Sequoiadendron giganteum*], standing in isolated groves in the southern Sierra Nevada, and the redwood, *Sequoia sempervirens,* occupying a narrow strip along the northern California coast, are the last representatives of a heroic race, the last of the true sequoias, a living link to the age of dinosaurs.

VERNA R. JOHNSTON

from SIERRA NEVADA: THE NATURALIST'S COMPANION

A professional biologist, ornithologist, and well-known wild-life photographer who taught at San Joaquin Delta College for nearly forty years, Verna R. Johnston brings the intimate knowledge of a lifetime of field experience to her work, and a sense of delight in nature as well. Her photography has appeared in numerous exhibitions, and she has written more than a hundred articles for Audubon, the Christian Science Monitor, the Encyclopedia Britannica, the New York Times, *and other publications. In this example, first pubished in 1970, she enumerates and appreciates the wildlife that lives among the big trees of the Sierra Nevada.*

Dawn is a magical time in the groves. As the first rays of sun strike the big-tree tops and lance down from one ruddy limb to another, the birds take over the forest. From still dim recesses ring out the robins' morning carols. The three-part song of the western tanager lends a strident base to the rapid bubbling warbles of California purple finches. Wood pewees dart about, snapping mandibles on tardy moths. A burst of melody hovers over the meadow—the black-headed grosbeak's morning flight song. On upturned finger-like roots of fallen sequoias, dark-sided juncos pipe out a dry trill. The day's foodlift recommences in the red-breasted nuthatch nesting hole in a white fir stump. The *yank-yank-yank* notes of busy parents rebound from insect-collecting forays up the higher trunks and branches of all the taller trees that furnish a foraging niche.

Sometimes the deep *kuk kuk kuk* of the West's largest woodpecker resounds throughout the forest, as the big black bird, nearly the size of a crow, wings its way to a favorite snag. Landing with flaming topknot erect, the male pileated woodpecker turns his striped red, black, and white head to right and left and goes to work. Tilting back his body, leaning on stiff tail, gripping tightly with the claws, he throws his heavy head and long sharp beak through an arc of eight to ten inches. As he bombards the trunk, striking first where wood is more decayed, his bill's hard glancing blows split off slivers a quarter-inch wide. Chips and flakes fly as the woods ring with the pummeling. The pileated woodpecker's Sierran niche includes dead trees of midmountain forests, where for rapid wood-cutting it is unexcelled; it has been known to dig out a hole large enough for concealment within thirty minutes in a dead but still firm sugar pine.

All woodpeckers possess extrapowerful neck muscles; the pileated can render a whack nearly equal to that of a person with an ordinary hammer. Its holes often measure six inches long, three inches wide, and three inches deep in trees or logs, where it drills to reach the boring beetle larvae and carpenter ants that form its major diet.

Occasionally it eats wild berries. This can be awkward for such a heavy bird. Ranger-naturalist Allen Waldo observed a pileated feeding on ripe blue elderberries, bending the branches over in so great an arc that the bird hung upside down as it cleaned off a berry clump at top speed. When eating was nearly finished, its feet suddenly slipped from the stem, and the woodpecker dropped to the ground flat on its back. It recovered immediately and flew off.

In spite of its size and power, the bird has enemies. Among avian predators, both goshawks and Cooper's hawks inhabit its range. Lowell Sumner and Joseph Dixon tell the story of a family of pileateds that suffered a tragic loss at the Parker Group of big trees in Sequoia National Park. A pair of these woodpeckers chiseled out a nest chamber at a height of twenty-four feet in a large fir stump above the camp kitchen of a troop of soldiers. The birds, wary at first, grew used to the men's presence and became quite tame. The soldiers, in turn, became greatly attached to the birds, naming them Cap and Phoebe.

Phoebe laid an egg a day from May 7 to May 10. The parents shared daytime incubation, "but at night Phoebe always occupied the nest, while Cap roosted in the doorway with his head outward." After the eggs hatched, both parents went far afield seeking food for their young. On the evening of June 16, as Phoebe was flying toward the nest, a Cooper's hawk struck and killed her and carried her to a nearby tree. Cap, who witnessed his mate's death, appeared to lapse into a state of shock. For a day and two nights he just sat in the door of his nest. On the morning of the eighteenth the continuous chirping of his extremely hungry brood seemed to rouse him, and he flew into the forest to quiet their appetites. From then on he was a diligent provider.

The task became more and more strenuous as the fuzzy fledglings grew large and waited, clamoring, at the nest door. On July 19, as Cap left the nest, "they all sailed out after him…and soon hit the ground with a thud." Cap collected them as best he could and led out into the forest, feeding on nearby stumps and logs, his brood scrambling and flapping along after him. For several days the procession remained around the camp, but finally the birds drifted away.

A companion woodpecker with feeding habits different from those of the pileated is the smaller white-headed woodpecker. Hopping up the trunks of conifers, it pries off thick bark scales to obtain insects living in the crevices. Its bill serves as a crowbar more than a hammer. White-heads sometimes tunnel nesting holes in spongy sequoia bark, which is thickest at the lower trunk levels that the birds prefer.

◆————————◆

Midday hours in the groves are a mingling of hot sun in the clearings, cool shade under the trees. The lupines, the crimson snow plants, the dogwoods of the forest understory pass from dazzling radiance to somber eclipse as the shadows come and go.

In depressions in some of the sequoia buttresses where bits of bark have accumulated, chipmunks, juncos, and robins take "bark baths," wallowing in the fine cinnamon dust, flipping it over their fur and feathers. Dust baths of any sort are thought to help animals clean their skin of oil, to discourage parasites, and to yield a pleasant sensation. Sequoia bark dust, impregnated with tannin, probably acts very much like insect powder. Tannin's astringency renders it unpalatable to most insects and antiseptic to most fungus diseases. In the huge sawdust piles along the Big Stump Trail, tannin is believed to be the ingredient that has inhibited plant growth on the piles for more than a century.

In July and August that lively little harvester of big-tree cones, the chickaree, goes into action, and any time of day a shower of two-inch bombs may thud to earth. This small, impish tree squirrel, also called the Douglas squirrel, is the Pacific Coast relative of the North American red squirrel. It frolics up and down sequoia trunks, peels off soft spongy bark strips for its nest, leaps from the high swaying branches of one tree to the next, explodes spontaneously in high-pitched squeals and scolds, and pops around trunks totally unexpectedly, its bushy short tail jerking and bright eyes bulging.

When it decides to harvest cones, several hundred feet up and out on the tip of a branch, the chickaree does it as though winter were closing in the next day. Its ivory incisors often snip off more than twenty cones a minute. Working at peak activity, it can drop a fusillade of thirteen green sequoia "grenades" in ten seconds. When enough have accumulated on the ground, it descends and stores them away, carrying one at a time to great caches in hollow logs, under prostrate trunks, in crevices or creeks. These moist, cool, and shady spots keep cones from opening for at least three years.

California ground squirrels and golden-mantled ground squirrels frequently run off with a share of the fallen harvest, but the chickaree manages to tuck away most of it. Naturalist Walter Fry watched one energetic chickaree cache more than thirty-eight barley sackfuls of cones in twelve days. From these, Fry extracted over twenty-six pounds of seeds.

With pine cones, chickarees discard the woody scales and eat the seeds. But the seeds of sequoia average ninety-one thousand to the pound; the seeds of a single cone weigh less than .06 ounce altogether, only a fraction of which is embryo food. What chickarees eat is the fleshy sequoia cone bract, which they strip while the cones are green and soft. Not all of the hidden cones are eaten during winter's scantier times. The chickaree's habit of storing big-tree cones alongside decaying logs at meadow edges has allowed many trees to sprout and grow over the centuries.

Chickarees favor sequoia cones that are two to five years old, and dislodge many seeds in their harvest. Older sequoia cones, aged four to nine, form a favorite egg-laying repository for the tiny, long-horned beetle (*Phymatodes nitidus*). As it tunnels into the cones, it often severs the water pipeline, creating cracks through which sequoia seeds can tumble out. Updrafts from fires also cause cones to pop open and release seeds.

◆————————◆

Sunset in the groves intensifies the burnt umber of the big-tree pillars, setting them off in bold relief against the lengthening shadows. This is the time when deer seek the meadows, when the last birdcalls rend the stillness. As night's cool air rises into a darkening forest, chipmunks retire to their burrows and the nocturnal mammals emerge.

The coyote trots out on its beat. Raccoons *(Procyon lotor)* amble along the creeks and through the campgrounds. The black bear *(Ursus americanus)* prowls, looking for promising morsels, rising on hind legs at certain preferred trees to reach high up and sharpen its claws on the bark. The bear manicure tree in Sequoia National Park is one of its favorites. Naturalist Ernest Thompson Seton believed that such trees were used as bear signboards, conveying through the bear's acute sense of smell pertinent facts about the tree's previous user—much the same as the urinary signal posts of dogs, wolves, and coyotes. The trees may be a kind of social register, telling a newcomer that his claw marks are the highest on the trunk or that a larger bear is boss of this domain.

All through the underbrush, in hollow logs, among rocks, in the myriad openings that tiny animals make use of, the most abundant mammals of the groves, the deer mice *(Peromyscus maniculatus)*, scamper on their nightly hunt for seeds and berries. Almost every bird and mammal predator feeds on these little mice, yet they are one of the most successful animals in the Sierra—indeed, in North America, if judged by numbers and wide range. Joseph Grinnell and Tracy Storer estimated that in Yosemite they nearly equaled in numbers all the other mammals of the area. Sumner and Dixon considered them the most widely distributed mammals in

Under the huge trees up come the small plant people, putting forth fresh leaves and blossoming in such profusion that the hills and valleys would still seem gloriously rich and glad were all the grand trees away. By the side of melting snowbanks rise the crimson sarcodes, round topped and massive as the sequoias themselves, and beds of blue violets and larger yellow ones with leaves curiously lobed; azalea and saxifrage, daisies and lilies on the mossy banks of the streams; and a little way back of them, beneath the trees and on sunny spots on the hills around the groves, wild rose and rubus, spirea and ribes, mitella, tiarella, campanula, monardella, forget-me-not, etc., many of them as worthy of lore immortality as the famous Scotch daisy, wanting only a Burns to sing them home to all hearts.

In the midst of this glad plant work, the birds are busy nesting, some singing at their work, some silent, others, especially the big pileated woodpeckers, about as noisy as backwoodsmen building their cabins. Then every bower in the groves is a bridal bower, the winds murmur softly overhead, the streams sing with the birds, while from far-off waterfalls and thunder clouds come deep rolling organ notes.

JOHN MUIR, "HUNTING BIG REDWOODS"

Sequoia and Kings Canyon National Park in the early 1950s. George Lawrence's live-trapping census of the mammals of Whitaker's Forest, in the same region, found them extremely abundant but cyclic. In many places where mammal surveys are made, deer mice are so numerous that it is necessary to trap them out before other species can be captured.

This elegant native is far different from the drab-colored, musky-smelling, city-dwelling house mouse. The soft brownish gray fur and pure white underparts of the deer mouse contrast cleanly. Its tail is well furred with dark hair above and white below. The large delicate ears and wide eyes surmount an inquiring face.

Deer mice in some forested regions of the United States perform a real service by feeding on larvae and pupae of insects detrimental to the trees. Whether similar ecological relationships exist in Sierran forests is yet to be determined, but the rodents are known to eat heavily of insects in the spring. In the summer and fall they turn to buds, nuts, berries, and seeds or, when within reach of cabins or campsites, meat, butter, and cheese. Throughout the long cold winters of the groves, the mice remain active underneath and above the snow, weaving a tracery of tiny footprints, living on large caches.

They climb trees readily, if slowly, and in emergencies jump into space from any height without hesitation. Sumner and Dixon watched deer mice fall thirty-eight feet and run away with no noticeable distress. "Since they are so light in relation to their surface, a fall usually has no serious consequences for them."

All their defenses cannot, of course, ward off the long-tailed weasel, striped skunk, and innumerable other enemies. Among the crawling predators is a native member of the boa family, the "two-headed snake," with a blunt tail that closely resembles the head and sometimes even moves and strikes like a head. Known as the rubber boa *(Charina bottae),* it both looks and feels to the touch like brown rubber, and is, like all Sierran snakes save the rattlesnake, harmless to humans. Sheltering by day in damp places under logs or rocks, often near streams, it produces in season up to eight young, born alive. Nightly at dusk its search for small mammals and lizards begins, a hunt that may require burrowing, swimming, or climbing to appease its hunger. A visitor who reported seeing "an eel" climbing a giant sequoia at twilight was among the few fortunate enough to watch a rubber boa in action. Although rated the most common snake in Yosemite's Mariposa Grove in a summer vertebrate survey, the boa, like most nocturnal creatures, is seldom seen by humans.

Nocturnal life has its sway in the groves; again comes the dawn. Over the centuries the wheel goes round and round. Individual chipmunks tumbling in their bark dust baths are here probably three years at most and gone; the woodpeckers, four years; mule deer, five years; humans, perhaps six decades. A three-thousand-year-old sequoia, the same solitary individual, lives on and on—through one thousand generations of chipmunks, seven hundred and fifty generations of woodpeckers, six hundred generations of deer, and fifty generations of humans.

ELNA S. BAKKER

from AN ISLAND CALLED CALIFORNIA

*Pioneering California naturalist Elna Bakker (1921–1995)
lived in southern California all her life. An expert on the ecology, geology, and anthropology of California, she patterned
An Island Called California (1971) after a series of exhibits
she consulted on for the Oakland Museum of California.
Presenting the ecological variety of California as an interde-
pendent whole, the exhibits led visitors through a "walk
across California" beginning at the Golden Gate, turning
south at Mono Lake, and ending in the deserts of southern
California, with a few side trips to other environments. In this
selection from the book she explores the coast redwood habitat.*

Many visitors to California redwood groves are depressed at first
by the dark and somber dignity of the forest, particularly in rainy
or cloudy weather. On bright days in spring and summer, however, the groves have color resources of their own. The pink petals
of oxalis (redwood sorrel) open tiny whorls among shamrock-
shaped leaves. Sword ferns arch green fronds over log and root.

Orange-bellied water dogs paddle about in the clear, shallow pools of the streams and rivers draining the coastal slopes, and the banks above are brocaded with five-finger and maidenhair fern. As the early sun burns through the morning mist, long shafts of light touch the flattened fanlike foliage with silver fire. In autumn the leaves of the vine maple blaze coal red through the shadows of the understory.

A relict like the fire pines, the redwood belongs to California, except for an eight-mile extension above the Oregon border. In a state which boasts of twenty-one coniferous natives, two have such outstanding features that they are the best known California trees. The coastal species—*Sequoia sempervirens,* or redwood—is the world's tallest tree, and its mountain relative—*Sequoiadendron giganteum,* or big tree—has the largest base circumference. Both have enviable records of longevity.

The tallest redwood was discovered only recently. For years Founders Tree near Dyerville in Humboldt County had this distinction, but its 364 feet have been overtopped by a giant more than 367 feet tall. Once on privately owned land near Orick in Humboldt County, it and several others almost as tall are protected in Redwood National Park. However, the distinguishing feature is not the unusual loftiness of several individuals but that the species as a whole is characterized by great height. Records have been claimed for Douglas fir and Australian eucalypts, but none standing today can match the redwoods. Big trees, whose sheer mass is most impressive, cannot come near their coastal relatives in height; too often their tops have been lightning blasted. But they outdo the redwoods when it comes to age. Though twenty-two hundred years of life, a coastal record, are venerable indeed, much longer lives have been noted for the big trees; however, these apparently have been bested by the bristlecone pines of the White Mountains in eastern California and other Great Basin ranges.

Though the largest groves and most magnificent stands are in the three northernmost coastal counties of the state, redwoods occur as far south as southern Monterey County, where little groups cluster in canyons opening out to the sea. At one time, they were part of the forest cover on most of the coastal hills from Santa Cruz north, but logging has removed them from many of their former habitats. The northern part of their range extends farther east than does the southern portion, which is confined to the western flanks and valleys of the outer Coast Ranges.

The beauty of their forests, their great height and long lives, their hardiness and the quality and durability of their lumber have put these giants into a very special category. They evoke a kind of reverence accorded no other American tree. Their groves have been called temples and their spires cathedral-like; every writer describing them is lavish with vocabulary borrowed from church architecture. But our task is to go beyond description and attempt to account for their lingering presence along the northern coast. There is fossil evidence that *Sequoia* and related genera were widespread over much of the Northern Hemisphere following the heyday of the dinosaurs. They flourished as part of the Arcto-Tertiary flora, the great plant group that thrived in the mild, humid climate then prevalent even in the Far North. The family, Taxodiaceae, in which this genus is placed, includes the bald cypress of the southeastern United States and Mexico, *Cryptomeria* of Japan, and a relict relative of the sequoia discovered not too long ago, the deciduous dawn redwood of China. California's two famed trees are not wholly alone in the world, ancient and isolated though they are.

If redwoods have died out elsewhere but continue to thrive in the coastal mountains, there must be some explanation why this is so, particularly since they have peculiarities. Their seedlings rarely survive in soils rich in the humus of undisturbed forest floors; fungi present in such soils are harmful to their roots. Instead they do well only on newly exposed soils where duff has been removed by fire or some other disturbance, or on recently deposited silt. A layer of topsoil is soon built, however, by decomposing needle drop. Redwoods as a species are relatively tolerant of shade. Seedlings apparently require full or partial sunlight; yet well-established youngsters flourish in the shade of the forest's interwoven canopy. This is not to say that the crowded trees do not respond to thinning. The increased light, nutrients, and moisture made available to the remaining trees result in growth spurts reflected by wider year rings of woody tissue.

One generally accepted characteristic of redwoods is their restriction to the fog belt of maritime central and northern California. Not only are the climatic conditions here most closely akin to the mild temperatures and humidity of the ancient Tertiary period, but redwoods, like all plants with foliage, lose water from their leaves by evaporation. The almost daily summer fogs are of inestimable value in reducing such water loss as they increase air humidity and decrease temperatures. An additional requirement limits the species. It does not fare well in soils having less than 18 percent available soil moisture in August, the critical month in California's dry summer climate. Fog drip contributes surprisingly large amounts of moisture to soil during the dry season, up to thirty or forty inches, it has been claimed, in some parts of the northern coast....

A number of features of endurance help offset the requirements of redwood. Like the fire pines, it is adapted to fire. Not only do its seeds flourish in the bare soil left by fire, but it root-sprouts and trunk-sprouts as well. Sprouting is the characteristic method of propagation where the soils are rich in humus or in heavily shaded areas where seedlings probably would not survive. Rings or straight rows of saplings are typical features of all the Pacific Northwest rainforests. So-called nurse trees are downed logs which are fertile substrate for seedlings growing like well-behaved schoolchildren in line on the upper surface of the decaying trunk. More typical of redwood are the circle of young trees which started as sprouts around a burned or injured parent tree. Fire usually is not fatal, however. Thick, fireproof, nonresinous bark; wood of high moisture content; and a humid environment limit its destructive ravages. Most burns heal over in time, and trees whose foliage and side branches have been destroyed may resprout as fire columns. The new shoots project from dormant buds as bushy twigs all along the tapered trunk.

One might say that the coast redwood seems disaster proof, up to a point. Floods, short of the rare catastrophes that undercut roots and topple trees, add silt to its substrate, encouraging seedlings and even invigorating the mature stands. The finest groves are on alluvial flats. They not only survive the low oxygen levels of flooded soils, but extend up to the new soil surface vertically oriented temporary roots from the old roots. Shortly after, they begin to spread horizontal root networks from newly buried portions of their trunks. The giants of alluvial terrain characteristically have several such systems from each successive flood.

Cut or burn them, and seedlings and sprouts soon form thickets of vigorous growth. Insects and decay rarely trouble them because of chemicals in the thick bark. Though high winds can fell them as they have shallow root systems, they are considered by foresters to be relatively wind-firm. Diehards they are, in their fog-frequented, wind-sheltered canyons or hillsides, when they have sufficient soil moisture to tide them over the summer season....

◆——————◆

A generalization often made about redwoods is that one seldom sees animal life deep in their mature groves. One may look and listen in vain for signs of birds and mammals other than *Homo sapiens*.

When by oneself the silence seems to have small sounds of its own. It is as though by listening hard enough one could hear the multiplying cells, the flowing sap, the stretching roots—the countless processes going on and on in these great trees, and around them, too, for a redwood forest is not quite the zoological desert it is often assumed to be. It is an ecosystem in its own right; and though animals such as black-tailed deer come and go in their constant quest for food, many others are at home in these shadowed stands.

Crested jays are the most easily recognized of several birds occurring in the dense foliage of coastal coniferous woods. Their cocky black crests, bright blue plumage, large size, and abrasive call are unmistakable. In a place where life seems to go about on hushed tiptoe, their boldness is refreshing. Any camp or picnic table will be under the surveillance of one or more of these friendly neighbors perched on a nearby limb, hoping to freeload off some generous visitor. Sit on a comfortable trailside log and watch quietly. Brown creepers and pygmy nuthatches will resume their appraisal of the insect population, apparently never stopping to rest during daylight hours, constantly pattering up and down the massive trunks and along the larger boughs. Chestnut-backed chickadees are on the same quest and work over the needled foliage. They often hang upsidedown as they probe with their bills into likely places. A large robinlike bird with a broad black *V* across its orange breast moves about quietly under shrubs or sits on lower limbs of trees. It is the varied thrush and belongs to the same family as the western robin. Winter wrens are even more ground-dwelling. They flit in and out of root tangles and rest occasionally to pour out the rivulets of song so typical of wrens. Golden-crowned kinglets flutter through the masses of limb and leaf pausing only to pick up a tasty insect.

Though mammals are harder to find in these dark groves, one species, the Roosevelt elk, has almost become a symbol of the northern redwoods. No doubt this is because of the fine herd maintained at Prairie Creek State Park in Humboldt County. Not mammals of the dark forest only, they browse their way in the more open glades and meadows, feeding on the vine maples and shrubs. Closely related to the Rocky Mountain elk, this particular subspecies is restricted to the humid forests of the Pacific Northwest. The Olympic elk of Walt Disney fame belongs to the same group. Many of the parks in Washington's rainforest are supposedly kept open by the browsing of the elk, for they spend the winter there when the higher ranges are snowbound.

At the other extreme in size is the Trowbridge shrew, a tiny fellow whose insect prey may be almost as large as the captor and whose runways tunnel the duff. Two kinds of chipmunks, Sonoma and Townsend, are redwood residents, and the western gray squirrel of the oak groves is also at home in coniferous forests. One would suppose the gray squirrel to be in severe competition with the agile chickaree or Douglas squirrel, but the latter's diet of cones and nuts is very different from that of its acorn-eating cousin. Chickarees often nest in woodpecker holes small enough to prevent entry by the larger carnivores, such as bobcats and mountain lions, and too high for gray foxes and skunks.

One of the most intriguing, if rarely seen, animals of the redwoods is the mountain beaver. It is not related to the true beaver except that it too is a rodent. Looking like an outsized gopher, it lives in a system of tunnels whose entrances are screened over with brushy cover, berry patches, fern fronds, salal, and the like. Plants make up its diet, which includes needles and leaves. It digs efficiently, and its task is made that much easier when it chooses to construct its tunnel maze in the damp earth of streamside, which it often does.

The many creeks, moist places, and rivers of the redwood country are home to amphibians of more than passing interest. The rosy-hued *Ensatina* and the ocelot-spotted giant salamander are common, as are several newts and other salamanders frequenting this damp habitat. *Ensatina* keeps undercover much of the time, in rodent burrows and hollow logs, under leaf litter, and in other hidden places. The giant salamander apparently prefers being close to water, for it seldom goes far from stream or creek. On occasion, however, it takes to climbing tree trunks.

Other oddities of the sequoia woods are the large banana slugs, shell-less land gastropods unable to live in drier environments or expose themselves to the direct sun for too long a time. Any desiccation of their mucus-covered skin would be fatal. They ooze about on the duff, feeding on vegetation and litter.

As with all biotic communities, the redwoods have their share of animals that feed on each other. Owls and the giant salamanders watch for amphibians, small reptiles, and rodents such as red tree and deer mice. Various insectivorous birds, shrews, and smaller salamanders hunt tiny game. Raccoons forage about in their favorite streamside haunts for frogs and other water dwellers including the young of fish such as steelhead and cutthroat trout and salmon which begin mature life by spawning in these coastal rivers. Regardless of the species discussed above, these great groves, it is true, do not support the animal life so rich in many other communities. Lack of variety in diet, scarcity of grass seeds, and the

REDWOOD HAIKU

Orange, the brilliant slug—
Nibbling at the leaves of
Trillium

LEW WELCH

absence of sheltering cover, particularly in the old-growth stands that are so impressive and dramatic, help account for the paucity of both individuals and species.

◇————————◇

Very little is written about redwoods without serious concern for their future. We know they are some of the most valuable timber resources, and provision must be made for their most efficient utilization. Esthetically we may deplore the ugly scars and slash piles of their harvesting, but we will not be able to prevent this major industry from operating in these coastal forests. Nor should we wish to stop its activities entirely. The wood is too useful and of too fine a quality for abandoning sequoia as a timber crop. Wise forestry practices should ensure a continuing supply from maturing second growth.

Be that as it may, we are the custodians of one of the world's most wonderful natural heritages, the proud old-growth redwood forests. Through the activities of various conservation groups, the American people have had the foresight to set aside a number of the virgin stands which invariably call forth wonder and admiration from all who come to stand at the feet of these great giants.

AUSTEN D. WARBURTON
AND JOSEPH F. ENDERT

from INDIAN LORE OF THE NORTH CALIFORNIA COAST

Austen Warburton (1918–1977), the great-great-grandson of one of the last governors of Spanish California, was a lifelong resident of Santa Clara, known for his contributions to the city's cultural programs and institutions. He was an attorney and also an avid historian and collector, fascinated not only by the history of Santa Clara and his own family, but by the native people of California. Here, he recounts some ancient redwood lore from the Yurok people of northwestern California.

The Redwood Tree (Keelch)

In the beginning when Wah-Peck-oo-May-ow permitted the spirits to decide what they wanted to be on earth, two of them chose to be Redwood Trees. There had to be at least two for propagation purposes. After they had grown to adulthood and were five or six feet in diameter, a great war between human beings raged around Cappel, a village on the Klamath River, and one of the trees was accidentally wounded. From the wounds came warm, red blood.

Now Wah-Peck-oo-May-ow, seeing this, decided he would do something to preserve the Redwoods. He decreed that in the future the Redwood must not be used for firewood but could be used by human beings to build their homes and their canoes. To prevent the burning, he gathered the bark of the Cascara, the dogwood bark, the fern bark, and other bitter barks and dried them in the hot sun and ground them into flour. To this he added swamp water and poured this medicine on the tops of the two Redwood Trees. This made the wood so bitter that fire would not eat it, and to this day, redwood does not burn easily.

In using the wood for building their homes and canoes, he required of the Indians that a portion of the Redwood spirit be transferred to the home and the canoe. So it is that in the home the spirit lives in the fire pit, which was lined with stone. So it is that in building a canoe the Indians must always leave a round knob about two or two and a half feet back from the bow on the bottom of the boat, depending on the size of the boat. This was supposed to be about six inches in diameter and six inches high, so that if a hole was to be drilled in it to seat a mast for sailing, there would still be plenty of room for the spirit to live.

If the Indians did not follow these instructions from Wah-Peck-oo-May-ow in the use of the Redwood, the owner of the canoe or the home would soon learn his mistake. The canoe, for example, would not be controllable with the paddle. If a right-handed stroke would be made with the paddle, the boat would swing to the left, and it would be difficult to bring it back on its straight course again. In addition it would tip over easily. It would not go up a riffle without being towed. The boat which has no "heart" and no place for the spirit to live would always be ruled by the devil (bad spirits).

The fire pit in the home answered the same purpose as the heart of the boat. The fire pit is the center of the Indian's home and is its heart. Here the cooking is done and the heat and comfort of the home are produced. The family talks, plans, and prays here, and the old grandmothers instruct the young children in the necessities of life and the legends which came to them from the beginning. So it is that by each fire pit in the home a slab of redwood is driven into the ground far enough back so as not to be burned but to accommodate the spirit of *Keelch*.

The Arrow Tree

In the beginning, when Wah-Peck-oo-May-ow populated the world with trees and mountains, and people and rivers, and all the things that came to be, he climbed a very high mountain which was always covered with snow, even in summer. From this mountain he could talk to all on the earth and see them milling around below him.

The redwood trees were made to be great warriors. Some received greater rank than others due to the fact that they were taller, straighter, of better color, with branches that began higher from the ground. These were considered the best warriors and were so designated by Wah-Peck-oo-May-ow.

Wah-Peck-oo-May-ow also urged all human beings to show great respect and courtesy to these redwood warriors. In time the Indian men, as they passed a particularly straight, tall redwood tree on the trail, would shoot an arrow high into the tree, just below the limbs. This was done as a salute, as a sign of recognition and loyalty. The Indian women also would remove their babies from the carrier baskets and hold them high, facing the warrior tree. If the baby was a boy baby and laughed and clapped its hands, it was an indication that the baby would grow tall and straight and be a brave warrior. Young women without children would sing softly a love song, making known to the warrior tree the admiration they had for him.

LUCY THOMPSON

from TO THE AMERICAN INDIAN

*Lucy Thompson (1853–1932) was born in Klamath River coun-
try, in the Yurok village of Pecwan. In her early twenties she
married Milton James Thompson, a timber cruiser from Ala-
bama. Although she lived much of her adult life in white society, she had an abiding passion for her own culture and was
annoyed and appalled by the inaccuracies in accounts of Yurok
ways written by white anthropologists. In 1916 she decided to
set the record straight and published* To the American Indian,
a detailed and unique survey of Yurok culture.

This happened during the early years of my grandmother's life and
concerns principally a family at Reck-woy village, at the mouth of
the river. On the south side of the river is a village named Wealth-
quow, and at this place the Indians gave a large entertainment,
where many guests had assembled to take part in the dance. This
dance is commonly known in the English language as the Brush
Dance. The Indians always begin dancing these dances after sundown and sometimes dance until late at night. Large crowds had
gathered at this dance, and among the guests were three girl friends
from across the river at Reck-woy, who joined the dancers in their

usual custom of holding a bunch of brush over their faces so no one would know who they were. All the dancers, both men and women, hold the bunch of brush over their faces, after the fashion of a masquerade ball.

While the dancers were making merry, two wild Indians came in and joined them with the brush over their faces, and nobody knew who they were. When the dancers finished for a short intermission, the three Reck-woy girls left the room and went down to the foot of the hill, about thirty yards away where a spring gushed out of the hillside. Laughingly, they had gone to get a drink of nice cold water from the spring and wash their faces in the cool, refreshing water. As the girls left the house, the two wild Indians followed them down to the spring, and upon reaching it, they sprang upon one of the girls, named Os-slook-o-may, and captured her, covering her mouth with their hands so she could not scream for help, and the other two girls made their escape back to the house to give the alarm. Everything being favorable for the wild Indians, as the thickets grew high and dense and the forests being near, they were soon lost in the inky shadows of the big trees, where they carried their captive. The two Indians traveled with the girl all night, going in a southerly direction away from the river, and as they went along through the darkness, she would take small pieces of her buckskin apron and tie them to the bushes, thus making a trail which aided her followers for a long distance. When the alarm was given that Os-slook-o-may had been captured by the wild Indians, the guests did not dance anymore, and all the men who were able went in pursuit of the wild Indians to rescue the girl. They lost her among the dark shadows of the trees, as they could not find any trail to follow that night, and the next morning they all started out in hot pursuit, soon finding the trail she had left. The girl's supply of strings had become exhausted, and therefore she had no means of leaving any further trace of the direction her captors were taking her. However, they searched the hills, creeks, and mountains for several days, but never found her trail again, and she was given up to the wilds; and the procession turned homeward, very sad and heartbroken.

Somewhere in the depths of a dark canyon among the redwoods, the wild Indians had carried Os-slook-o-may. When they reached their hiding place, one of the Indians made her his wife, after the fashion of a primeval wedding. The wild Indians are always very rich in all kinds of Indian wealth, and this wild Indian dressed his bride in the most beautiful of Indian dresses, made of buckskin and ornamented with shells, and lavished wealth upon her. A little son came to their home in the wilds, of which they were both very proud, and they watched the little baby grow into a robust, handsome little fellow who by nature inherited the ways of his father as soon as he was big enough to walk and talk. He would run away from his mother and skip among the trees, romp among the bushes, and seemingly never grow tired of his wild revelry; he would talk and whistle to himself; and this grieved his mother very much, as she had tried every plan to subdue him from his wild romping, but of no avail.

When the boy was about six years of age, his mother became very lonesome for her people and wished very much to see them again, so one day she summoned up the courage to ask her husband to allow her to return to her home on a visit, as she said her folks were mourning for her as lost, having given up hopes of seeing her alive. He consented to let her go home on a visit, and said that she could take her little boy with her, so they began to make ready for the journey, as it was a long distance and the country was very rough. The O-ma-ha (Devil) husband, who was immensely rich, dressed his wife in one of the most beautiful of Indian dresses, and the little boy was also richly clad, and so they started on their journey to Reck-woy. The wild man guided and accompanied them until they neared the village of Wealth-quow, the village from which he had stolen her on the night of the dance, and here, as they came into a small open space overlooking the village, he parted from his wife and little son, and they crossed the river and went into her native village. As she entered the village, she was most beautiful to behold, dressed in the most gorgeous Indian dress, with her little son by her side; and startled friends and relatives, who had mourned her as dead, greeted her with much surprise, as they had mourned her loss for nearly nine years.

Her folks were overjoyed to find their long-lost child restored to them, and with hearty greetings and a royal welcome, she found herself back in the village of her birth. With breathless interest they sat listening to her wonderful tales concerning her life in the solemn wilds, how she had been carried over mountain and crag, and through the huge forests, to a strange home in the cave in a cliff of rocks, where one of the wild men had made her his wife. In this strange cave she had enjoyed the comforts of a luxuriant home, for her husband was exceedingly rich and was very kind to her and their child. From her description, it seemed this cave was located at the source of Redwood Creek, which we call Cho-lu-wer-roy, in a dark canyon which is perhaps over a distance of sixty miles from Reck-woy, off in a southerly direction. In a cave of this dark canyon, surrounded on every side by the giant redwoods, she had spent nine years of her life listening to the sigh of the wind among the trees and strange enchantment of the babble of the brooks down the rocky canyon. Safe in her cave and lonely, with nothing but nature and a wild man to comfort her, she had grown more lonely as the years crept by in her desire to see her people once more. How they had traveled on their journey back along the creekbeds for a long distance, over high mountains and around sheer walls of great bluffs, and through the awful calm of dense forests and overhanging thickets! She had at last reached the home of her birth. Parting from her devoted husband for the first and last time, she faithfully promised to meet him again at the close of her visit and return with him again to the cave in the wilds. During the first days of her visit, she encouraged her boy to associate with the children of the village. But he could not resist the calling of that wild nature he had inherited from his father, and all of his mother's pleadings proved of no avail in changing his character. He would watch his opportunity and run away from the other children and play by himself, among the dense bushes, jumping and whistling as he would go. His mother gave up in despair in her efforts to change his ways.

She remembered the day and place where she had promised to meet her husband and return with him to their home, but she refused to go and meet him at the appointed time and place, as she said she never intended to return, and had merely made him the promise in order to get back to her people; and now that she was with them she would never leave them again.

He waited in vain at the appointed place as she came not to meet him, and after waiting a long time he came to the conclusion that she had made him a false promise, so he crept cautiously down to the river and swam across to Reck-woy village, where he knew his wife was staying. When he reached the other side, he crept up the hillside and concealed himself in a dense clump of bushes, where he could look down upon the house where he knew she was staying, and watched for her. His wife seldom ventured out of the house, as she was afraid that he would get her again, so she kept close indoors that he might not have any chance of getting her away again. One day he managed to attract the attention of his little son, and he came up to his father and they talked together. He directed the son to go and tell his mother to come to him, as he was waiting for her.

When the son delivered the message to his mother, she replied that she did not believe this to be true, so he returned to his father, telling him what his mother had said. He immediately sent him back to her, imploring that she come to him. The mother looked puzzled at the boy and said that he must be mistaken, but he said that he knew his father, and pleaded earnestly for her to return to their home in the canyon. Studying the boy's eager face a few moments, she replied by saying that he could choose between her and his father; he could remain with her or go with his father, back into the lonesome wilds. The boy at once preferred his father and bade his mother farewell. Father and son returned to their hiding place, and the mother, who had once cheered them in the lonesome wilds, never saw them again; they had gone out of her life forever, like a dream that had come and gone, and faded again, with the closing day, back into the primeval redwoods, where you may see father and son staying together among the mystic shadows of dreamland mountains.

JUAN CRESPI, MIGUEL DE COSTANSO,
AND PEDRO FONT

from DIARIES OF THE PORTOLA AND ANZA EXPEDITIONS

In 1769 an expedition under the command of Gaspar de Portolá set out from Baja California to explore California from San Diego north. One of its goals was to find Monterey Bay, which Sebastián Vizcaíno had found, named, and determined to be an important port sixty-seven years before. Besides Portolá, two other members kept diaries of the expedition: Miguel Costansó, the engineer, and Juan Crespí, a priest who had been appointed by the Franciscans to be the group's official recorder. Although they found Monterey Bay, Portolá's group did not realize they were there; it may be that their view was obscured by fog and they thought they were seeing just another stretch of coastline. Six and a half years later, the Anza expedition traveled through the same territory, with Fray Pedro Font as diarist. In the following excerpts from the diaries, all three offer brief remarks about the astounding redwood trees, though only Crespí calls them "redwoods." Costansó calls them "sabins," and Font considers them to be spruces. In the first excerpt, the Portolá expedition, which set out from San Diego in July, is headed north, searching for Monterey.

◇————————————————————————————————◇

From the diary of Miguel Costansó of the Portolá Expedition:
October 4 [1769]—Our commander…determined to call a meeting of his officers to consider what action was most suitable in the present exigency. He drew attention to the scarcity of provisions that confronted us; to the large number of sick we had among us (there were seventeen men half-crippled and unfit for work); to the season, already far advanced; and to the great sufferings of the men who remained well, on account of the unlimited work required in looking after the horses and watching them at night, in guarding the camp, and in the continual excursions for exploration and reconnaissance. The meeting was held after we had heard the mass of the Holy Ghost, and all the officers voted unanimously that the journey be continued, as this was the only course that remained, for we hoped to find—through the grace of God—the much desired port of Monterey, and in it the packet *San Joseph,* which would relieve our needs; and, if God willed that in search for Monterey we should all perish, we would have performed our duty towards God and man, laboring together until death for the success of the undertaking upon which we had been sent.

October 5—The scouts set out early in the morning to examine the country so that we might continue our journey.

October 6—The scouts returned in the afternoon with very pleasant news. They had found a river of great verdure and with many trees of Castile [the Pajaro River valley], and they believed that they had seen another point of pines to the north (it was afterwards known, however, that they had been deceived because it was very foggy). They likewise saw tracks of large animals with split hoofs and thought they might be bison; and a populous village of Indians who lived in huts covered with thatch, and who, according to what they said, must have numbered over five hundred souls. These Indians had no notice of our coming to their lands, as our men could see from the consternation and fright that their presence caused; amazed and confused, without knowing what they did, some ran for their weapons, others shouted and yelled, and the women burst into tears. Our men did all they could to quiet them, and succeeded with great difficulty. The sergeant of the presidio of Loreto, who was in command of the party, dismounted and approached them with signs of peace. The Indians did not allow him to reach their village; they made him signs to stop, and, at the same time, taking their arrows they stuck them all, point first, into the ground; they did the same with other darts and plumes, which they brought immediately. They withdrew afterwards, and as the scouts understood that this had been done as a sign of peace, several of them dismounted and took some of these arrows and darts. The natives were very much pleased, and applauded this act of our men, who, to assure them still further that their intention was not to injure them, but rather to seek their friendship, asked them by signs for food. Upon this the contentment of the Indians was increased, and their women immediately set themselves to grind seeds, from which they made some round pats which they gave to our men. The sergeant gave the Indians some glass beads, and they were well satisfied and content....

October 9—The short and cloudy days did not give the scouts opportunity to examine the country, especially as we arrived somewhat late at the camping place. This obliged us to rest here in order to give the scouts time to make their exploration. They left early in the morning and were given the day for this purpose.

They examined the country for [a distance equal to] two days' march of the pack animals, and returned without any information of importance—which greatly depressed us, considering the scarcity of the provisions and the embarrassment caused by the sick, who could not shift for themselves, the number of the ailing increasing every day.

October 10—We left the Río del Pájaro and proceeded for one league over level ground, not being able to continue the march farther, as the sick were already exhausted, falling down from their mules. We halted near a small pond formed between some low hills—a place with plenty of water and pasture....

⋄———⋄

From the diary of Juan Crespí of the Portolá expedition:
October 10 [1769]—About eight in the morning we set out northwest. We could not make the march as long as was intended, because the sick men were worse, and each day their number increased, so we must have traveled but little more than one league, over plains and low hills, well forested with very high trees of a red color, not known to us. They have a very different leaf from cedars, and although the wood resembles cedar somewhat in color, it is very different, and has not the same odor; moreover, the wood of the trees that we have found is very brittle. In this region there is a great abundance of these trees and because none of the expedition recognizes them, they are named redwood from their color. We stopped near a lagoon which has much pasture about it and a heavy growth of the redwoods. In this march many tracks of animals

resembling those of domestic cattle have been encountered, and there is some discussion as to whether they may not be buffalo. Some very large deer have also been seen, which they call stags to differentiate them from ordinary deer. The droppings of some mulelike animals have also been found. Bands of them have been seen, and it is said that they are long eared and have short, flat tails. In the lagoons many cranes are also seen. The explorers say that near here they have seen many chestnut trees which are in flower, and they brought some few nuts, which we tasted, and they truly are chestnuts, the only difference noticed being that they have a thicker shell than those of Spain.

◦———————◦

From Costansó's diary:
October 15 [1769]—We set out from the Laguna del Corral—a name given to it on account of a piece of fence that was constructed between the lake and a low hill in order to keep the animals penned by night with few watchmen. We marched very slowly so as to cause the sick as little distress as possible; we contrived to carry them on sidesaddles, as the women in Andalusia travel. We proceeded for a league and a half and halted near another small pond in the bottom of a narrow and very pleasant little canyon, with plenty of firewood and pasture.

The road was somewhat difficult. We directed our course to the north-northwest, without withdrawing far from the coast, from which we were separated by some high hills very thickly covered with trees that some said were savins. They were the largest, highest, and straightest trees that we had seen up to that time; some of them were four or five yards in diameter. The wood is of a dull, dark, reddish color, very soft, brittle, and full of knots.

This canyon was given the name of La Lagunilla....

October 23—We moved the camp a distance of two leagues from the Cañada de la Salud, and camped near an Indian village, discovered by the scouts, situated in a pleasant and attractive spot at the foot of a mountain range and in front of a ravine covered with pine and savin, among which descended a stream from which the natives obtained water. The land appeared pleasant; it was covered with pasture, and was not without firewood. We traveled part of the way along the beach; the rest, from the point of rocks previously mentioned, to the village, over high, level land with plenty of water standing in pools of greater or less extent.

The Indians, advised by the scouts of our coming to their lands, received us with great affability and kindness, and, furthermore, presented us with seeds kneaded into thick pats. They also offered us some cakes of a certain sweet paste, which some of our men said was the honey of wasps; they brought it carefully wrapped in the leaves of the carrizo cane, and its taste was not at all bad.

In the middle of the village there was a large house, spherical in form and very roomy; the other small houses, built in the form of a pyramid, had very little room, and were built of split pine wood. Because the large house so much surpassed the others, the village was named after it.

Note: The point of rocks that we left behind is the one known as the Punta de Año Nuevo. Its latitude is, with a slight difference, the same as that of the Cañada de la Salud....

◇———◇

From Crespí's diary:
October 24 [1769]—We set out at half past eight with two heathen of this village who came to guide us, taking a northerly direction, in sight of the sea, over high, broad hills of good land, but all burned over and despoiled of trees. Only through the openings is to

be seen the Sierra Blanca which still remains with us, but after half a league's travel there were some groves of redwoods. We crossed two arroyos, each one of which carried more than a buey of water. In two leagues we crossed two valleys with very good land and an abundance of running water in each....One of them...has a fair-sized lagoon. This is a fine place, with good lands and an abundance of water, where a good mission could be placed....

It is a pleasure to see the great number of blackberries in this place, so thick that they prevent us walking. After traveling seven hours...we arrived at the camping place, which is in a small valley with a good village of heathen, who received us with much friendliness. They are fair, well formed, and some of them are bearded. They have their village near the beach...but they also have their little houses in this valley, and at present are living in them. The valley has a great deal of land...[and] an arroyo with plenty of running water which goes to the beach....The only shortcoming...was the scarcity of wood, but the mountains are near, and there is plenty of brush from the redwoods. I believe the place is a good site for a mission, for which purpose I dedicated it to our Father Santo Domingo, so that the conversion of this village may proceed under his patronage.

◇————◇

From Costansó's diary:
November 5 [1769]—We followed the coast of the estuary, although we did not see it because we were separated from it by the low hills of the canyon that we were following in a south-southeasterly direction. We traveled for three leagues. The country was pleasant. The hills west of the canyon were crowned with savins, low live oaks, and other smaller trees. There was sufficient pasture. We halted on the bank of a stream of good water. Some of the natives were

seen; they invited us to go to their villages, and offered us their presents of seeds and fruits...

November 6—Without leaving this canyon we marched, in the same direction, for three more leagues over pleasanter land, more thickly covered with savins, white oaks, and live oaks loaded with acorns. Two very numerous bands of Indians met us on the road with presents of *pinole* and some large trays of white *atole,* which supplied in large measure the needs of our men. These natives requested us earnestly to go to their villages, offering to entertain us well; they were disappointed because we would not yield to their solicitations. Some of the men asked them various questions by means of signs, in order to obtain from them information they desired, and they were very well satisfied with the grimaces and the ridiculous and vague gestures with which the natives responded—a pantomime from which, truly, one could understand very little, and the greater part of the men understood nothing. Meanwhile we arrived at the end of the canyon where the hilly country, which extended to our left and lay between us and the estuary, terminated. At the same time the hills on our right turned towards the east, and closed the valley that contained the waters of the estuary. We likewise directed our course to the east. We proceeded for a short stretch in this direction and halted on the bank of a deep stream, which descended from the mountain range and flowed precipitately to the calm waters of the estuary....

◇————————◇

From the diary of Pedro Font of the de Anza expedition:
March 26 [1776]—We reached the arroyo of San Francisco, on whose banks we saw a village. The Indians came out to us on the road, and the commander went with me to the village and gave the

women some glass beads, and I counted about twenty-five huts. We crossed the arroyo and found the holy cross which Father Palóu set up on its bank last year. On the arroyo there are various laurels, ash, and other trees, and a few spruce trees which they call redwood, a tree that is certainly beautiful; and I believe that it is very useful for its timber; for it is very straight and tall....

March 28—About five o'clock in the afternoon the commander and the lieutenant returned from their exploration very well pleased, for they had found more than they had expected in the vicinity of these hills....On them and in their canyons they found plentiful timber and firewood, much water in several springs or lakes, abundant lands for raising crops, and finally, a vast supply of pasturage in all the country, so that the new settlement will be able to have plentiful fuel, water, and grass or pasturage for the horses, all near by....

March 29—We went a little further, and from a small elevation there I observed the trend of the port in this direction. I saw that its extremity was toward the east-southeast, and that a very high redwood, which stands on the bank of the arroyo of San Francisco, visible from a long distance, rising like a great tower in the Llano de los Robles, and whose height I afterward measured, lay to the southeast*....

The commander decided to go to explore a nearby valley called San Andrés, which is in the range of the spruce trees, also called redwoods, which ends at the Punta de Almejas...to see if it had good timber for the settlement at the port....In it we saw, as we went through, extensive groves with many and various trees of good timber, such as live oaks, madroños, spruce, and also cottonwoods and

---

*This was the "palo alto," or tall pole, for which the South Bay town of Palo Alto was named.

other trees, with much brush on the banks of the arroyo, or long and narrow lake, which runs through this valley and forms the arroyo of San Matheo, which runs out upon the plain by a narrow pass through some hills, and consists of two arroyos that join before emerging....

About a league before this there came out on our road a very large bear, which the men succeeded in killing. There are many of these beasts in that country, and they often attack and do damage to the Indians when they go to hunt, of which I saw many horrible examples. When he saw us so near, the bear was going along very carelessly on the slope of a hill where flight was not very easy. When I saw him so close and that he was looking at us in suspense I feared some diaster. But Corporal Robles fired a shot at him with aim so true that he hit him in the neck. The bear now hurled himself down the slope, crossed the arroyo, and hid in the brush, but he was so badly wounded that after going a short distance he fell dead. Thereupon the soldiers skinned him and took what flesh they wished. In this affair we spent more than an hour here. The commander took the hide to give as a present to the viceroy. The bear was so old that his eye teeth were badly decayed and he lacked one tooth, but he was very fat, although his flesh smelled much like a skunk or like musk. I measured this animal and he was nine spans long and four high [over six feet long]. He was horrible, fierce, large and fat, and very tough....

We now traveled...to the east-southeast and considering the exploration of this valley sufficient, since there was nothing else in it to see, it was decided to go to the camp...at the arroyo of San Matheo. The Indians of this village were very attentive and obliging, and even troublesome, for they had so attached themselves to the camp that when it was already very late it was necessary to drive them out in order that we might get some sleep. So I think that it would be easy to establish them in a mission.

AUGUSTE DUHAUT-CILLY

from A VOYAGE TO CALIFORNIA

August Duhaut-Cilly (1790–1849), master of the trading ship
Héros, *spent the better part of 1827 and 1828 along the coast*
of Alta and Baja California trying to sell or trade his cargo so
that he and his crew could return to France. His diary, in
which he recorded his impressions of the region's natural his-
tory and his encounters with the residents, is now considered
to be one of the most important accounts of California before
the American conquest. In the following passage from his visit
to the Russian colony of Fort Ross, north of the San Francisco
and Bodega Bay, we find the beginnings of the redwood log-
ging industry.

On June 2nd toward evening we found ourselves a few leagues
from land on that part of the coast where I supposed the Russian
colony to be, and in fact we discerned with the telescope something that resembled a group of houses. At sunset we lay closer.
Convinced now that we were not mistaken, I ran up the flag and
shot off a cannon. Almost at once a puff of white smoke told us
that they were responding in the same way, and we could make
out a Russian flag. But since it was too late for a landing before

47

nightfall, we shortened sail and maintained our position until the following day.

On the morning of the 3rd, as we were lying to at a distance of several miles, examining the coast without discerning any opening or recess that might indicate a harbor, we suddenly noticed three bidarkas [sealskin boats] coming toward us, each carrying three persons. Several minutes later these boats arrived alongside, and we were paid a visit by the Russian commandant himself, Paul Shelekhov, to whom I communicated my reasons for coming there. At the same time I requested permission to anchor in his harbor in order to display those things in the cargo that might suit him. Although he was not in need of much and was rather short of trading goods, he welcomed my proposal and, ordering one of his men to serve us as pilot, he said he would accompany me to the port of Bodega, the only anchorage in use by the colony. He sent two of the boats back to shore and asked me to have the other hoisted on board, after which we took our way parallel to the coast.

From where we had been lying to, the settlement had quite a different look from that of the presidios of California, models of rude design and indifferent execution. Houses of elegant shape with roofs well constructed, fields well planted and surrounded by palisades gave this place an appearance that was quite European. After fifteen miles we reached a small peninsula that sheltered the roadstead of Bodega....

Toward evening, Commandant Shelekhov returned to shore, where horses had been brought for him, having made me promise to visit him the next day. On the morning of the 4th...mounting our horses, we began the journey, accompanied by several Russians and by our pilot; after having performed skillfully his nautical functions on the previous day, he steered us equally well over a different element, bearing now the modest title of guide. Having crossed the isthmus of the peninsula, we rode for a league along a fine sandy beach and then ascended a cliff of moderate height. After that we took our way over an esplanade carpeted with grass mixed with strawberry plants bearing fruit and ensplendored with a multitude of flowers of every color. The sea was breaking at the base of the cliff, its snow-white foam contrasting with the dark color of the rocks and the rich green of the fields which our horses trod with no more sound than if they had been stepping on eiderdown. Two leagues along this plain brought us to the bank of a considerable river [the Russian River], called Sacabaya by the Indians and Slavianka by the Russians. It was too deep even in the summertime to be forded, and in winter it becomes fearsome, swiftly carrying off immense tree trunks uprooted by storms. The retreating water had left some huge ones on both banks.

The crossing has been disastrous for many travelers; two years before this, an American captain was drowned here. As for us, we passed over safely enough in a bidarka that Mr. Shelekhov had sent for the purpose. Since this boat, made of sealskin, held only two persons, it was necessary to make a trip for each one of us. Conducted skillfully by a Kodiak Islander, it had more than one point of resemblance to the bark of old Charon. Its lightness and instability could make one think that it was meant only for the transporting of shades, and the guttural grunting of the Kodiak when he pointed out the person who was to enter the bidarka with him must have sounded like the hoarse voice of the pitiless boatman of Hades, scolding souls on the banks of the Styx.

One had to exercise great care in sliding oneself into a round hole up to the middle of the body, when the slightest movement to right or left was enough to make the light craft tip in a disquieting way. Nevertheless, I had no wish to sit idly while we crossed, and in my capacity of seaman I seized a paddle and wielded it in a way to satisfy the old pilot of the Slavianka. It is in these cockle boats of skin that the natives of the Aleutian Islands, braving the high seas, hunt the Saricovian otter [sea otter] and do battle with the most monstrous whales, whose flesh and oil are their favorite food and drink....

Our horses were accustomed to the passage of the river and they swam across by themselves as soon as they were relieved of their saddles. Starting out once more we ascended by so steep a road that we found it hard to believe that the horses could avoid falling back on their riders.

The mountain whose summit we reached, not without difficulty and even some danger, was covered with enormous conifers, mixed with sycamores, bay trees, and several species of oaks. At a height of two thousand feet we looked out over the sea, which was beating against the land below; the waves, silent at this distance, looked like small whitish patches scattered over a cloth of azure....

At eleven in the morning we arrived at the colony called Ross by the Russians....All the buildings at Ross are of wood but well built and well maintained. In the apartment of the governor are found all the conveniences valued by Europeans but still unknown in California. Outside the compound are lined up or scattered the pretty little houses of sixty Russian colonists, the flat huts of eighty Kodiaks, and the conical huts of as many native Indians.

East of the settlement the land rises gradually to great heights covered with thick forests that block the wind from the north to the southeast. All these slopes are partitioned into fields of wheat, beans, oats, potatoes, and the like, fenced off to protect the crops not from thieves but from farm animals and wild beasts.

In spite of its military appearance the colony is a commercial establishment owned, along with those of Sitka and Kodiak Island, by a company of merchants. It appears, however, that the emperor has granted it great privileges, and that many in the Russian court own an interest, large or small....

Although this colony, in existence for fifteen years, appears to lack nothing, it cannot be of great account to the company that founded it. As the principal source of revenue they counted on the hunt for sea otters and seals. The first of these is nearly exhausted and no longer provides anything; as for the second, the governor keeps about a hundred Kodiaks on the Farallones throughout the year...but that hunt, once quite productive, declines with every passing day and in a few more years will amount to nothing. Looking on these products as now secondary, the governor has for several years concerned himself primarily with husbandry. Not only does he grow the wheat and vegetables that were once obtained from California, but he also provisions the larger colony of Sitka. With only six hundred cows he was producing more butter and cheese than all of Alta California with its countless herds....

We went with Mr. Shelekhov to view his timber production. In addition to the needs of his own settlement he cuts a great quantity of planks, beams, timbers, and the like, which he sells in California, in the Sandwich Islands, and elsewhere; he even builds entire houses and ships them disassembled. The trees felled are almost all conifers of several kinds and especially the one called *palo colorado* (redwood). The only virtues of this tree are that it is quite straight and splits easily; for the rest, it has little resin and is very brittle. It is the largest tree that I have ever seen. Mr. Shelekhov showed me the trunk of one that had been felled recently; it was twenty feet in diameter, measured two feet from the ground and from one burl or buttress to the other; the main trunk was more than thirteen feet in width. I measured two hundred and thirty feet from the stump to the crown, lying where it had been parted from the bole. Imagine what a huge quantity of boards can be obtained from a tree of this size. The stacks of them from one such covered a considerable stretch of ground. Not all the *palos colorados* are this prodigious, but one can see many that three men would have difficulty stretching their arms around and that would make, as a single piece, the lower masts of our largest ships of war.

Mr. Shelekhov treated us with the most refined hospitality, and we passed a comfortable night with him. Unfortunately neither Dr. Botta nor I understood Russian, and the governor spoke neither French nor English nor Spanish. This inconvenience caused us to miss much of the charm that his company should have provided. It was in Spanish that we made ourselves understood best. I did only a little business with him; an American ship had preceded me here and had taken nearly all the pelts possessed by the establishment. I sold him only the value of a few hundred sealskins. Arising early the next day I positioned myself on a hillside to the east and sketched the citadel....After breakfast we mounted our horses to return to the port, from where we set sail the next morning.

WILLIAM TAYLOR

from CALIFORNIA LIFE ILLUSTRATED

William Taylor (1821–1902) was a minister specializing in street preaching in Baltimore and Washington, D.C., when the Methodist Church sent him to California as a missionary evangelist in 1849. He stayed in the West for seven years and then traveled throughout the world, serving as the Methodist Missionary Bishop for Africa before returning to California, where he spent the last seven years of his life. California Life Illustrated *(1858), a memoir of Taylor's first trip to California, gives details of family life, social life, politics, and Church history in San Jose, Santa Cruz, and Sacramento. Here he describes finding and cutting redwoods, "in the territory of grizzly bears and wild cats," to build a house for his family.*

We spent the following week in learning California prices and modes of life and in trying to secure a house in which to live. Captain Wilson kindly invited us to remain aboard ship until we could make arrangements for housekeeping and allowed us the free use of his boat in passing to and from the land. The lowest price of boat hire for the shortest distance was one dollar per passenger. We learned prices in part by little experiments in buying. Mrs. Taylor said to a dealer in potatoes, "How much do you ask per peck for your potatoes?"

"We sell nothing by measure here," replied he, "for man or beast. Everything is bought and sold by weight, ma'am."

"Well, what do you ask per pound for potatoes?"

"Fifty cents per pound, ma'am."

"I'll take a pound to begin with," said she, laying down the money; and he gave her for fifty cents but one potato.

I priced some South American apples, nearly as tough as leather; fifty cents apiece. We ascertained that fresh beef was selling for fifty cents per pound; dried apples, seventy-five cents per pound; Oregon butter, two dollars fifty cents per pound; flour, fifty dollars per barrel; and provisions of every kind proportionably high. None of these things moved us, however, for we had brought with us a year's supply of all the substantials of life. The only difficulty with us was to get a house in which to live. Reverend O. C. Wheeler, I learned, was paying five hundred dollars a month rent for such a house as we needed, a small one-and-a-half-story house, containing four or five rooms. That was frightful, for I only had money enough, including the missionary appropriation for our support for a year—seven hundred and fifty dollars—to pay rent, at that rate, for about two months.

There stood in the neighborhood of our chapel a one-story, rough board shanty, about twelve feet square, with a shed roof of the same material, promising altogether but very little protection from the storms of approaching winter; but I thought as a last resort I would try and get my wife and babes into it till something better could be obtained. I learned that the rent for the shanty was forty dollars per month. I immediately applied for it, but lo! it had been secured for the personal occupancy of a reverend Episcopal brother in "the regular succession"; and I, a poor irregular, was left to do the best I could.

I then spoke of building a little house, but lumber was selling for from three hundred to four hundred dollars per thousand feet. To pay such prices and build a house with my little stock of funds was out of the question.

In the meantime I had my household goods and provisions taken ashore, paid ten dollars per dray load to have them hauled up on the hill near the chapel, and there they lay piled up in the open air for a fortnight. That was prior to the advent of petty rogues in California.

On my second Sabbath, at eleven A.M., I again occupied the pulpit of Brother Wheeler, and had a gracious meeting. At three P.M. we had another great class meeting in the "shanty with the blue cover." Many of the brethren with whom we had prayed, and sung, and shouted the Sabbath before had gone to parts unknown; but a new recruit had come in of the same sort. After class the question was raised, "How shall our preacher get a house to live in?" It was decided that the only way was to build one; and then an effort was made in the class to see how much could be raised toward that desirable end. But the sojourners *"were strapped,"* and the resident brethren had subscribed all they felt able to give toward the chapel and could do but little for a parsonage, so the effort resulted in a subscription amounting to twenty-seven dollars, perhaps enough to buy the nails and hinges. The prospect for a residence in the land of our adoption, as we supposed for life, was very dark; but I never had doubted that God sent me to California and felt a comfortable assurance that in some way he would provide for us.

Captain Otis Webb, son of old Father Daniel Webb of the Providence Conference, though nothing himself but a high-minded outsider (the Lord bless the outsiders! I have found among them some of the best friends I ever had in my life), hearing of our situation, sent us word that he was building a house near our chapel, which would be finished in a week, and that we were welcome to the use of it, rent free, for a month. So after remaining a fortnight in port aboard ship, enjoying the hospitality of Captain Wilson, we moved into the new house of Captain Webb, a one-and-a-half-story house, containing five rooms, [which] would have rented for about four hundred dollars a month. Thus the evil day, in regard to shelter, was postponed for a month at least....

The question now was, "What shall we do at the end of the month?" Some said, as the Missionary Society had sent us there, they would be bound to support us. I replied that the Missionary Society never had, and never could, support a man at California rates; that my rent alone for a year would be about five thousand dollars, to say nothing of other expenses; that the society, moreover, was in debt; and that I never expected to draw on them for a dollar while in California. I said to the brethren that if nothing better opened I would take my ax and wedge and go to the redwoods, fifteen miles distant across the bay, and get out lumber for a house, and build it myself. They said I could not do it but could suggest no other way of getting a house.

A brother who had located from the traveling ranks to try his fortunes in California said, "Poor Brother Taylor will work himself sick, and that will end the matter. It had been better for him to come to California on his own hook as I did." I said that I had come in the order of Providence and that I did not believe that God would allow my family to suffer for want of shelter.

I saw no other way, however, but to go to the redwoods and leave the result with the Lord. Alexander Hatler, a brother from Missouri who, with his good wife, had emigrated to that land before gold was discovered, said he would go with me and help me get out lumber. So on Tuesday, the 10th of October, we set sail for the redwoods, in company with some of Father White's family, who had a shanty in the woods, where the old man and his sons spent much of their time, getting out and hauling lumber.

We landed where the town of San Antonia is now located. We then had five miles to walk, and climb a mountain, carrying our packs of blankets, provisions, and working tools. We reached the shanty a little after dark. Brother Hatler and I put our stock of provisions into the family mess and were admitted as guests, with the privilege of wrapping in our own blankets and sleeping on the ground, under the common shelter. After supper we listened to Father White's thrilling backwoods stories till bedtime; and then, at the family altar, we made the tall forests vocal with our song of praise.

The next morning Brother Hatler and I found a large log that some woodsman had abandoned, which we thought could be worked to good advantage. We drove all our wedges into it, but could not split it, so it took us till noon to chop our wedges out. A heavy rain then set in, which continued till the next morning.

On Thursday we worked till noon on another log. Being very large, we had to bore it and burst it open with powder; but it was too cross-grained for our purpose. We then selected a large tree and chopped at it till dark. The next morning brought our giant of the forest to the ground but, alas! we could not work it. It was difficult to find a tree with straight grain and easy to split; but the trees were so large, many of them measuring twelve feet in diameter, that when a good one was opened, it yielded almost a yardful of lumber. But we did not succeed in getting the right tree.

On Friday P.M. we returned to the landing, so as to take the land breeze early on Saturday morning and be in the city in time for the appointments of the Sabbath. We lay on the beach that night, in the open air, to gaze at the stars, listen to the howling of the coyotes (a small species of wolf), or the gabble of multiplied thousands of wild geese and the quacking of wild ducks, or meditate, or sleep, as we felt inclined. I took my turn at each of these, especially the last.

The city brethren were not at all disappointed with the result of our trip to the woods. It was just as they expected; but I surprised them by telling them that I was not at all discouraged and meant to try it again the next week.

That was my fourth Sabbath in the city, and the second to preach in our new chapel. It was crowded that day, and we had a memorable season. I made provision for my appointments on the following Sabbath, so as not to be under the necessity of returning from the woods for a fortnight. Brother Hatler could not leave his business to return with me to the redwoods, so I had to depend on my own muscles and skill alone. That week I wrought very hard and was a little scared one night, as the following extract from my journal will show:

Friday, October 19, 1849—We are here on the territory of grizzly bears and wild cats, which are frequently seen by the woodchoppers. I had some expectation of a visit from a grizzly last night. We butchered a calf in the evening, which we had purchased from a Spaniard, and had it in the shanty. I lay before the open door and thought if bruin should come in to get some veal, I would have the honor of his first salutation. But, thought I, the God who saved me from the dangers of the deep will surely keep the bears off me. With these reflections I fell into a sweet sleep.

After midnight I was suddenly awakened by a noise outside the hut. I sprang up, saying to myself, "There's the bear, sure enough!" when in he came; but, to my comfort, I found it one of the men of the shanty. Such are many of the dreadful bears we encounter in this life....

It may not be amiss here to insert another bit of experience from my journal:

Sunday morning, October 21, 1849—For retirement and meditation, I have strolled out to the top of a high hill. The sky is clear as crystal, and the sun is shining with a California radiance, unknown in other lands....

Looking eastward I see a dense forest of huge redwood timber, doubtless the veritable cedars of Lebanon. West and north, hills and mountains stretch to the uttermost line of the ken of vision, and the scene, in its barrenness and sterility of appearance, is only relieved here and there by a small oasis and by the herds of cattle feeding on the dry grass. Southward the whole valley, for fifty miles, is filled with fog. It looks as though a firmament of white, broken clouds had dropped from the heavens and settled over the whole region of the bay of San Francisco and its adjacent vales....

I may here add that I preached that Sunday under the shade of a large redwood tree to twenty-five woodsmen. One of my hearers, a man of forty-five years, heard preaching that day for the last time. He soon afterward took suddenly ill, and died, and was added to the two lonely strangers on the neighboring hill. The ensuing week I finished my work in the woods. My scantling, which I bought in a rough state, split out like fence rails, I hewed to the square with my broadax. I got my joists from a man who had a saw pit. I made three thousand shingles, and gave them for twenty-four joists, seventeen feet long. I bought rough clapboards six feet long, and shaved them down with my drawknife for weatherboarding; and thus got in the woods all the materials for a two-story house sixteen by twenty-six feet, except flooring, doors, and windows. I bought the doors from a friend at a reduced price, eleven dollars per door. The windows one dollar per light, ten by twelve inches. It cost me twenty-five dollars per thousand feet to get my lumber hauled to the landing, and the regular price of freight from there to the city was forty dollars per thousand feet; but by hiring a boat and working myself, I got it done for less than half that price…

I have gone thus into detail, not to exhibit mine as a peculiar case, for it was not so, but simply to illustrate California life. As for sufferings, I had none. My labors in house building were simply a good acclimating process, which increased my physical power and prepared me the more effectively to endure the ministerial toil to which I was called. As for comforts, I was better off than most of my neighbors. We had a comfortable home, while the great mass of our "city folks" lived in very inferior shanties and tents.

I have often gone out in the morning after a stormy night and found whole rows of tents lying flat on the ground, and scattered in every direction by the merciless blasts of winter; and many of my brethren in the ministry, at a later day, suffered probably greater trials and hardships than I did at the beginning. The Lord bless and reward them, for he only knows how great and varied have been the trials of missionary life in California.

WALT WHITMAN

SONG OF THE REDWOOD-TREE

Writing in an ecstatic voice that often echoed the prophetic diction and drama of the Old Testament, Walt Whitman (1819–1876) was known for liberating verse from the confines of meter and rhyme and choosing elements of real life—ordinary people, work, and the human body—as subjects for poetry. "Song of the Redwood-Tree," a hopeful vision of "a swarming and busy race settling and organizing" in the West, was first published in "Centennial Songs" as part of Two Rivulets, *a collection of poetry and prose from 1876. Ever the symbolic idealist, Whitman expressed the feelings of trees he had only imagined; he never visited a living redwood tree.*

1

A California song,
A prophecy and indirection, a thought impalpable to breathe as air,
A chorus of dryads, fading, departing, or hamadryads departing,
A murmuring, fateful, giant voice, out of the earth and sky,
Voice of a mighty dying tree in the redwood forest dense.

Farewell my brethren,
Farewell O earth and sky, farewell ye neighboring waters,
My time has ended, my term has come.

Along the northern coast,
Just back from the rock-bound shore and the caves,
In the saline air from the sea in the Mendocino country,
With the surge for base and accompaniment low and hoarse,
With crackling blows of axes sounding musically driven by strong
    arms,
Riven deep by the sharp tongues of the axes, there in the redwood
    forest dense,
I heard the mighty tree its death-chant chanting.

The choppers heard not, the camp shanties echoed not,
The quick-ear'd teamsters and chain and jack-screw men heard not,
As the wood-spirits came from their haunts of a thousand years to
    join the refrain,
But in my soul I plainly heard.
Murmuring out of its myriad leaves,
Down from its lofty top rising two hundred feet high,
Out of its stalwart trunk and limbs, out of its foot-thick bark,
That chant of the seasons and time, chant not of the past only but
    the future.

You untold life of me,
And all you venerable and innocent joys,
Perennial hardy life of me with joys 'mid rain and many a
    summer sun,
And the white snows and night and the wild winds;
O the great patient rugged joys, my soul's strong joys unreck'd by man,
(For know I bear the soul befitting me, I too have consciousness, identity,

And all the rocks and mountains have, and all the earth,)
Joys of the life befitting me and brothers mine,
Our time, our term has come.

Nor yield we mournfully majestic brothers,
We who have grandly fill'd our time;
With Nature's calm content, with tacit huge delight,
We welcome what we wrought for through the past,
And leave the field for them.

For them predicted long,
For a superber race, they too to grandly fill their time,
For them we abdicate, in them ourselves ye forest kings!
In them these skies and airs, these mountain peaks, Shasta,
        Nevadas,
These huge precipitous cliffs, this amplitude, these valleys, far Yosemite,
To be in them absorb'd, assimilated.

Then to a loftier strain,
Still prouder, more ecstatic rose the chant,
As if the heirs, the deities of the West,
Joining with master-tongue bore part.

Not wan from Asia's fetiches,
Nor red from Europe's old dynastic slaughter-house,
(Area of murder-plots of thrones, with scent left yet of wars and
        scaffolds everywhere,)
But come from Nature's long and harmless throes, peacefully builded
        thence,
These virgin lands, lands of the Western shore,
To the new culminating man, to you, the empire new,
You promis'd long, we pledge, we dedicate.

You occult deep volitions,
You average spiritual manhood, purpose of all, pois'd on yourself, giving
*   not taking law,*
You womanhood divine, mistress and source of all, whence life and love
*   and aught that comes from life and love,*
You unseen moral essence of all the vast materials of America, (age upon
*   age working in death the same as life,)*
You that, sometimes known, oftener unknown, really shape and mould
*   the New World, adjusting it to Time and Space,*
You hidden national will lying in your abysms, conceal'd but ever alert,
You past and present purposes tenaciously pursued, maybe unconscious
*   of yourselves,*
Unswerv'd by all the passing errors, perturbations of the surface;
You vital, universal, deathless germs, beneath all creeds, arts, statutes,
*   literatures,*
Here build your homes for good, establish here, these areas entire, lands
*   of the Western shore,*
We pledge, we dedicate to you.

For man of you, your characteristic race,
Here may he hardy, sweet, gigantic grow, here tower proportionate to
*   Nature,*
Here climb the vast pure spaces unconfined, uncheck'd by wall or roof,
Here laugh with storm or sun, here joy, here patiently inure,
Here heed himself, unfold himself, (not others' formulas heed,) here fill
*   his time,*
To duly fall, to aid, unreck'd at last,
To disappear, to serve.

Thus on the northern coast,
In the echo of teamsters' calls and the clinking chains, and the
 music of choppers' axes,
The falling trunk and limbs, the crash, the muffled shriek, the
 groan,
Such words combined from the redwood-tree, as of voices ecstatic,
 ancient and rustling,
The century-lasting, unseen dryads, singing, withdrawing,
All their recesses of forests and mountains leaving,
From the Cascade range to the Wahsatch, or Idaho far, or Utah,
To the deities of the modern henceforth yielding,
The chorus and indications, the vistas of coming humanity, the
 settlements, features all,
In the Mendocino woods I caught.

　　　2
The flashing and golden pageant of California,
The sudden and gorgeous drama, the sunny and ample lands,
The long and varied stretch from Puget Sound to Colorado south,
Lands bathed in sweeter, rarer, healthier air, valleys and mountain
 cliffs,
The fields of Nature long prepared and fallow, the silent, cyclic
 chemistry,
The slow and steady ages plodding, the unoccupied surface ripening,
 the rich ores forming beneath;
At last the New arriving, assuming, taking possession,
A swarming and busy race settling and organizing everywhere,
Ships coming in from the whole round world, and going out to
 the whole world,

To India and China and Australia and the thousand island paradises
    of the Pacific,
Populous cities, the latest inventions, the steamers on the rivers,
    the railroads, with many a thrifty farm, with machinery,
And wool and wheat and the grape, and diggings of yellow gold.

   3
But more in you than these, lands of the Western shore,
(These but the means, the implements, the standing-ground,)
I see in you, certain to come, the promise of thousands of years,
    till now deferr'd,
Promis'd to be fulfill'd, our common kind, the race.

The new society at last, proportionate to Nature,
In man of you, more than your mountain peaks or stalwart trees
    imperial,
In woman more, far more, than all your gold or vines, or even
    vital air.

Fresh come, to a new world indeed, yet long prepared,
I see the genius of the modern, child of the real and ideal,
Clearing the ground for broad humanity, the true America, heir of
    the past so grand,
To build a grander future.

THE BIG TREES

J. M. HUTCHINGS

from SCENES OF WONDER AND CURIOSITY IN CALIFORNIA

*When English writer and editor J. M. Hutchings (1820–1902)
arrived in California in 1849, he intended to search for gold but
instead continued his career in letters, founding* Hutchings'
California Magazine *and writing travel books. One was*
Scenes of Wonder and Curiosity in California *(1870),
from which the following selection about one of the first
encounters between Europeans and the big trees is taken.*

*Hutchings first visited Yosemite in 1855, as a tourist. In
1863 he brought his wife to the Yosemite Valley and began operating a hotel. A few years later, he built a sawmill. Learning
that John Muir was a millwright as well as a botanist,
Hutchings gave Muir the job of installing the machinery and
running it.*

In the spring of 1852, Mr. A. T. Dowd, a hunter, was employed by
the Union Water Company of Murphy's Camp, Calaveras County,
to supply the workmen engaged in the construction of their canal
with fresh meat, from the large quantities of game running wild on
the upper portion of their works. Having wounded a bear, and

J. M. HUTCHINGS

while industriously following in pursuit, he suddenly came upon one of those immense trees that have since become so justly celebrated throughout the civilized world. All thoughts of hunting were absorbed and lost in the wonder and surprise inspired by the scene. "Surely," he mused, "this must be some curiously delusive dream!" But the great realities standing there before him were convincing proof, beyond a doubt, that they were no mere fanciful creations of his imagination.

When he returned to camp, and there related the wonders he had seen, his companions laughed at him and doubted his veracity, which previously they had considered to be very reliable. He affirmed his statement to be true, but they still thought it "too much of a story" to believe—thinking that he was trying to perpetrate upon them some first of April joke.

For a day or two he allowed the matter to rest—submitting with chuckling satisfaction to the occasional jocular allusions to "his big tree yarn," and continued his hunting as formerly. On the Sunday morning following, he went out early as usual, and returned in haste, evidently excited by some event. "Boys," he exclaimed, "I have killed the largest grizzly bear that I ever saw in my life. While I am getting a little something to eat, you make preparations to bring him in. All had better go that can possibly be spared, as their assistance will certainly be needed."

As the big tree story was now almost forgotten, or by common consent laid aside as a subject of conversation; and, moreover, as Sunday was a leisure day—and one that generally hangs the heaviest of the seven on those who are shut out from social intercourse with friends, as many, many Californians unfortunately are—the tidings were gladly welcomed; especially as the proposition was suggestive of a day's excitement.

Nothing loath, they were soon ready for the start. The camp was almost deserted. On, on they hurried, with Dowd as their

70

guide, through thickets and pine groves; crossing ridges and canyons, flats and ravines; each relating in turn the adventures experienced, or heard of from companions, with grizzly bears and other formidable tenants of the forests and wilds of the mountains; until their leader came to a dead halt at the foot of the tree he had seen and to them had related the size. Pointing to the immense trunk and lofty top, he cried out, "Boys, do you now believe my big tree story? That is the large grizzly I wanted to you see. Do you still think it a yarn?"

Thus convinced, their doubts were changed to amazement, and their conversation from bears to trees; afterward confessing that, although they had been caught by a ruse of their leader, they were abundantly rewarded by the gratifying sight they had witnessed; and as other trees were found equally as large, they became willing witnesses, not only to the entire truthfulness of Mr. Dowd's account, but also to the fact that, like the confession of a certain Persian queen concerning the wisdom of Solomon, "the half had not been told."

Mr. Lewis, one of the party above alluded to, after seeing these gigantic forest patriarchs, conceived the idea of removing the bark from one of the trees, and of taking it to the Atlantic states for exhibition, and invited Dowd to join him in the enterprise. This was declined; but, while Mr. Lewis was engaged in obtaining a suitable partner, someone from Murphy's Camp, to whom he had confided his intentions and made known his plans, took up a posse of men early the next morning to the spot described by Mr. Lewis, and, after locating a quarter section of land, immediately commenced the removal of the bark, after attempting to dissuade Lewis from the undertaking...

from AT HOME AND ABROAD

It was when Bayard Taylor (1825–1878) first began to write for the New York Tribune *that the paper's editor, Horace Greeley, charged him with the task of reporting on the California gold rush. The result, published in 1850 in book form as* Eldorado, *secured his literary reputation. He had earlier written a guidebook to Europe and subsequently wrote a number of other travelogues detailing impressions of Africa and the Orient.* At Home and Abroad, *from which this account of a trip to the redwoods is excerpted, was published in 1859. Taylor wrote prolifically in many genres, including fiction, poetry, and drama, and continued to write for the* Tribune *throughout his life.*

Like many writers after him, Taylor immediately thought of Genesis when he first saw the big trees: "There were giants in the earth in those days." Although this verse first referred to superhumans who lived on earth before the Flood, applying it to sequoias is not so strange in light of their age and immensity.

At Vallecitos (where we had dined the previous day, in the Valhalla of the Teutonic gods), we were but twenty miles from the grove of giant trees, in Calaveras County. This grove was one of the things which I had determined to see before setting out for California. I have a passion for trees, second only to that for beautiful human beings and sculpture. I rank arboriculture as one of the fine arts. I have studied it in all its various schools—the palms of Africa, the cypresses of Mexico, the banyans and pipals of India, the birches of Sweden, and the elms of New England. In my mind there is a gallery of masterpieces, which I should not be afraid to place beside those of the Vatican and the Louvre. Types of beauty and grace I had already—the Apollo, the Antinous, the Faun, even the Gladiator—but here were the Heraclidae, the Titans!

Besides, on the American continent, trees are our truest antiquities, retaining (as I shall show) the hieroglyphics, not only of Nature but of Man during the past ages. The shadows of two thousand years sleep under the boughs of Montezuma's cypresses at Chapultepec: the great tree of Oaxaca is a contemporary of Solomon, and even the sculptured ruins of Copan, Palenque, and Uxmal are outnumbered in years by the rings of trunks in the forests which hide them. In California, the only human relics of an earlier date than her present Indian tribes are those of a race anterior to the Deluge; but those giants of the Sierra Nevada have kept, for forty centuries, the annual record of their growth. As well think of going to Egypt without seeing the pyramids, as of visiting California without making a pilgrimage to her immemorial trees!

I procured a two-horse team, with driver, in Sonora, regardless of expense. Mr. E., whose labors were now drawing to a close, also accompanied us. We had but two days for the trip—in all, sixty miles of very rough mountain road—and therefore started with the first peep of dawn. As far as Vallecitos, our road was that which we had traversed in coming from San Andreas, crossing the great chasm of the Stanislaus. The driver, however, took another route to Columbia, leading through a still more terribly torn and gashed region, and approaching the town from the eastern side. Here were huge artificial chasms, over which the place seemed to hang, like Fribourg over its valley. The multitude of flumes, raised on lofty trestle-work, which crossed these gulfs; the large waterwheels; the zigzag sluices below; and the cart roads running on narrow planes of different elevation into the various branches of the mines, with distorted masses of primitive rock sticking up here and there, formed, altogether, a picture so vast and grotesque as to make us pause in astonishment. I remember nothing like it in any other part of the world.

We breakfasted at the Broadway Hotel and then hastened on, in order to reach Murphy's by noon. The gulf of the Stanislaus was crossed without accident, as it was rather too early for any other teams to be abroad on the road. The possibility of meeting another vehicle is the one great risk which haunts you during such transits. Near Vallecitos, while crossing one of the primitive bridges, our "off" horse got his leg into a hole, injuring it rather severely, though not so as to prevent his going on. The miners carry their ditches and sluices across a road just as they please, and in order to save a few planks, bridge them with rough logs and the branches of trees, interspersed with irregular boulders, to hold them. "When a stick is too crooked for anything else, they make a bridge of it," growled the driver, who threatened to tear up a fence or a flume, and would have done so, had not the bridge been mended on our return.

At Vallecitos, we left the road to San Andreas and took a trail leading eastward to Murphy's, an old mining camp, four or five miles distant. We passed through a succession of shallow valleys, which in spring must be lovely, with their scattered trees, their flowery meadows, and the green of their softly rounded, ridged hills. They were now too brown and dry—not golden with wild oats, like the Coast Mountains—but showing the dull line of the naked soil. In one of the broadest of these valleys lay Murphy's—a flourishing village until ten days previous, when it was swept away by fire. This was the *fourth* mining town destroyed during our visit! The cottage residences, standing alone in the midst of their gardens, escaped; but the business portion of the place, including the hotel, was utterly consumed.

The proprietors of the hotel, the Messrs. Perry, are also the owners of the big trees. They enjoy a wide reputation for their enterprise and the good fare wherewith they regale the traveler. They had already erected a shanty among the ruins, and promised us dinner while the horses were feeding. My wife was kindly received by Mrs. Perry, and I was overwhelmed with cordial invitations to stop and entertain the Murphyites—which, to my regret, was impossible. We had, in fact, a miraculous dinner—everything was good of its kind, and admirably cooked. What more can be said? The claret was supreme, and the pears which we purchased for dessert dissolved in inexpressible fragrance upon the tongue. The farmer from whom we procured them presented me with a watermelon, Mr. P. added some fresh meat for our supper at the forest hotel, and we went our way rejoicing.

In the outskirts of the village were encamped companies of newly arrived emigrants, among their shattered wagons and their weary cattle, and we met numbers of others on the way. From Luther's Pass at the head of Carson Valley, a trail turns southward, crosses the Sierra, and passing down the ridge above Silver Valley to the big trees, forms the most direct road from Carson River to the southern mines. These emigrants were now at the end of their toil and sufferings; but, instead of appearing rejoiced at the deliverance, their faces wore a hard and stern expression, with something of Indian shyness. The women, as if conscious that their sunbrowned faces and their uncombed hair were not particularly beautiful, generally turned their heads away as we passed. Dirty, dilapidated, and frowsy as many of them were, they all wore hoops! Yes, even seated in the wagons, on the way, their dusty calicoes were projected out over the whiffletrees [harness bars] by the battered and angular rims of what had once been circles! It was an exhibition of sacrifice to fashion, too melancholy for laughter.

The valley of Murphy's is two thousand feet above the sea and lies at the foot of those long, lateral ridges which connect the broken ranges called the foothills with the central ridge of the Sierra Nevada. The distance to the big trees is fifteen miles, with an additional ascent of twenty-five hundred feet. Immediately on leaving the village, we entered a close, wooded canyon, down the bottom of which rushed the water of a canal, as if in its natural bed. It was delightful to drive in the shade of the oaks and pines, with the clear waters of a roaring brook below us—*clear* water being the rarest sight in these mountains. Gaining the summit of the ridge, we drove for miles over an undulating, but rapidly ascending road, deep in dust and cut into disagreeable ruts by the wheels of emigrant wagons. Huge shafts of fir, arborvitae, and sugar pine arose on all sides, and the further we advanced the grander and more dense became the forest. Whenever we obtained an outlook, it revealed to us hills similarly covered; only now and then, in the hollows, were some intervals of open meadow. The ditch, coming from far up in the mountains, still kept beside us, sometimes carved in the steep side of the hill and sometimes carried across a valley on a wooden framework a hundred feet high.

The air perceptibly increased in coolness, clearness, and delicious purity. The trees now rose like colossal pillars, from four to eight feet in diameter and two hundred feet in height, without a crook or a flaw of any kind. There was no undergrowth, but the dry soil was hidden under a bed of short, golden fern, which blazed like fire where the sunshine struck it. We seemed to be traversing some vast columned hall, like that of Karnak, or the Thousand

Columns of Constantinople—except that human art never raised such matchless pillars. Our necks ached from the vertical travels of our eyes, in order to reach their tops. Really, the Western hyperbole of tall trees seemed true: that it takes two men to see them—one beginning where the other leaves off.

Our progress, from the ascent and the deep dust which concealed the ruts, was slow and would have been tedious, but for the inspiring majesty of the forest. But when four hours had passed and the sun was near his setting, we began to look out impatiently for some sign of the trees. The pines and arborvitae had become so large that it seemed as if nothing *could* be larger. As some great red shaft loomed duskily through the shadows, one and then another of us would exclaim, "There's one!"—only to convince ourselves, as we came nearer, that it was not. Yet, if such were the courtiers, what must the monarchs be? We shall certainly be disappointed: nothing can fulfill this promise. A thick underwood now appeared, radiant with the loveliest autumnal tints. The sprays of pink, purple, crimson, and pure gold flashed like sprinkles of colored fire amid the dark green shadows. "Let us not ask for more," said I, "nothing can be more beautiful."

Suddenly, in front of us, where the gloom was deepest, I saw a huge *something* behind the other trees, like the magnified shadow of one of them, thrown upon a dark red cloud. While I was straining my eyes in questioning wonder, the road made a sharp curve. Glancing forward, I beheld two great circular—shot towers? Not trees, surely!—but yes, by all the dryads, those are trees! Aye, open your mouth, my good driver, as if your two eyes were not sufficient, while we sit dumb behind you! What can one say? What think, except to doubt his senses? One sentence only comes to your mind: "There were giants in those days."

Between these two colossi, called the Sentinels, ran our road. In front, a hundred yards further, stood the pleasant white hotel, beside something dark, of nearly the same size. This something is only a piece of the trunk of another tree which has been felled, leaving its stump as the floor of a circular ballroom, twenty-seven feet in diameter. Dismounting at the door, we were kindly received by the doctor, and assured of good quarters for the night. The sun was just setting, and we were advised to defer the inspection of the grove until morning. Seating ourselves in the veranda, therefore, we proceeded to study the Sentinels, whose tops, *three hundred feet* in the air, were glowing in the golden luster, while the last beam had passed away from the forest below them.

To my astonishment, they did not appear so very large, after all! Large they were, certainly, but nothing remarkable. At first, I was puzzled by this phenomenon, but presently remembered that the slender saplings (apparently) behind them, were in themselves enormous trees. In dwarfing everything around, they had also dwarfed themselves. Like St. Peter's, the pyramids, and everything else which is at once colossal and symmetrical, the eye requires time to comprehend their dimensions. By repeatedly walking to them, pacing round their tremendous bases, examining the neighboring trees, and measuring their height by the same comparison, I succeeded in gradually increasing the impression. When the last gleam of twilight had gone and the full moon mounted above the forest, they grew in grandeur and awful height, until the stars seemed to twinkle as dewdrops on their topmost boughs. Then, indeed, they became older than the pyramids, more venerable than the trine idol of Elephanta, and the secrets of an irrecoverable past were breathed in the dull murmurs forced from them by the winds of night.

"Thank God that I have lived to see these works of his hand!" was the exclamation with which I turned away, reluctantly driven indoors by the keen, frosty air. Before a cheerful fire the doctor related to us the history of the discovery of the grove. When I was on the Mokelumne, in 1849, its existence was unknown. At the close of that year, some miners, prospecting high up in the mountains, are reported to have come upon some of the trees, and to have been laughed at and called hard names by their friends, on account of their incredible stories. In the spring of 1850, however, a company on a tour of prospecting, hunting, and general speculation happened to encamp in a valley about four miles distant. One of the men, pushing up the ridge alone, found himself at last in the midst of the monstrous grove. He was at first frightened (I can well imagine it), then doubtful, then certain. Returning to the camp, he said nothing about the trees, knowing that he would only be called a liar, but informed the leader of the party that he had found signs of gold, or of deer, higher up and offered to guide them. By this device he brought them all to the grove—and the story of the big trees soon afterward astonished the world.

But with discovery came also ruin. After the first astonishment was over came the suggestion of a speculative mind: "Can't some money be made out of this here thing?" A plan was soon formed. One of the biggest trees must be cut down, barked, and the pieces of bark numbered, so that when put together again in the same order, they would, externally, exactly represent the original tree. Take them to New York, London, Paris—and your fortune is made. How to get the tree down? was the next question. A mass of solid wood, *ninety feet* in circumference, was clearly beyond the powers of the ax. Where was the saw, or the arms to wield it, which could do the work? But the prospect of money sharpens the wits, and this difficulty was finally overcome. Pump augers were the thing! By piercing the trunk with a great number of horizontal bores, side by side, it might finally be cut asunder. Augers were therefore procured, and two sets of hands went to work.

After a steady labor of six weeks, the thing was done—but the tree stood unmoved! So straight and symmetrical was its growth, so

immense its weight, and so broad its base, that it seemed unconscious of its own annihilation, tossing its outer branches derisively
against the mountain winds that strove to overthrow it. A neighboring pine, of giant size, was then selected, and felled in such a
way as to fall with full force against it. The top shook a little, but
the shaft stood as before! Finally the spoilers succeeded in driving
thin wedges into the cut. Gradually, and with great labor, one side
of the tree was lifted; the line of equilibrium was driven nearer and
nearer to the edge of the base; the mighty mass poised for a
moment, and then, with a great rushing sigh in all its boughs, thundered down. The forest was ground to dust beneath it, and for a
mile around, the earth shook with the concussion.

Yet, perhaps, it is as well that *one* tree should be felled. The
prostrate trunk illustrates the age and bulk of these giants better
than those which stand. We learn from it that the wood was sound
and solid throughout; that the age of the tree was thirty-one hundred years; that it contained two hundred and fifty thousand feet of
timber, and that, a thousand years ago, the Indians built their fires
against its trunk, as they do now. The stump, as I said before, is the
floor of a ballroom; higher up (or, rather further off), is a bowling
alley. The pine trees, forming the forest around the house, though
apparently so small, average six feet in diameter and over two hundred in height.

Our quarters at the little hotel were all that could be desired.
Pure, ice-cold water, venison, delicious bread and butter, and clean
beds all combined to make us regret that our stay was so limited. At
daybreak the doctor summoned us, and we prepared for a stroll
through the grove before sunrise. The great trees, to the number of
ninety, are scattered through the pine forest, covering a space about
half a mile in length. A winding trail, ascending one side of the glen
and descending on the other, conducts to the principal trunks. They
have all received names, more or less appropriate. Near the house

is the "Beauty of the Forest," really a paragon of colossal elegance though comparatively young. Her age is probably not more than two thousand years.

How cool, and silent, and balmy was the stupendous forest, in the early morn! Through the open spaces we could see a few rosy bars of vapor far aloft, tinted by the coming sun, while the crimson and golden sprays of the undergrowth shone around us, like "morning upbreaking through the earth!" The dark red shafts soared aloft rather like the great, circular watchtowers of the Middle Ages than any result of vegetable growth. We wandered from tree to tree, overwhelmed with their bulk, for each one seemed more huge than the last. Our eyes could now comprehend their proportions. Even the driver, who at first said, "They're not so—*condemned* big, after all!" now walked along silently, occasionally pacing around a trunk, or putting his hand upon it, as if only such tangible proof could satisfy him.

We first visited the "Three Graces," then the "Miners' Cabins" and "Uncle Tom's Cabin." The two last are hollowed out at the bottom by Indian fires, which have burned themselves central chimneys far up the trunk. Either of them would give shelter to a family of moderate size. The next group bore the traces of fools. Some lovesick blockhead, visiting the grove in company with three ladies, one of whom looked coldly upon his suit, another sang, and another did something else, has fastened upon three of the trees marble tablets, inscribed severally, in letters of gold, "The Marble Heart,"(!) "The Nightingale," and "The Salem Witch." I said to the doctor: "Have you a ladder and a hammer about the house?" "Yes—why?" "Because if I were to remain here tonight, you would find those things smashed tomorrow morning." His furtive smile assured me that the search for the trespasser would not be very strict. Miss Avonia Jones, an actress who was there a short time previous, bestowed her own name upon a tree and likewise had a marble tablet prepared, regardless of expense. Fortunately the tablet happened to reach Murphy's, on its way to the grove, just before the fire and was destroyed. Fancy one of those grand and awful trees bearing the name of "Avonia Jones"! Even Senator Gwin, as I was informed, had his name cast on an iron plate and sent to the Mariposa Grove, to be placed on one of the largest trees. Oh! the pitiful vanity of our race!

At the top of the glen stands the "Mother of the Forest," ninety-three feet in circumference and three hundred and twenty-five feet high. Her bark, which has been stripped off to a height of one hundred and ten feet, now represents her in the Crystal Palace at Sydenham. This was wanton wickedness. She now stands blasted, stretching her bare, reproaching arms high over the forest. She forms part of what is called the "Family Group," numbering twenty-four trees. Here we commenced the return trail, and soon came upon the "Father of the Forest," which surpasses everything else by his tremendous bulk. He lies upon the earth, as he fell, centuries ago. His trunk is one hundred and ten feet in circumference at the base, and his original height is estimated to have been four hundred and fifty feet! In contemplating him, one almost refuses to credit the evidence of one's senses. By counting a few of the rings, and making a rough estimate, I satisfied myself that his age could not have been less than *five thousand years!* The interior of the trunk is burned out, forming a lofty, arched passage through which you walk for one hundred and eighty feet, and then emerge from a knothole! Not far off is another prostrate trunk, through which a man may ride on horseback for more than a hundred feet.

There are a variety of trees named after various states, also the "Old Maid" and "Old Bachelor," two lonely, leaning, dilapidated figures, and "Pike," a, tall, gaunt trunk, not so inappropriately named. The largest of all the living trees is called "Hercules," and is, if I mistake not, ninety-seven feet in circumference. I suggested that his name should properly be changed to "the Patriarch." Young trees, sprung from the seed, are seen here and there, but the soil seems insufficient to nourish many of them until the older race passes away. The doctor called my attention to a new and curious fact. In the earth, completely covered by the gradual deposits of centuries of falling leaves, are the trunks of the progenitors of these giants. The wood is almost black and has a dry, metallic sound. In one place a living tree, between two and three thousand years old, is found to be planted astride of another trunk, entirely hidden in the soil! It is evident that eight or perhaps ten thousand years have elapsed since this race of trees first appeared on the earth. One is bewildered by the reflections which such a discovery suggests.

During our walk, we watched the golden radiance of the sun as, first smiting the peaks of the scattered giants, it slowly descended, blazing over a hundred feet of their massive foliage before the tops of the enormous pines were touched. This illumination first gave us a true comprehension of their altitude. While sketching the Sentinel afterwards from the veranda, the laws of perspective furnished a new revelation. The hostess and my wife, standing together at the base of a tree, became the veriest dwarfs. Beyond them was what appeared to be a child's toy cart—in reality the wagon of an emigrant family, which had arrived the evening before! Some of the young "Pikes," expert with their rifles, brought down a few cone-bearing twigs, two of which the doctor presented to me, together with a large stick of timber and a piece of bark, four inches thick, of a golden brown color and with the softness and luster of velvet.

Botanists have now decided that these trees are akin to the California redwood, *Sequoia sempervirens,* and they will henceforth be known as the *Sequoia gigantea,* thereby settling the national quarrel as to whether they shall be called *washingtonia* or *wellingtonia.* It is singular that this discovery should not have been sooner made: a single glance at the cone is enough. It is very small, not one-fourth the size of a man's fist, containing a few thin, laminar seeds, something like those of a parsnip. As the tree will bear a degree of cold equal to zero, it may be successfully grown in the latitude of Washington. The growth is slow at first—so the gardeners in Sacramento and San Francisco inform me—but increases rapidly as the tree gains root.

Since the discovery of this grove, three others have been found, showing that the tree is not phenomenal in its appearance. One of these groves, near the headwaters of the Tuolomne, lies at an altitude of six thousand feet, and contains about four hundred trees, but few of which are thirty feet in diameter. The Mariposa trees, on the road to the Yosemite Valley, number about three hundred, one of which is said to be one hundred and two feet in circumference. Visitors are divided in opinion as to which grove is grandest and most impressive in its character. But he who would not be satisfied with the Calaveras trees is capable of preferring his own nondescript cottage to the Parthenon, and his own crooked legs to those of the Apollo Belvedere.

Taking a last look at these immemorial giants of the forest, as they stretched their tufted boughs silently in the sunshine over the heads of the vassal trees, we drove down the mountain through the aisles of pine and between the gemlike sprays of the thickets. In four hours we reached Murphy's, dined again luxuriously, and then sped away for Columbia, where my evening's work awaited me.

from "MAMMOTH TREE FROM CALIFORNIA"

In 1853, the tree that A. T. Dowd had discovered was felled by five men who, lacking a saw big enough for the task, spent twenty-two days drilling holes with long-handled pump augers. The rings were counted and it was found to be 1,244 years old—relatively young for such a large redwood.

In 1854, North Grove's largest sequoia, called the "Mother of the Forest," was stripped of its bark, which was eventually reassembled as the centerpiece of the Crystal Palace exhibition hall in New York City. In 1857 the exhibit was reassembled in England's Crystal Palace, where it remained on display for several years.

The tree at present on exhibition at the Crystal Palace was called the "Mother of the Forest" and was the largest perfect tree in the grove and contains far more timber than any other....

The bark was removed in sections by means of scaffolding around the tree, in the summer of 1854. The sections are eight feet in length, and the pieces vary in width from two to five feet. Four months were occupied in its removal from the tree, after which it was carefully boxed up and carted overland eighty miles to Stockton, whence it was shipped down the river to San Francisco, and thence on a clipper vessel around Cape Horn to New York, where it was exhibited during the past season at the Crystal Palace, and has now, after a journey of twenty thousand miles, found its home at the Crystal Palace at Sydenham, the only place in the world at all capable of exhibiting its magnificent proportions. Every piece was carefully marked and numbered at the time of its removal, so that it can be put up in precisely the same manner that it came from the tree. Over one hundred feet in height of the trunk has been erected in the North Transept, and gives one an exact idea of the tree as it stood in all its majesty upon its native mountains, such as no description of tongue or pen can convey....

What a stupendous monument raised by the hand of Almighty God is this? The oldest and largest living thing upon the earth; a tree that had beheld the glory and fall of Greece and Rome; the destruction of Jerusalem, of Babylon, and Palmyra; that saw the flight of Paris with Helen; that knew of the wanderings and trials of Ulysses; that had witnessed the incarnation, miraculous mission, crucifixion, and ascension of the Messiah; a tree that had

It is a comfort to know that the vandals who bored down with pump augers the largest of the Calaveras trees, in order to make their fortunes by exhibiting a section of its bark at the East, have been heavy losers by their villainous speculation.

HORACE GREELEY, AN OVERLAND JOURNEY

seen the conflicts and success, the defeats and triumphs of Christianity and freedom for ages; that watched the career of that mysterious person, the wandering Jew, for eighteen centuries; that saw the Hegira of Mahomet, the rise and glory of Herculaneum and Pompeii, and their final disappearance in a tomb of fire—could it not tell us of many mighty events now lost to the history of the world which can never be known? Think of it—this stately monarch of the forest and memorial of the past, fresh and vigorous even now, not a mark of decay upon trunk, limb or leaf, has been reserved until the nineteenth century, and a portion now removed to enable the world to look upon a monument coeval with the Deluge....

Its trunk is now blackened from a million fires that have been kindled by the children of two hundred generations, until, finally, modern innovation has dismantled its centurian garb to please the fastidious and curious in the midst of this great mart of commerce and civilization.

from "HUNTING BIG REDWOODS"

John Muir (1838–1914) was born in Scotland and grew up in Wisconsin under the stern care of Calvinist parents. He transformed a religious heritage of scrupulous conscience and piety into a passionate devotion to nature that combined scientific precision, poetic mysticism, and political activism. Though he started publishing relatively late in life, his literary output was enormous, ranging from essays and autobiography to poetry and political tracts. He founded the Sierra Club, established Yosemite as a nationally protected monument, and influenced several U.S. presidents to embrace environmental policies that saved countless acres of wilderness. From the time he first encountered them until his death, the Sierran sequoias were his most cherished botanical species.

Who of all the dwellers of the plains and prairies and fertile home forests of roundheaded oak and maple, hickory and elm ever dreamed that earth could bear such growths—trees that the familiar pines and firs seem to know nothing about, lonely, silent, serene, with a physiognomy almost godlike; and so old, thousands of them still living had already counted their years by tens of centuries when Columbus set sail from Spain and were in the vigor of youth or middle age when the star led the Chaldean sages to the infant Saviour's cradle! As far as man is concerned they are the same yesterday, today, and forever, emblems of permanence.

No description can give any adequate idea of their singular majesty, much less of their beauty. Excepting the sugar pine, most of their neighbors with pointed tops seem to be forever shouting Excelsior, while the big tree, though soaring above them all, seems satisfied, its rounded head, poised lightly as a cloud, giving no impression of trying to go higher. Only in youth does it show like other conifers a heavenward yearning, keenly aspiring with a long, quick-growing top. Indeed the whole tree for the first century or two, or until a hundred to a hundred and fifty feet high, is arrowhead in form, and, compared with the solemn rigidity of age, is as sensitive to the wind as a squirrel tail. The lower branches are gradually dropped as it grows older, and the upper ones thinned out until comparatively few are left. These, however, are developed to great size, divide again and again, and terminate in bossy, rounded masses of leafy branchlets, while the head becomes dome shaped. Then poised in fullness of strength and beauty, stern and solemn in mien, it glows with eager, enthusiastic life, quivering to the tip of every leaf and branch and far-reaching root, calm as a granite dome, the first to feel the touch of the rosy beams of the morning, the last to bid the sun good-night.

Perfect specimens, unhurt by running fires or lightning, are singularly regular and symmetrical in general form, though not at all conventional, showing infinite variety in sure unity and harmony of plan. The immensely strong, stately shafts, with rich purplish brown bark, are free of limbs for a hundred and fifty feet or so, though dense tufts of sprays occur here and there, producing an ornamental effect, while long parallel furrows give a fluted, columnar appearance. It shoots forth its limbs with equal boldness in every direction, showing no weather side. On the old trees the main branches are crooked and rugged, and strike rigidly outward, mostly at right angles, from the trunk, but there is always a certain measured restraint in their reach which keeps them within bounds. No other Sierra tree has foliage so densely massed or outline so finely, firmly drawn and so obediently subordinate to an ideal type....

The root system corresponds in magnitude with the other dimensions of the tree, forming a flat, far-reaching, spongy network two hundred feet or more in width without any taproot, and the instep is so grand and fine, so suggestive of endless strength, it is long ere the eye is released to look above it. The natural swell of the roots, though at first sight excessive, gives rise to buttresses no greater than are required for beauty as well as strength, as at once appears when you stand back far enough to see the whole tree in its true proportions. The fineness of the taper of the trunk is shown by its thickness at great heights—a diameter of ten feet at a height of two hundred being, as we have seen, not uncommon. Indeed the boles of but few trees hold their thickness as well as sequoia. Resolute, consummate, determined in form, always beheld with wondering admiration, the big tree always seems unfamiliar, standing alone, unrelated, with peculiar physiognomy, awfully solemn and earnest. Nevertheless, there is nothing alien in its looks....The sequoia, with all its strangeness, seems more at home than any of its neighbors, holding the best right to the ground as the oldest, strongest inhabitant. One soon becomes acquainted with new species of pine and fir and spruce as with friendly people, shaking their outstretched branches like shaking hands, and fondling their beautiful little ones; while the venerable aboriginal sequoia, ancient of other days, keeps you at a distance, taking no notice of you, speaking only to the winds, thinking only of the sky, looking as strange in aspect and behavior among the neighboring trees as would the mastodon or hairy elephant among the homely bears and deer....

The bark of full grown trees is from one to two feet thick, rich cinnamon brown, purplish on young trees and shady parts of the old, forming magnificent masses of color with the underbrush and beds of flowers. Toward the end of winter the trees themselves bloom while the snow is still eight or ten feet deep. The pistillate flowers are about three-eighths of an inch long, pale green, and grow in countless thousands on the ends of the sprays. The staminate are still more abundant, pale yellow, a fourth of an inch long; and when the golden pollen is ripe they color the whole tree and dust the air and the ground far and near.

The cones are bright grass green in color, about two and a half inches long, one and a half wide, and are made up of thirty or forty strong, closely packed, rhomboidal scales with four to eight seeds at the base of each. The seeds are extremely small and light, being only from an eighth to a fourth of an inch long and wide, including a filmy surrounding wing, which causes them to glint and waver in falling and enables the wind to carry them considerable distances from the tree.

The faint lisp of snowflakes as they alight is one of the smallest sounds mortals can hear. The sound of falling sequoia seeds, even when they happen to strike on flat leaves or flakes of bark, is about as faint. Very different is the bumping and thudding of the falling cones. Most of them are cut off by the Douglas squirrel and stored for the sake of the seeds, small as they are. In the calm Indian summer these busy harvesters with ivory sickles go to work early in the morning, as soon as breakfast is over, and nearly all day the ripe cones fall in a steady pattering, bumping shower. Unless harvested in this way, they discharge their seeds and remain on the trees for many years. In fruitful seasons the trees are fairly laden. On two small specimen branches, one and a half and two inches in diameter, I counted four hundred and eighty cones. No other California conifer produces nearly so many seeds, excepting perhaps its relative, the redwood of the Coast Mountains. Millions are ripened annually by a single tree, and the product of one of the main groves in a fruitful year would suffice to plant all the mountain ranges of the world.

The dense, tufted sprays make snug nesting places for birds, and in some of the loftiest, leafiest towers of verdure thousands of generations have been reared, the great, solemn trees shedding off flocks of merry singers every year from nests, like the flocks of winged seeds from the cones....

Little...is to be learned in confused, hurried tourist trips, spending only a poor noisy hour in a branded grove with a guide. You should go looking and listening alone on long walks through the wild forests and groves in all the seasons of the year. In the spring the winds are balmy and sweet, blowing up and down over great beds of chaparral and through the woods now rich in softening balsam and rosin and the scent of steaming earth. The sky is mostly sunshine, oftentimes tempered by magnificent clouds, the breath of the sea built up into new mountain ranges, warm during the day, cool at night, good flower-opening weather. The young cones of the big trees are showing in clusters, their flower time already past, and here and there you may see the sprouting of their tiny seeds of the previous autumn, taking their first feeble hold of the ground and unpacking their tender whorls of cotyledon leaves. Then you will naturally be led on to consider their wonderful growth up and up through the mountain weather, now buried in snow bent and crinkled, now straightening in summer sunshine like uncoiling ferns, shooting eagerly aloft in youth's joyful prime, and towering serene and satisfied through countless years of calm and storm, the greatest of plants and all but immortal....

In summer the days go by in almost constant brightness, cloudless sunshine pouring over the forest roof, while in the shady depths there is the subdued light of perpetual morning. The new leaves and cones are growing fast and make a grand show, seeds are ripening, young birds learning to fly, and myriads of insects glad as birds keep the air whirling, joy in every wingbeat, their humming and singing blending with the gentle ah-ing of the winds; while at evening every thicket and grove is enchanted by the tranquil chirping of the blessed hylas, the sweetest and most peaceful of sounds, telling the very heart-joy of earth as it rolls through the heavens.

In the autumn the sighing of the winds is softer than ever, the gentle ah-ah-ing filling the sky with a fine universal mist of music, the birds have little to say, and there is no appreciable stir or rustling among the trees save that caused by the harvesting squirrels. Most of the seeds are ripe and away, those of the trees mottling the sunny air, glinting, glancing through the midst of the merry insect people, rocks and trees, everything alike drenched in gold light, heaven's colors coming down to the meadows and groves, making every leaf a romance, air, earth, and water in peace beyond thought, the great brooding days opening and closing in divine psalms of color.

Winter comes suddenly, arrayed in storms, though to mountaineers silky streamers on the peaks and the tones of the wind give sufficient warning. You hear strange whisperings among the treetops, as if the giants were taking counsel together. One after another, nodding and swaying, calling and replying, spreads the news, until all with one accord break forth into glorious song, welcoming the first grand snowstorm of the year, and looming up in the dim clouds and snowdrifts like lighthouse towers in flying scud and spray. Studying the behavior of the giants from some friendly shelter, you will see that even in the glow of their wildest enthusiasm, when the storm roars loudest, they never lose their godlike composure, never toss their arms or bow or wave like the pines, but only slowly, solemnly nod and sway, standing erect, making no sign of strife, none of rest, neither in alliance nor at war with the winds, too calmly, unconsciously noble and strong to strive with or bid defiance to anything. Owing to the density of the leafy branchlets and great breadth of head the big tree carries a much heavier load of snow than any of its neighbors, and after a storm, when the sky clears, the laden trees are a glorious spectacle, worth any amount of cold camping to see. Every bossy limb and crown is solid white, and the immense height of the giants becomes visible as the eye travels the white steps of the colossal tower, each relieved by a mass of blue shadow.

In midwinter the forest depths are as fresh and pure as the crevasses and eaves of glaciers. Grouse, nuthatches, a few woodpeckers, and other hardy birds dwell in the groves all winter, and the squirrels may be seen every clear day frisking about, lively as ever, tunneling to their stores, never coming up empty mouthed, diving in the loose snow about as quickly as ducks in water, while storms and sunshine sing to each other.

One of the noblest and most beautiful of the late winter sights is the blossoming of the big tree like gigantic goldenrods and the sowing of their pollen over all the forest and the snow-covered ground—a most glorious view of Nature's immortal virility and flower-love.

One of my own best excursions among the sequoias was made in the autumn of 1875, when I explored the then unknown or little known sequoia region south of the Mariposa Grove for comprehensive views of the belt, and to learn what I could of the peculiar distribution of the species and its history in general. In particular I was anxious to try to find out whether it had ever been more widely distributed since the glacial period; what conditions favorable or otherwise were affecting it; what were its relations to climate, topography, soil, and the other trees growing with it, etc.;

and whether, as was generally supposed, the species was nearing extinction....

Nearly all my mountaineering has been done on foot, carrying as little as possible, depending on campfires for warmth, that so I might be light and free to go wherever my studies might lead. On this sequoia trip, which promised to be long, I was persuaded to take a small wild mule with me to carry provisions and a pair of blankets. The friendly owner of the animal, having noticed that I sometimes looked tired when I came down from the peaks to replenish my bread sack, assured me that his "little Brownie mule" was just what I wanted, tough as a knot, perfectly untirable, low and narrow, just right for squeezing through brush, able to climb like a chipmunk, jump from boulder to boulder like a wild sheep, and go anywhere a man could go. But tough as he was and accomplished as a climber, many a time in the course of our journey when he was jaded and hungry, wedged fast in rocks or struggling in chaparral like a fly in a spider web, his troubles were sad to see, and I wished he would leave me and find his way home alone.

We set out from Yosemite about the end of August, and our first camp was made in the well-known Mariposa Grove. Here and in the adjacent pine woods I spent nearly a week, carefully examining the boundaries of the grove for traces of its greater extension without finding any. Then I struck out into the majestic trackless forest to the southeastward, hoping to find new groves or traces of old ones in the dense silver fir and pine woods about the head of Big Creek, where soil and climate seemed most favorable to their growth, but not a single tree or old monument of any sort came to light until I climbed the high rock called Wamellow by the Indians.... Away toward the southwest, on the verge of the glowing horizon, I discovered the majestic domelike crowns of big trees towering high over all, singly and in close grove congregations. There is something wonderfully attractive in this king tree, even when beheld from afar, that draws us to it with indescribable enthusiasm; its superior height and massive, smoothly rounded outlines proclaiming its character in any company; and when one of the oldest attains full stature on some commanding ridge it seems the very god of the woods. I ran back to camp, packed Brownie, steered over the divide and down into the heart of the Fresno Grove. Then choosing a camp on the side of a brook where the grass was good, I made a cup of tea, and set off free among the brown giants, glorying in the abundance of new work about me....

The Fresno big trees covered an area of about four square miles, and while wandering about surveying the boundaries of the grove, anxious to see every tree, I came suddenly on a handsome log cabin, richly embowered and so fresh and unweathered it was still redolent of gum and balsam like a newly felled tree. Strolling forward, wondering who could have built it, I found an old, weary-eyed, speculative, gray-haired man on a bark stool by the door, reading a book. The discovery of his hermitage by a stranger seemed to surprise him, but when I explained that I was only a tree lover sauntering along the mountains to study sequoia, he bade me welcome, made me bring my mule down to a little slanting meadow before his door and camp with him, promising to show me his pet trees and many curious things bearing on my studies....

The name of my hermit friend is John A. Nelder, a fine, kind man, who in going into the woods has at last gone home; for he loves nature truly, and realizes that these last shadowy days with scarce a glint of gold in them are the best of all. Birds, squirrels, plants get loving, natural recognition, and delightful it was to see how sensitively he responds to the silent influences of the woods.... He led me to some noble ruins, remnants of gigantic trunks of trees that he supposed must have been larger than any now standing, and though they had lain on the damp ground exposed to fire and the weather for centuries, the wood was perfectly sound. Sequoia timber is not only beautiful in color, rose red when fresh, and as easily worked as pine, but it is almost absolutely unperishable. Build a house of big tree logs on granite and that house will last about as long as its foundation. Indeed fire seems to be the only agent that has any appreciable effect on it. From one of these ancient trunk remnants I cut a specimen of the wood, which neither in color, strength, nor soundness could be distinguished from specimens cut from living trees, although it had certainly lain on the damp forest floor for more than three hundred and eighty years, probably more than thrice as long. The time in this instance was determined as follows: when the tree from which the specimen was derived fell, it sunk itself into the ground, making a ditch about two hundred feet long and five or six feet deep; and in the middle of this ditch, where a part of the fallen trunk had been burned, a silver fir four feet in diameter and three hundred and eighty years old was growing, showing that the sequoia trunk had lain on the ground three hundred and eighty years plus the unknown time that it lay before the part whose place had been taken by the fir was burned out of the way, and that which had elapsed ere the seed from which the monumental fir sprang fell into the prepared soil and took root. Now because sequoia trunks are never wholly consumed in one forest fire and these fires recur only at considerable intervals, and because sequoia ditches, after being cleared, are often left unplanted for centuries, it becomes evident that the trunk remnant in question may have been on the ground a thousand years or more.

Similar vestiges are common, and together with the root bowls and long straight ditches of the fallen monarchs, throw a sure light back on the postglacial history of the species, bearing on its distribution. One of the most interesting features of this grove is the apparent ease and strength and comfortable independence in which the trees occupy their place in the general forest. Seedlings, saplings, young and middle-aged trees are grouped promisingly around the old patriarchs, betraying no sign of approach to extinction. On the contrary, all seem to be saying, "Everything is to our mind and we mean to live forever." But, sad to tell, a lumber company was building a large mill and flume nearby, assuring widespread destruction.

JOHN MUIR

YOSEMITE, EMERSON, AND THE SEQUOIAS

John Muir gave the following account of his 1871 meeting with the American philosopher Ralph Waldo Emerson in his after-dinner remarks when Harvard conferred an honorary master's degree on him in 1896. It was later published by William Frederic Badè in The Life and Letters of John Muir.

I was fortunate in meeting some of the choicest of your Harvard men, and at once recognized them as the best of God's nobles. Emerson, Agassiz, Gray—these men influenced me more than any others. Yes, the most of my years were spent on the wild side of the continent, invisible, in the forests and mountains. These men were the first to find me and hail me as a brother. First of all, and greatest of all, came Emerson. I was then living in Yosemite Valley as a convenient and grand vestibule of the Sierra from which I could make excursions into the adjacent mountains. I had not much money and was then running a mill that I had built to saw fallen timber for cottages.

When he came into the valley I heard the hotel people saying with solemn emphasis, "Emerson is here." I was excited as I had

never been excited before, and my heart throbbed as if an angel
direct from heaven had alighted on the Sierran rocks. But so great
was my awe and reverence, I did not dare to go to him or speak to
him. I hovered on the outside of the crowd of people that were
pressing forward to be introduced to him and shaking hands with
him. Then I heard that in three or four days he was going away, and
in the course of sheer desperation I wrote him a note and carried it
to his hotel telling him that El Capitan and Tissiack demanded him
to stay longer.

The next day he inquired for the writer and was directed to
the little sawmill. He came to the mill on horseback attended by
Mr. Thayer and inquired for me. I stepped out and said, "I am Mr.
Muir." "Then Mr. Muir must have brought his own letter," said Mr.
Thayer, and Emerson said, "Why did you not make yourself known
last evening? I should have been very glad to have seen you." Then
he dismounted and came into the mill. I had a study attached to the
gable of the mill, overhanging the stream, into which I invited him,
but it was not easy of access, being reached only by a series of sloping planks roughened by slats like a hen ladder; but he bravely
climbed up and I showed him my collection of plants and sketches
drawn from the surrounding mountains, which seemed to interest
him greatly, and he asked many questions, pumping uncon-
scionably.

He came again and again, and I saw him every day while he
remained in the valley, and on leaving I was invited to accompany
him as far as the Mariposa Grove of big trees. I said, "I'll go, Mr.
Emerson, if you will promise to camp with me in the grove. I'll
build a glorious campfire, and the great brown boles of the giant
sequoias will be most impressively lighted up, and the night will be
glorious." At this he became enthusiastic like a boy, his sweet perennial smile became still deeper and sweeter, and he said, "Yes, yes, we
will camp out, camp out"; and so next day we left Yosemite and

rode twenty-five miles through the Sierra forests, the noblest on the face of the earth, and he kept me talking all the time, but said little himself. The colossal silver firs, Douglas spruce, libocedrus [incense cedar] and sugar pine, the kings and priests of the conifers of the earth, filled him with awe and delight. When we stopped to eat luncheon he called on different members of the party to tell stories or recite poems etc., and spoke, as he reclined on the carpet of pine needles, of his student days at Harvard....

Early in the afternoon, when we reached Clark's Station, I was surprised to see the party dismount. And when I asked if we were not going up into the grove to camp they said, " No; it would never do to lie out in the night air. Mr. Emerson might take cold, and you know, Mr. Muir, that would be a dreadful thing." In vain I urged that only in homes and hotels were colds caught, that nobody ever was known to take cold camping in these woods, that there was not a single cough or sneeze in all the Sierra. Then I pictured the big climate-changing, inspiring fire I would make; praised the beauty and fragrance of sequoia flame; told how the great trees would stand about us transfigured in purple light, while the stars looked down between the great domes; ending by urging them to come on and make an immortal Emerson night of it. But the house habit was not to be overcome, nor the strange dread of pure night air, though it is only cooled day air with a little dew in it. So the carpet dust and unknowable reeks were preferred. And to think of this being a Boston choice. Sad commentary on culture and the glorious transcendentalism.

Accustomed to reach whatever place I started for, I was going up the mountain alone to camp, and wait the coming of the party next day. But since Emerson was so soon to vanish, I concluded to stop with him. He hardly spoke a word all evening, yet it was a great pleasure simply to be with him, warming in the light of his face as at a fire. In the morning we rode up the trail through a noble forest of pine and fir into the famous Mariposa Grove, and stayed an hour or two, mostly in ordinary tourist fashion—looking at the biggest giants, measuring them with a tape line, riding through prostrate fire-bored trunks, etc., though Mr. Emerson was alone occasionally, sauntering about as if under a spell. As we walked through a fine group, he quoted, "There were giants in those days," recognizing the antiquity of the race. To commemorate his visit, Mr. Galen Clark, the guardian of the grove, selected the finest of the unnamed trees and requested him to give it a name. He named it Samoset, after the New England sachem, as the best that occurred to him.

The poor bit of measured time was soon spent; and while the saddles were being adjusted I again urged Emerson to stay. "You are yourself a sequoia," I said. "Stop and get acquainted with your big brethren." But he was past his prime, and was now a child in the hands of his affectionate but sadly civilized friends, who seemed as full of old-fashioned conformity as of bold intellectual independence. It was the afternoon of the day and the afternoon of his life, and his course was now westward down all the mountains into the sunset. The party mounted and rode away in wondrous contentment, apparently, tracing the trail through ceanothus and dogwood bushes, around the bases of the big trees, up the slope of the sequoia basin, and over the divide. I followed to the edge of the grove. Emerson lingered in the rear of the train, and when he reached the top of the ridge, after all the rest of the party were over and out of sight, he turned his horse, took off his hat and waved me a last good-bye. I felt lonely, so sure had I been that Emerson of all men would be the quickest to see the mountains and sing them. Gazing awhile on the spot where he vanished, I sauntered back into the heart of the grove, made a bed of sequoia plumes and ferns by the side of the stream, gathered a store of firewood, and then walked about until sundown. The birds, robins, thrushes, warblers, etc., that had kept out of sight came about me, now that all was quiet, and made cheer. After sundown I built a great fire and as usual had it all to myself. And though lonesome for the first time in these forests, I quickly took heart again—the trees had not gone to Boston, nor the birds; and as I sat by the fire, Emerson was still with me in spirit, though I never again saw him in the flesh....

BURNETTE G. HASKELL

from "KAWEAH: HOW AND WHY THE COLONY DIED"

The utopian Kaweah Colony, founded in 1885 in eastern Tulare County, was led by Burnette G. Haskell and James J. Martin, activists from San Francisco. The colonists planned to establish a cooperative lumber company governed by the principles of Marxian socialism and using the labor-check, a system of currency based on units of work performed. In 1890 the Kaweah colonists lost all claims to their land when Congress established Sequoia National Park, and the community soon disbanded.

Burnette G. Haskell (1857–1907), born in Downieville, California, was a labor organizer and editor of the journal Truth, whose motto was "Truth is five cents a copy and dynamite is forty cents a pound." The Kaweah Colony came about as his politics moved from communist-anarchist toward the cooperativist ideas of Edward Bellamy. Here, he details the downfall of the utopian community in the sequoias.

When John Swinton, the Friend of the Poor, asked Karl Marx, the Man of Earthquakes, on the sands of Ramsgate: "What *is?*" Marx responded, *"Struggle."*

Kaweah Colony failed—but it struggled.

Those who had believed that they would be burglars of paradise, that they would reach upon this earth to the kingdom of heaven, have abandoned their purpose and are routed and disorganized, babbling many tongues. "And so the Lord scattered them abroad from thence upon the face of all the earth; and they left off to build the city."

The full history of the Tower of Babel may not be condensed within these limits, and perhaps also the time is not yet ripe for a thoroughly wise and critical survey of the whole experiment; yet some of the facts, heretofore concealed, now in honor should be stated, and even now lessons may be drawn from this tale of work and idleness, noble purpose and weakly practice, joy, faith, sorrow and disaster—all so human and so true—that may enlighten or warn, as well as interest the people of these United States. For this experiment was purposeful, and had it won it would have set its seal upon the future of this country, and perhaps its failure as well may count in some way as affecting the destiny of events....

Having been identified with Kaweah from the first, I know its plans and purpose and why and when and where it failed. It was one of the hopes of my life. And seeing it now, lying dead before me, knowing that its own hands assisted in strangling it, knowing that the guilt of its death rests upon nearly all of its members, myself far from being excepted, the faltering steel that cuts the epitaph chisels as well *"peccavi"* [I have sinned].

I look out the window of my mountain cabin and the sky is full of winter storm. I hardly know how to begin to tell you the story.

How the Colony Started

My attention was turned to the labor question in 1882. I participated in most of its phases until 1885, when, in company with a number of others who had also dipped into the study of political economy, we arrived at what was conceived to be a solution to the problem of poverty and wealth, the inequalities of destiny and fortune, and had found, we believed, a road to human happiness.

The labor movement is profoundly impressed with the spirit of the age. Whether it knows it or not, the bugle of evolution has given the guide to every file of its broadening and marching flank that is sweeping around the corner of the future on to the broad plains of coming democracy; and we, its dreamers, were but a skirmish line of the main body. Though swept away, there are divisions and divisions behind. If we fell from the ambush perhaps this salutation that we make to death may warn the next thin line of the rifle pits that bar this way and teach them another road to the open fields. We were not fit to survive, and we died. But there is no bribe money in our pockets, and beaten and ragged as we are, we are not ashamed.

We were of the opinion—as are two millions of American farmers and mechanics today—that the abolition of poverty, if accomplished, meant the happiness of the people. When answered that "human nature" itself was the gate that shut out heaven, we retorted, in our pride, that this selfish nature was but the product of conditions, and that when these were altered human disposition would change. We believed our species sufficiently civilized to change environment at once, readapt ourselves without delay to new forces and conquer the subtle spell of heredity in one generation.

But how where we going to abolish poverty? We were but a score or so, poorly equipped with money, but having clear-cut convictions that will bear the closest theoretical attack.

We knew that wealth was produced by the application of human labor to the raw material provided by nature. We had the labor; we must get the land; this to abolish the landlord tax on tools and soil. But we must, in inaugurating production, choose some product which from its natural scarcity would command a market; we must find a locality where this market was at our doors, otherwise our surplus labor would fall into the purse of the transportation lords; we must provide our own medium of exchange, so as to avoid the interest tax. We must work cooperatively to escape profit and to enforce the necessity and beauty of human brotherhood. Thus founded, our state, however small at first, would grow in strength and loveliness until all men should heed, and the whole world should follow our guidons [flags] in one resistless advance.

This was the purpose for which Kaweah was founded, and upon which it was carried out. It never was a private moneymaking scheme nor a mere project for creating individual homes but always had this quasi-public character. It was for propaganda, and not for pelf [riches], that it existed. I know that there are tales afloat of "fortunes gulled from the credulous public," and so forth, but these are idle and silly lies....

Honorable Erskine M. Ross, of the United States District Court, in the last case against the colonists (where the trustees were charged with obtaining money through the mails for their own profit) instructed the jury to acquit upon the grounds that the accounts of the colony showed a most marvelous economy, a perfectly honest administration, and a devotion and self-sacrifice unexampled in business affairs. For five years, three hundred men, women, and children were supported on an average of five dollars a month each. And this included clothes, tools, powder, books, music, schools, printing press, art and music lessons, and physical training. The trustees received thirty cents an hour; so did the sawyer at the mill. "Where was the chance for theft?" as Judge Ross asked. Yet that idiot's lie is still alive today....Summarizing finances, let me say this: from all sources the colony received in cash and material sixty thousand dollars. For this sum, for five years it supported three hundred people and built a road to the giant forest that the government engineers say now could not be built under the competitive system for less that three hundred thousand. There was not an opportunity for robbery. But there was no possible inclination. Why, we had with us men like Whittier, Thoreau, and Dana; we had Swinton, Grönlund, Buchanan, Owen, Vrooman, Debs....

The fates seemed to smile upon the enterprise at first. A location was found. On the Sierra slopes of the western borders of Tulare County, beneath the shadow of Mount Whitney, grew a vast body of timber, some of it of giant growth, but the largest portion of merchantable pine, fir, and redwood. It had been offered to the people by the United States for years, but remained unentered. The lumber monopolists of that section had surveyed and pronounced it "inaccessible," it being nearly two miles high, crowning an abrupt range to which it was believed impossible to build a road. But the great San Joaquin Valley needed this timber and would be its natural market. Its treeless plains were being made into orchard homes, and lumber was requisite as much as water for the soil. A vast population, ever growing, would during this generation occupy these plains and look to these forests for their natural wood supply. It could be teamed to the valley if but a road could be built. This forest lies at the headwaters of the North Fork of the Kaweah River.

Our people heard of it; some of them visited and surveyed and reported the facts; their eyes, sharpened by faith, had seen a way to build the road. The matter was discussed and at last decided. That road should be built to the forest if human labor could do it. We located the land—land which, remember, had been declared worthless and inaccessible—and filed our claims properly at the land office. Forty-three people went down from San Francisco to Visalia on the same day and made entries.

We purposed, after building our road, to produce lumber ourselves and to sell it to the farmers in the valley at cost. But having our own banking system, the time check, for which alone we intended to sell, we calculated that the very fact of our notes having a greater purchasing power for this staple article, lumber, would give them a premium over coin throughout the whole valley. The farmer having been taught thus their value would receive them thereafter for his labor and food, and through their use we planned that the people themselves should build a canal through the center of the valley along the San Joaquin to tide-water, owned by the ones who built it. This successfully accomplished, we hoped that the people would have learned from experience the way out from the exactions of monopoly, and that step would follow step until we should have established justice and abolished alike the tramp and the millionaire.

This was our plan. And while accomplishing it we meant to create amid the hills an ideal commonwealth, the Fraternal Republic, of which the world will always dream.

Visalia is a curious town, but probably not more so than any other country place. The advent of so many people filing upon "worthless" land aroused suspicion at once. The story went abroad that the Southern Pacific [railroad] was behind the move. A protest naturally went to Washington. The entries were suspended on mere suspicion and kept so for five years. But relying upon the faith of the government so often pledged to protect the actual settler, the little band went to work to make their road. They issued a pamphlet explaining their views, asking recruits and money. From first to last about five hundred others joined them, some from almost every state in the Union, and many from countries of Europe. This list of membership itself is a curious study. It is the United States in microcosm; among the members are old and young, rich and poor, wise and foolish, educated and ignorant, worker and professional man, united only by the common interest in Kaweah. There were temperance men and their opposites, churchmen and agnostics, Darwinists and Spiritualists, bad poets and good, musicians, free-thinkers, artists, prophets, and priests. There were dress-reform cranks and phonetic spelling fanatics, word purists and vegetarians. It was a mad, mad world, and being so small, its madness was the more visible; but in its delirium it did some noble work, and per-haps—perhaps it was not quite a failure after all.

Thus much generally of the people. Let me now speak of the location. The canyon of the North Fork is more than an ordinarily beautiful place. The climate is agreeable, the soil productive, the scenery exquisitely lovely. To follow the road up to the pines is to take a journey connected with which there is singular charm. Arriving at the summit of the pine ridge, one crosses into the for-est a saddle not wider than fifty yards, on each side of which is a sheer descent of thousands of feet; one slope is that of East Branch canyon, the other that of the Marble Fork, where its fourteen falls tumble in weird beauty to unmeasured chasms below. From here to the west one can look over the tops of mountains far out into the San Joaquin Valley; yes, on a clear day you can see the surf at Santa Cruz, white as a bosom unloosened from its bodice; to the east the glacial peaks of Tyndall and Whitney pierce the skies. You are above the clouds and can view the storms raging beneath you.

By a detour north of some miles over a rough and difficult trail one can cross the Marble Fork and enter upon the plateau whence rise the monster stems of the giant forest. This grove is of primeval grandeur; trees in diameter from eighteen to thirty-five feet, and in height from two to three hundred, and so many of them that the sense of their size is lost in their number. Throughout the forest one remarks a solemn silence, not almost but absolutely deathly in its quiet. It is a vast solitude without a sign of bird or animal life. Magnificent glades covered with rich grass, the sites of ancient lakes, are interspersed here and there, and in the center of each a bursting spring, from which wanders, like the Meander, a babbling brook.

Above and beyond the forest and the timber line are the forty Sierra lakes, unsounded and of amethyst hue, so deep are they, the sources of the rivers that drain their waters to the fertile Italian valley below.

Mountains of marble, quarries of lime, and mines of many metals were among the resources of the locality. They waited only for the hand of well-directed labor to make them sources of progress, wealth, and civilization....

The great majority of colonists, I am fully persuaded, joined Kaweah to escape the grind and worry of the outside world, to secure social advantages and harmonious surroundings, and to realize the ideal of a fraternal and happy life. That they failed to have these things is not their fault. The capitalist press used their banal reporter's English to stab us to death; the lumber monopoly of the San Joaquin went to Congress behind our back and made a park of the forest we had saved from flame. The machinery of the law was used to take us three hundred miles to meet charges in court without one single jot of evidence, while gigantic lumber thieves were looting the forests of Humboldt and the authorities winked their eye. We were poor. We were ignorant. We were jeered at. But no man dare say but we were honest.

At the time of the breaking up of the colony, the population was about one hundred and fifty. It had been as high as three hundred, and altogether probably four hundred of the members have at various times visited or resided upon the grounds....

Until December 1890 all of the houses were tents. The tent town of Advance was the home of the families from April 1887 until December 1889; the town of Kaweah, then established six miles farther down the canyon, was built of rough lumber and tenting combined. Some of the dwellings were mere hovels and some were furnished and decorated with considerable taste. William Christie, the treasurer, lived with his family in a tent that was open, top and sides, to wind and weather; many of the unmarried workers slept for months in the hay piled in an open barn.

Various attempts were made to organize a band and an orchestra, but the membership changed so often that nothing permanent resulted. A Sunday school and church existed for a while, but finally died. Literary and scientific classes were started but petered out from lack of interest. A "home circle" that met every Saturday night was often interesting, but finally ceased when the men folks went up to Atwell's to work. A series of "mothers' meetings" broke up through bickerings and want of something definite to do. Dances were occasionally had, though they met with strenuous opposition from a few who believed dancing a sin.

Instead of the fraternal, friendly feeling hoped for, one found Kaweah divided into factions and fractions of factions. Discussions about what Brown had to eat, and how Smith was pretending to be sick to escape work were met with, instead of an interest in literature and art. Miss Doe had been seen walking with Richard Roe, and Mrs. Poe quarreled with her husband; Master Brown had been ignored at the children's party and had no chance to speak his piece, and Miss Mary's poem had been rejected by the editor of the colony paper out of the merest jealousy.

It was a huge family, and everybody seemed to have the business of everybody else nearest his heart. Whenever the mail arrived, all crowded around the postmaster to see who had letters from whom and to wonder what they contained. People who had extra supplies bought with their private means brought them in closed boxes marked "furniture," and consumed them in secret for fear of adverse comment. As one said, "Why, here they snuff the smoke that comes from my chimney to see what I had for dinner." And yet really until the last six months there was no real lack of plain and wholesome food, and there was never any real suffering for the necessities of life.

The tendency to gossip appears to be inherent in human nature, and otherwise good people seem to take a delight in finding flaws in their neighbors. One really estimable lady wrote to the press that drunkenness prevailed at Kaweah, and when reproached with the misstatement, which arose from the drinking at a farmhouse of a glass of poor mountain wine, declared in defense that a "single drop intoxicates as much as a barrel." Scores of instances like this could be cited. Mr. Martin, the secretary, was accused over and over again, secretly, behind his back, with having "made thousands and thousands of dollars out of commissions on the purchase of supplies." As a matter of fact the Visalia merchants always gave us, on time, to help us out, cash discounts, and these were always taken in extra supplies. But though this lie was exposed over and over again, it was continually the subject of repetition and comment. In this and a hundred similar things gossip and tittle-tattle were almost unbearable. It was kick, kick, kick, until one longed again for the large city, where one's next-door neighbor is unknown.

These little pinpricks were of the things that killed the noble purpose and enthusiasm of the enterprise and slowly drained its life away.

Another hope of the colonists was that of educational facilities. And the opportunity existed for having the best. But removed from the restraints of the competitive world, parents and children alike were unable to distinguish between liberty and license. The schools established—common school, kindergarten, music classes, and art school—were colony enterprises, and would have succeeded had not every person had to have a finger in the pie. The teachers found it impossible to enforce discipline when a child, who deemed himself aggrieved, would in the class openly threaten that he would go home and get his father to call a meeting and remove the instructor. The boys and girls alike called the teachers by their first names, and came to school or not just as they pleased. Complaints made to the parents were of no avail whatever, corporeal punishment of children being a "relic of barbarism." One teacher was found objectionable because she would not permit religious songs to be sung in school, and two or three others were requested to resign for other frivolous reasons. Whenever anybody had a grievance they had only to "call a meeting" and the offensive pedagogue had to quit his desk and go back to the pick and shovel. The natural jealousy and envy of the man "who held down the soft job" came at once into play and the means were right at hand to carry out the leveling process.

I have no words except of praise for the women of Kaweah; the men did most of the gossiping, kicking, and loafing; the women were uniformly kind, cheerful, hardworking, and patient. They cooked, washed, baked, sewed, canned fruit, and on one notable occasion, when the mill camp was deserted by the men who went below "to attend a meeting," they fought a forest fire for twenty hours and by their heroic work, attested by burned and bleeding hands and faces, saved that glorious plateau for posterity.

An accomplished landscape artist worked for months at the washtub; a graduate of three conservatories of music did the cooking for days when there was a strike in the restaurant. Every year others picked and canned hundreds of pounds of fruit for the winter on shares from adjacent ranches. Others packed shingles, kept vegetable gardens, raised chickens, and set type in the printing office. I have seen a woman getting in firewood with an ax and bucksaw in plain sight of thirteen men gathered for six solid hours

around a stump excitedly discussing a rule of order improperly con-
strued at the last meeting.

Not All Misery and Meanness
But all has not been miserable and mean at Kaweah. There were
warm and noble friendships, sweet romances, times of firm faith
and courageous daring, laughter, pleasure, and weeks of perfect,
lovely peace. To see the crowds afield, with fingers stained with
wild grapes and arms full of fragrant flowers; to hear the merry
shouts of the bathers in the warm summer water of the river; to
gather in the open air on moonlit nights and listen to the orchestra
playing old, sweet tunes; to watch the fall of some toppling pine
beneath the flashing axes of our woodmen—these were joys to all
of us. And did we not cheer when brave Christie rode into the
foaming waters, rapidly risen, that had cut us off from the world,
on his desperate ride to Visalia for aid? There was, despite our
meannesses, a charm as of heaven around this place, and those who
went out still longed to come back and see the old scenes once
again. It is right to say also that our faults have been petty and
venial; among all here there has been no crime, no immorality, no
corruption.

But it was in the conduct of its political and business life that
Kaweah was more notably a failure. In the former its purpose was
in terms to put in practice the idea of social democracy, to found a
collective state ruled by no class but by the people. Officers were
elected by the majority and held office until removed by the power
that elected them. Meanwhile they were to be obeyed implicitly.
This was the theory, but it never was nor could be put in practice,
and for this reason, that no power existed to *compel* obedience.
Every member legally was an equal partner, and while theoretically
he was bound to obey his selected chief, practically he only did so

when he pleased. His officer had no power to compel obedience and no remedy against insubordination except his own resignation.

Every man who came here, with but few exceptions, came under the belief that his particular talents and abilities had not been properly recognized in the outside world; that a capitalist cabal or conspiracy there existed against him, and that here in Kaweah his merits would be instantly noted, and that he would at once assume his natural position as a leader of affairs. And if such recognition were not quickly made he assumed that the "corrupt influence of capitalism" had pursued him here, and that he was still a "victim." Then he went to the general meeting for redress and generally got it, with power to act, until he, in turn, was pulled down through the same process by another. This general meeting, which assembled monthly, assumed like the Athenian popular assemblies, to deal with *details,* and it made confusion worse confounded. Members drew pay while attending it, and at one time it lasted four days at a stretch. Generally what one month's meeting ordered the next would rescind. Under its domination we suffered from all the evils of popular assemblages such as we read of in the books. We had not believed what we read; now we knew they did not tell the half of it.

Too Many "Average" Men
In the outside world all of us had been mere citizens not charged with the management of affairs; here we were the state and running the machine ourselves. The conditions were entirely novel. To have managed them successfully we should have had a good supply of Caesars, Cromwells, and Jeffersons; instead, we had the average man. The result was absolute anarchy tempered by occasional streaks of despotism. Of all the leaders, H. T. Taylor was the only one whose gifts fitted him at all to cope with the situation, and so long as he directed the material work, it went on in a fairly successful way. When, after the road was finished, he tired of the bickering

and resigned as general superintendent, absolutely unable to bear the burden longer, the ship was rudderless and went adrift.

I remember that when objectors used to urge that at Kaweah there would be laziness, we used to answer that such was impossible because every man was an equal partner working for himself; and of course partners would not "soldier" upon each other. But they did. Not all of them by any manner of means. But there were enough lazy men to aggravate and discourage the good ones; and many of them used to loaf with their mouths full of phrases about "living upon the spiritual plane and loving your brother."

A ditch was surveyed and built, and then the water would not run in it; a planing-mill foundation was dug out of solid granite where power could not be got to the machines; trees and vines were planted out and left without water and died; and any amount of other useless and foolish work was done, every bit of it the result of a varied, vacillating, and truly democratic system of direction. Three different bookkeepers had three different systems of entry of their own, and as one succeeded the other in power, the books under their control would give points to the wisest advocate of "the old, corrupt capitalist system of double entry." There was a time, too, when even the women were affected; they cut off their skirts, made leggings of them, and called it "dress reform." But the men laughed this fad down, from jealousy, and thereafter secured the monopoly of original "progressive" ideas to themselves.

In June 1890 a small mill was put at the end of the road, and the cutting of lumber for actual business necessities began. A total of about twenty thousand feet (at ten dollars per thousand) was cut during a three months' run with a mill whose capacity was three thousand feet a day; the actual cut averaged one hundred and ninety-three feet per day—less than a tenth of what ought to be done—and this mill was not run shorthanded. It is true that most of the time it did not run; that the loggers were inexpert; that the mill was small and old; that picnics had to be organized; that the men had to come down for "general meeting"; that this foreman was bad and that foreman was worse; that the timber was small; that the oxen were lame; and a hundred other reasons; but the fact remains that results were not attained as they are in the competitive world.

The Beginning of the End

At this juncture the United States government unwisely, unjustly, and meanly stepped in, reserved the locality for a park and arrested the trustees for cutting timber on alleged government land. The agents of Uncle Sam could not see the monster lumber thieves in every other canyon of the Sierra, but they could see us who, in good faith, were trying to do honest work upon what we believed to be ours in equity, and is today ours in law.

A long and expensive trial, ending in conviction on a technical point and continuing until May 1891, was the result. The trustees were sentenced to fine or imprisonment and appealed, which appeal was dismissed in 1900, and the trustees then "pardoned" by President McKinley.

Thereafter at Atwell's Mill the colony leased some timber land and began a struggle for mere existence. Although this mill was on patented land, the government tried also to interfere here, and once closed down the mill with troops. This was a persecution that they were finally forced to reconsider, and the cavalry was withdrawn. But we were now starving. We had lost our nerve and our grit.

The last of June 1891, noting the same vacillation and want of method and results as had occurred before obtaining the Atwell lease, the trustees issued to the resident members an imploring circular, urging the workers to more active and persistent effort at the mill, and begging the nonworkers to keep from picnics and other action that impeded the work. But this appeal had no permanent effect except to arouse antagonism. Work still continued in the same desultory fashion until the last of July, when Taylor was sent up to the mill. While there, he discovered by a survey that the force had, with the willful carelessness of children, cut over their line on to government land, thus again exposing the trustees to arrest and prison, and more than this, that they had concealed from the trustees the fact of having done so. This was more than they could bear, and all of them, except Mr. Martin, at once resigned. At the November meeting a report of the season's work at Atwell's—five months—showed that instead of cutting 2.5 million feet, as a private enterprise with driven men would easily have done, Kaweah had cut only one-tenth of that; instead of its being produced for ten dollars a thousand or less, it had cost from eighteen to twenty dollars, and it was sold for ten dollars! Comment is superfluous, and whatever excuses may be made, the business failure is flat.

The Colony Dissolved
In October 1891 upon the recommendation of the new treasurer, A. M. White, in his final report, the facts were notified to the world and proceedings taken to dissolve the colony.

The enterprise is a dreary failure, and so must we conclude from its history will be any other similar attempt at present at productive cooperation. Distributive cooperation has over and over again proved a success, but productive never yet, and I think that this history shows the reason why. Under the competitive system men produce because they must work to the highest pitch or starve, and they are under competent leadership. Under the cooperative there is no such prodding incentive to toil, no probability of such leadership, and men are not yet civilized enough to do right for right's sake alone and to labor for the love of production itself.

A few more than half of the resident members at the November meeting, 1891, abolished the time checks, took possession of the machinery and land of the colony, repudiated the credits of the old workers, and decided to continue the struggle as a small enterprise under the absolute power of one man. It is needless to say now (1902) that this attempt was as well a failure. They hoped to make a living here as small farmers thus cooperating. Whether this plan would have succeeded cuts no figure whatever with this history. We can leave them quarreling over the little property left, as we leave coyotes quarreling over a carcass.

One duty only remains to those whose hearts were with Kaweah as a cooperative experiment; it is to let the truth be known.

And is there no remedy, then, for the evils that oppress the poor? And is there no surety that the day is coming when justice and right shall reign on earth? I do not know; but I believe, and I hope, and I trust.

THE COAST REDWOODS

L. K. WOOD

from LURE OF HUMBOLDT
BAY REGION

At about the time that A. T. Dowd found the big trees of the
Sierra, European Americans were also finding their way to the
northern California coast. In 1849, L. K. Wood was part of a
group that traveled west from the Trinity River to find
Humboldt Bay. The following selection recounts their arduous
passage through the immense trees, dense shadows, and fallen
logs of the redwood forest.

Wood is better known for an expedition that took place
the following year. In 1850, the Josiah Gregg party set out to
find a route from the Trinity gold fields to San Francisco. After
a dispute over which route to take, Wood and four others
headed south. When they came to what is now called Salmon
Creek in Humboldt Redwoods State Park, they found a group
of eight grizzly bears. They began shooting and two of the
bears attacked them. Wood was mauled by the bears but managed, with the rest of the group, to get to the Mark West
Ranch near Sonoma, where he recovered.

The month of October 1849 found me on Trinity River, at a point now called Rich Bar. How I came there and from whence, over what route, by what conveyance, or for what object, it matters not; suffice it to say that I was there, and that too, without provisions, poorly clad, and, worse than all, in this condition at the commencement of a California winter. The company at this place numbered some forty persons, the most of whom were in much the same situation and condition as myself. Near this bar was an Indian ranch, from which, during the prevalence of the rain that was now pouring down as if in contemplation of a second flood, we received frequent visits. From them we learned that the ocean was distant from this place not more than eight days' travel, and that there was a large and beautiful bay, surrounded by fine and extensive prairie lands.

The rainy season having now to all appearances set in, alternate rain and snow continually falling—a scanty supply of provisions for the number of persons now here, and scarcely a probability of the stock being replenished before the rains should cease—the idea was conceived of undertaking an expedition with the view to ascertaining whether the bay of which the Indians had given a description, in reality existed....

The day of departure arrived, but with it came no change in the weather, save an occasional change from rain to snow. Many of the party now began to exhibit marked symptoms of a desire to withdraw and abandon the expedition. The two Indian guides refused to go, assigning as a reason that the great storm we had experienced on the river had been a continuous snowstorm in the mountains, and that the depth of the snow would present an insuperable barrier to our progress, and endanger the safety of the whole party to attempt the passage. This was sufficient for those who had manifested a desire to withdraw; and the number of the company was speedily reduced to eight men, including the captain, whose determination was only the more fixed because so large a number had abandoned the expedition....

Owing to this great diminution in the number of the party, it became necessary before setting out to examine the condition of our commissary department—from which it was ascertained that the stock of provisions had suffered even greater diminution than had the company in point of numbers. The articles found were flour, pork, and beans, and of these scarcely sufficient for ten days' rations. Notwithstanding this, an advance was determined upon, and accordingly, we broke up camp. Here commenced an expedition, the marked and prominent features of which were constant and unmitigated toil, hardship, privation, and suffering. Before us, stretching as far as the eye could reach, lay mountains, high and rugged, deep valleys, and difficult canyons, now filled with water by the recent heavy rains....

Nothing beyond the ordinary routine of constant traveling by day, and stretching our wearied limbs upon the snow or cold, wet ground by night, occurred during the succeeding four days worthy of notice.

Toward the evening of the next day, while passing over a sterile, rugged country, we heard what appeared to be the rolling and breaking of the surf upon the distant seashore, or the roaring of some waterfall. A halt was therefore determined upon, and we resolved to ascertain the cause of this before proceeding further and here pitched our camp.

Early the next morning Mr. Buck left camp alone, for the purpose above expressed, and before night returned bringing with him a quantity of sand which from its appearance, as well as that of the place where it was gathered, he thought indicated the presence of gold; but not being on a gold-hunting expedition, we thought it the better discretion to use all possible dispatch in reaching the coast. The result of his search was that he found a stream at the foot of a rugged descent whose now swollen waters rushed with terrific speed and violence. This, then, was what we heard. The gleam of hope that for the moment animated us was soon dispelled. This stream is the South Fork of Trinity.

Having ascertained that it was impossible to effect a crossing at or near this place, we continued on down, keeping as near it as was possible, until we came to its junction with the Trinity River.

Here we succeeded in crossing. Upon gaining the opposite shore, we had a steep bank to ascend. As we reached the top of this bank, we came suddenly upon an Indian rancheria....It had been our intention to follow the river down, although its course, being from this point northwest, was not in the direction we desired to take. Against this, however, the Indians cautioned us, asserting that there were numerous tribes scattered along the river to its mouth who would certainly oppose our passing through their country; besides, on being made to understand the object we had in view, they informed us that our best route, both in point of distance and on account of the Indians, was to leave the river and strike westward.

This advice we, upon the whole, thought the most prudent to follow, and accordingly commenced the ascent of the mountain that now lay in our path.

The night of the second day after leaving the river, having pitched our camp, we set about preparing a supper. I would not consume the time in detailing so minutely these unimportant items, but a portion of the material of that night's meal, although a morsel delicate and palatable in comparison with some of which we partook later in our journey, and it being the first time within my experience where necessity had reduced me to a like extremity, it made an impression upon my mind which today is as fresh as if it occurred but yesterday. Our stock of flour was exhausted; the almost continual rain, however, had so saturated our entire camp equipment, the flour among the rest, that there had formed, on the inner surface of the sacks in which it had been carried, a kind of paste which the dampness had soured and moulded.

This paste was carefully peeled off, softened with water, and equally divided among the party—when each one, after the same had been submitted to a process of hardening before the fire, devoured his portion with an avidity that would have astonished and shocked mortals with appetites more delicate than ours. Nothing now remained of the stock of provisions that constituted our outfit—flour, pork, beans—all were gone. The night of the 13th of November we were compelled to retire to our blankets supperless. Our animals, however, had been without feed for the previous two days but now were luxuriating in fine grass, which fact tended to render our situation the more supportable, for the preservation of our animals, next to food for ourselves, was of the highest importance, because upon them we depended for the packing of our blankets and provisions, when fortunate to find any of the latter....

In the morning all the party, save a guard for the camp, started out in search of food, and after a short hunt succeeded in killing several deer. A quantity of venison steak, broiled or cooked in the ashes, soon appeased the extreme hunger from which we were suffering. Here we remained several days for the purpose of recovering our nearly exhausted strength. During our stay at this place, we cured a quantity of venison with which, upon resuming our journey, we packed the animals and proceeded on foot ourselves, thinking that by so doing we could certainly take sufficient to last, if not until we should get through, at least until more should be obtained. But no; on we toiled, faithfully and constantly, until the last of the venison was consumed, and the first, and second, and third day of fasting came and passed.

During all this time our animals suffered intensely from want of food. The only kind that could be obtained for them was leaves, and in places even these could be procured only by cutting down trees. Two of them, however, were too far reduced to go further, and we were compelled to leave them behind.

Again we had the good fortune to reach a piece of mountain prairie where we found an abundance of game for ourselves and plenty of grass for the animals. At this place we remained three days, collecting and preparing meat for use while traveling. We had now two animals less in number, and consequently were obliged to increase the loads of those remaining in order to pack sufficient to keep soul and body together for a reasonable length of time, for when we left one camping place, when or where another would be found was of course uncertain, and to pack our provisions ourselves was a thing out of the question in our present condition.

Having prepared as large a quantity of meat as our animals could carry, on we went. Disappointment seemed to be our constant companion. Without following us day after day in our zigzag course and detailing the occurrences that transpired, suffice it to say ten days passed away without our being favored with the sight of any living thing that could be made available or useful for food. Again our stock of provisions was exhausted. For several days we subsisted upon a species of nut resembling the acorn, but far more bitter and unpalatable. The only way they could be used was by roasting them in the fire until crisped and dry. A dose of these was found to be from six to ten, and to be taken every fifteen minutes—a larger dose or oftener was sure to operate as an emetic. Our drink was, for the greater part of the time, a tea made of yerba buena—an herb resembling mint. It seemed that each scene of toil and suffering which we had been compelled to undergo after leaving these recruiting places—that were to us like oases to the traveler across the sandy desert—was but the prelude to another of a worse and more trying character. Not one was without its quota of hardship, privation, and almost starvation. At length we reached another opening in this world-wide forest, and without first selecting a camping place, as was usual with us, we hastened to search for food. We ascended a rocky eminence that overlooked the country for a considerable distance around. Upon gaining the summit one of the most attractive and inviting scenes opened to our view. To us it was unquestionably more interesting from the fact that we were laboring under the not very agreeable sensations produced by two days and a half's total abstinence from food. On one side were feeding little knots of deer, on another and nearer to us was a large herd of elk, and still in another direction both were to be seen. After a few moments' consultation we determined to attack the elk and accordingly separated in order to approach them from opposite directions.

Scarcely a half-hour had elapsed before I heard the report of a rifle and two more in quick succession. From the direction I supposed it to be Van Duzen, and from the rapid succession in which the shots were fired, I was fearful that some danger had befallen him and immediately hastened to his assistance. I shall not soon forget the scene that was here presented to me. There stood Van Duzen reloading his rifle; nearby lay three grizzly bears, two dead and the third with his back broken. Two others stood near by, grinning and snarling in a most unamiable manner, looking first upon their fallen companions and then upon us. As this was my first introduction to Bruin, and the meeting being so sudden and unexpected, I hesitated a moment whether to approach and become better acquainted or remain a spectator. There was a certain something in their appearance that involuntarily brought to mind the many tales I had heard related of their ferocity when disturbed and, particularly, when wounded. I, however, concluded to venture a shot at one of them, and with that intention advanced toward them. Van Duzen, perceiving this, called on me to stop, fearing that we might get into trouble. Heedless of this caution, I approached slowly, intently watching their movements, until within fifteen steps of one of them, when I stopped and fired. The shot was a fatal one—the shaggy monster fell, with a howl, dead upon the ground. At the same moment Wilson, whom the frequent firing had likewise attracted to the spot, set a ball through the heart of the remaining bear with a similar result. This you will say was pretty good shooting, to kill five grizzly bears with as many shots out of one band. But it is nevertheless true. As for myself, I can say without boasting— although it was my first experience in hunting this kind of game, and although I was conscious of the fact that should my shot fail to be a fatal one, the bear would in all probability be upon me before I could get ten steps from where I stood—that I felt indifferent to danger. Our situation had become so desperate, the conviction fast settling upon our minds that each day passed in the mountains lessened the probability of reaching any settlement in safety, that recklessness and indifference had become second nature with me.

Our attention having been so completely engrossed in the encounter with the grizzlies, the herd of elk were forgotten, and we lost the opportunity of getting any of them. However, before night we succeeded in bringing several deer into camp. At this place we remained five days, feasting and fattening on bear meat, and preparing venison for future use.

Our progress up to this time had been very slow. The distance traveled per day did not exceed an average of seven miles. The appearance of the country now seemed to change—the mountain ridges were less high and abrupt than those over which we had passed, but much more densely covered with timber. Our belief now was that twelve miles' further travel would bring us, if not to the coast, at least to a more level country where our advance would be more rapid and attended with less difficulty and suffering. We therefore resumed our journey with lighter hearts and more buoyant hopes.

Our calculation of the distance to the coast or valley subsequently proved to be not far from correct. The redwood forests, however, through which we had to pass were more dense and difficult to penetrate than any before; consequently our progress was in proportion retarded. Dr. Gregg frequently expressed a desire to measure the circumference of some of these giants of the forest, and occasionally called upon some one of us to assist him. Not being in the most amiable state of mind and feeling at this time, and having neither ambition to gratify nor desire to enlighten the curious world, we not infrequently answered his calls with shameful abuse. His obstinate perseverance, however, in one or two instances, resulted in success. One redwood tree was measured whose diameter was found to be twenty-two feet, and it was no unusual thing to find these trees reaching the enormous height of three hundred feet. This may excite incredulity abroad, but trees have since been found in the redwood forest of much greater dimensions.

Through this forest we could not travel to exceed two miles a day. The reason of this was the immense quantity of fallen timber that lay upon the ground in every conceivable shape and direction, and in very many instances one piled upon another so that the only alternative left us was literally to cut our way through. To go around them was often as impossible as to go over them. We were obliged, therefore, constantly to keep two men ahead with axes, who, as occasion required, would chop into and slab off sufficient wood to construct a sort of platform by means of which the animals were driven upon the log and forced to jump off on the opposite side. There was not the least sign indicative of the presence of any of the animal creation; indeed, it was almost as impenetrable for them as for us, and doubtless was never resorted to save for purposes of shelter.

On the evening of the third day from our bear camp, as we called it, our ears were greeted with the welcome sound of the surf rolling and beating upon the seashore. There was no doubt or mistake about it this time. The lofty tops caught the sound, which the deep stillness of a night in a forest rendered the more plainly audible, and echoed back to our attentive ears....

At an early hour in the morning we resumed our journey with renewed spirits and courage. For three long days did we toil in these redwoods. Exhaustion and almost starvation had reduced the animals to the last extremity. Three had just died, and the remainder were so much weakened and reduced that it constituted no small part of our labor and annoyance in assisting them to get up when they had fallen, which happened every time they were unfortunate enough to stumble against the smallest obstacle that lay in their path, and not one single effort would they make to recover their feet until that assistance came. At length we issued from this dismal forest prison, in which we had so long been shut up, into the open country, and at the same instant in full view of that vast world of water—the Pacific Ocean. Never shall I forget the thrill of joy and delight that animated me as I stood upon the sandy barrier that bounds and restrains those mighty waters.

NINETTA EAMES

from "STAGING IN THE MENDOCINO REDWOODS"

Ninetta Eames, the aunt and guardian of Jack London's second wife, Charmian, was also editor of Overland Monthly *and, for a time, Jack London's literary agent. Amid the picturesque details of "Staging in the Mendocino Woods," one of many articles she wrote for* Overland Monthly *in the period from 1887 to 1900, she describes some of the elaborate measures that had been developed by lumber companies in a period of less than fifty years to exploit coastal resources.*

Seven miles south of Mendocino City, we crossed the Albion River, a pretty stream averaging a width of a hundred yards for a mile or two up its abrupt, wooded banks. The immediate coastline is bare of trees, its sharply indented wall bordered for miles by outlying rocks. In the shoal ground off the south point of the little harbor is Pinnacle Rock, standing in range of the smokestack of the sawmill. In the throat of the inner cove, Mooring Rock is seen, girdled by a rusty mooring chain. Vessels of ninety tons burden, and drawing six and a half feet of water, are loading off the mill wharf, while lighters are used for transferring freight to large schooners lying at

Mooring Rock. The forests accessible to Albion Cove are almost exhausted, and the quaint old mill stands in a wasteful disorder of logs and lumber.

We passed stock ranches next the bluffs, with dwarf pines straggled about. The low hills on the east were blotched with burnt stumps, indicating the one-time existence of vast numbers of trees. There was no longer a lavish outspread of flowers, though many painted blooms still nodded to us behind the moss-grown rails of the fences. The handsomest of these, and for that matter the most beautiful flower we had yet seen, was the *Rhododendron californicum,* which is said not to grow farther south than Mendocino. The people hereabout call them "wild oleanders." The flaring, roseate blossoms form compact clusters on the branchlets of a large evergreen shrub whose peculiar habitat is the well-drained peat of these bench lands.

The country grew more hilly as we journeyed north and was frequently cut through by gorges dark with pine and redwood, or canyons whose streams dance to the sea under the lightsome foliage of alders or spicy nutmeg trees and lithe-limbed spruce. In many localities the soil is rich and friable, presenting to the eye a varied landscape of billowy pasture lands alternating with squares of plowed patches and fields of waving oats....

A mile below Little River Harbor is Stillwell Point, a bold cliff two hundred feet high. Soon after passing this conspicuous landmark we sighted the pretty town of Little River. When our horses came to a slow climb, we took advantage of the lull to question the driver and learned that the lumber industry here is reduced to the shipping of ties. The sawmill was silent, the swampy boom gorged with whitening logs, and the yards stacked with discolored lumber and the debris of past milling. A number of coasting schooners have been built here and brought out at high water....

From the tableland lying between Little River and Mendocino Bay one has the first glimpse of Mendocino City, the oldest and most picturesque of all the coast towns. It occupies the rolling bench on the north side of the ragged curve of the bay. Viewed from a distance on shore or at sea, the city seems to have an imposing array of cupolas, which are in reality water tanks, with windmills of every known pattern. There is in fact an individuality about the waterworks of this town not found in any other place of its size. Every family or group of families has its separate well and windmill, thus obviating the necessity of a general source of water supply. One sees windmills painted in red, white, or blue, or dark shades of maroon and yellow, and still others so ancient and wind-tortured that their distinctive color can only be guessed.

When the wind blows, and there is rarely a day here that it does not, these various windmills set up a medley of discordant creaks and groans, each pitched in a different key, and, whether heard singly or collectively, all equally nerve-rending. It is presumable one could get used to the constant slapping, straining, and screeching, for nowhere are there people more serene, healthy, and home-loving than in this breezy town of Mendocino....

The first settler on the present site of Mendocino City was one William Kaston, a voyager up the coast in 1850, who was forced by stress of weather to seek shelter in the bay. It was not known why he concluded to take up his abode on a bleak, isolated headland, or whether he had companions other than the Indians who hunted and fished along this beautiful river.

A year or two after the arrival of Kaston, a richly laden vessel from China was driven on the beach at the mouth of the Noyo, and parties came up from Bodega to gather salvage from the wreck. These men took back glowing accounts of the wonderful forests at Big River, and their contiguity to a good port—a desideratum of special moment at a time when the price of lumber was greatly out of proportion to the wages paid for hire.

The first to avail himself of this immense timber wealth was Harry Meiggs, who in 1852 brought, in the brig *Ontario,* a crew of men and the machinery necessary to erect a sawmill on the point flanking the north side of the harbor. The oxen used to draw the logs to this mill were sent overland from Bodega. A village sprung up which was called in those days "Meiggsville," or Big River Landing....

The lumber interests of Big River are at a standstill. No smoke issues from the enormous brick chimney of the sawmill. Unless a moneyed company buys the mill and builds railroads to the uncut forests higher up the stream, this charming seaside town must share the decline of her sister villages. Her horticultural resources are not sufficient in themselves to support the present population, and a return to prosperity must depend upon the further development of her timber industry. There is plenty of good land here, but the near indestructibility of the redwood stumps and roots renders its clearing a difficult undertaking.

A day spent in rowing up and down Big River is an enviable pastime, especially in latter May, when not even the feather of a cloud mars the lovely blue of the sky, and water and woods are aglow in a downpour of sun-gold.

The day after the river excursion I took the delightful ten-mile ride up the coast to Fort Bragg. Every bight of the sea on the way had its stream and sawmill, though only the Caspar mill was running, Fort Bragg being the Aaron's rod that had swallowed all the others. This lively lumber town was full of excitement over the prospective launching of a "cigar raft," which lay in its cradle upon ways 600 feet long. The raft itself measured 365 feet in length, with a diameter of 21 feet. It was equipped with rudder and steering gear and had a pilot house perched on top from which a flag floated. The raft contained more than 1.2 million feet of piling, saw logs, and ties, all bound together in the shape of a cigar by means of wire ropes placed 12 feet apart, with a core or center chain of solid stud link cable, by which it was to be towed.

For the three months previous, the building of this raft, the first of the kind ever attempted on the Pacific Coast, was the one absorbing topic of interest to lumber companies. Should the venture prove successful, they would duplicate their mills in the large seaport cities, where all the refuse lumber could be sold for fuel. The carrying out of this plan would not appreciably diminish the work done at the present mills, as only the smaller logs can be made into rafts, thus utilizing trees which are either burnt or left standing.

Unfortunately, the Fort Bragg raft was not launched in deep enough water, and the bow struck the sand when the stern still rested upon a hundred feet of ways. It took days of perplexing labor to get her fairly afloat, by which time the strain had so loosened her bands that she parted at sea, and thousands of dollars' worth of logs were lost. The experiment, though a failure in this instance, has at least demonstrated that this manner of raft can be built and launched at certain lumber ports along the Pacific, if the ways are made to run far enough back, and have sufficient elevation to secure the right momentum to the sliding raft....

The trip back to Ukiah was taken by way of Mendocino City, and thence the road climbs to the Mendocino Barrens, through redwood and pine, with here and there a rhododendron, like a huge bouquet stuck in the somber background of their foliage. Upon gaining the ashen soil of the highland, the forest thins to a few meager trees raising distorted limbs above the thorny clumps of chamise. The Barrens indeed would be unspeakably monotonous if it were not for the rhododendron, which here holds queenly sway, transforming the arid stretch into a wonderful profusion of blooms which look for all the world like vast gardens of roses.

Shortly after entering an unbroken wilderness of stately timber, a man stepped quickly out of the shade and signed to the driver to take him aboard. The Wells, Fargo messenger who was the sole occupant of the interior of the stage made an instinctive clutch at his gun, and glanced askance at the stranger, who composedly took the seat by his side. In the conversation that followed, we learned that the newcomer was a woodcutter on his way to an upper logging camp.

There was something about this young woodsman, who could hardly have been much past twenty, that aroused interest. It might have been a touch of daring in the keen, dark eyes, or a hint of concealment in the handsome mouth. His manner and speech were respectful and intelligent, and his voice betrayed a curious mingling of suavity and insistence. Though he conversed with modesty and apparent candor, one felt that he was withholding more than he imparted.

"I commenced as a water slinger, when I was a boy," he replied in answer to a question from the messenger, "and have been in logging camps ever since. The work ain't so bad, if the men were treated right. They have to work twelve hours out of the twenty-four, and have only a half hour for dinner. Their pay comes every three months, and then in drafts on San Francisco banks, which takes time and money to cash. Now this ain't fair treatment, for we men pay back at least three-fourths of our wages into the company's stores, so they ain't losing nothing on us. We sent them respectful petitions to correct these things, but they don't pay no attention, and what we've got to do is to unite and compel them to give us our rights. It took me three months to get the first thirty names on our list, and now we have fourteen hundred names, all of Mendocino woodsmen. I don't work in a place only just long enough to let the men understand what we want 'em to do. The Russians held out the longest, but they're now coming in fast. The

Humboldt companies all give their men what we're asking for. We only want our rights, and we don't mean to do anything that ain't peaceable to get 'em," with a contradictory flash of his dark eyes.

There was a rude eloquence in this recital of grievances, and I had reason to know the facts of the case had not been exaggerated. In further discussion, the young man had the fairness to admit that there was something to be said on the side of the companies.

"They ain't any of 'em much more'n making expenses, but all the same they ought to be fair with us," he added stubbornly.

With the present limited market, there is no doubt California's lumber trade is greatly overstocked. This depression would not continue if cheaper methods of transportation were brought about, whereby redwood and other valuable timber in the state could be shipped to the East and elsewhere.

When the woodsman was about to leave us, it was not in human nature to refrain from asking his name.

"I'm a Master Workman, madam," with a smile and bow of no mean grace, and the somber wood shut in his upright figure.

Look as intently as we might, we could detect no sign of house or camp, only the crowding of gigantic, corrugated pillars, and a stillness that was awesome even at midday. In Tom Bell Gulch the grandeur of the redwoods exceeded anything we had yet seen. The entire length of this supremely picturesque canyon, we rode through lofty branchless columns keeping their ranks closed in and supporting a plumy roof more than two hundred feet above us.

EDWARD MARKHAM

A MENDOCINO MEMORY

*While technological innovations and the ever present lust for
wealth continued to deplete California's redwood forests, there
was nonetheless a keen appreciation for the power and stateli-
ness of the trees, as evidenced in this poem by Edwin Markham.*

*Markham (1852–1940) had been a teacher in and around
the San Francisco Bay Area and sometimes published poet for
some twenty years when, in 1898, acclaim for his poem "The
Man with the Hoe," a protest against the exploitation of
laborers, brought him sudden, unanticipated fame. In 1922
William Howard Taft invited him to read his poem "Lincoln,
the Man of the People" at the dedication of the Lincoln
Memorial. "A Mendocino Memory" was published in* Lincoln
and Other Poems.

Once in my lonely, eager youth I rode,
With jingling spur, into the clouds' abode—
Rode northward lightly as the high crane goes—
Rode into the hills in the month of the frail wild rose,
To find the soft-eyed heifers in the herds,

Strayed north along the trail of nesting birds,
Following the slow march of the springing grass,
From range to range, from pass to flowering pass.

I took the trail: the fields were yet asleep;
I saw the last star hurrying to its deep—
Saw the shy wood-folk starting from their rest
In many a crannied rock and leafy nest.
A bold, tail-flashing squirrel in a fir,
Restless as fire, set all the boughs astir;
A jay, in dandy blue, flung out a fine
First fleering sally from a sugar pine.

A flight of hills, and then a deep ravine
Hung with madroño boughs—the quail's demense;
A quick turn in the road, a wingèd whir,
And there he came with fluted whispering,
The captain of the chaparral, the king,
With nodding plume, with circumstance and stir,
And step of Carthaginian conqueror!

I climbed the canyon to a river-head,
And looking backward saw a splendor spread,
Miles beyond miles, of every kingly hue
And trembling tint the looms of Arras knew—
A flowery pomp as of the dying day,
A splendor where a god might take his way.

And farther on the wide plains under me,
I watched the light-foot winds of morning go,
Soft shading over wheat-fields far and free,
To keep their old appointment with the sea.

And farther yet, dim in the distant glow,
Hung on the east a line of ghostly snow.

After the many trails an open space
Walled by the tules of a perished lake;
And there I stretched out, bending the green brake,
And felt it cool against my heated face.
My horse went cropping by a sunny crag,
In wild oats taller than the antlered stag
That makes his pasture there. In gorge below
Blind waters pounded boulders, blow on blow—
Waters that gather, scatter and amass
Down the long canyons where the grizzlies pass,
Slouching through manzanita thickets old,
Strewing the small red apples on the ground,
Tearing the wild grape from its tree-top hold,
And wafting odors keen through all the hills around.

Now came the fording of the hurling creeks,
And joyous days among the breezy peaks,
Till through the hush of many canyons fell
The faint quick tenor of a brazen bell,
A sudden, soft, hill-stilled, far-falling word,
That told the secret of the straying herd.

It was the brink of night, and everywhere
Tall redwoods spread their filmy tops in air;
Huge trunks, like shadows upon shadow cast,
Pillared the under twilight, vague and vast.
And one had fallen across the mountain way,
A tree hurled down by hurricane to lie

With torn-out roots pronged-up against the sky
And clutching still their little dole of clay.

Lightly I broke green branches for a bed,
And gathered ferns, a pillow for my head.
And what to this were kingly chambers worth—
Sleeping, an ant, upon the sheltering earth,
High over Mendocino's windy capes,
Where ships go flying south like shadow-shapes—
Gleam into vision and go fading on,
Bearing the pines hewn out of Oregon.

ROBERT LOUIS STEVENSON

from THE SILVERADO SQUATTERS

The tremendously prolific Scottish author Robert Louis Steven-
son (1850–1894) came to California in 1879, following Fannie
Vandegrift Osborne, whom he had met and fallen in love with
in 1876. They married soon after she was divorced and spent
their honeymoon in an abandoned silver-mining camp on the
slopes of Mount St. Helena. The Silverado Squatters, pub-
lished in 1883, is based on Stevenson's journal of their stay.

We drove off from the Springs Hotel about three in the afternoon.
The sun warmed me to the heart. A broad, cool wind streamed
pauselessly the valley, laden with perfume. Up at the top stood
Mount St. Helena, a bulk of mountain, bare atop, with tree-fringed
spurs, and radiating warmth. Once, we saw it framed in a grove of
tall and exquisitely graceful white oaks, in line and color a finished
composition. We passed a cow stretched by the roadside, her bell
slowly beating time to the movement of her ruminating jaws, her
big red face crawled over by half a dozen flies, a monument of
content.

A little farther, and we struck to the left up a mountain road,
and for two hours threaded one valley after another, green, tangled,

full of noble timber, giving us every now and again a sight of Mount St. Helena and the blue hilly distance, and crossed by many streams, through which we splashed to the carriage step. To the right or the left, there was scarce any trace of man but the road we followed; I think we passed but one ranchero's house in the whole distance, and that was closed and smokeless. But we had the society of these bright streams—dazzlingly clear, as is their wont, splashing from the wheels in diamonds and striking a lively coolness through the sunshine. And what with the innumerable variety of greens, the masses of foliage tossing in the breeze, the glimpses of distance, the descents into seemingly impenetrable thickets, the continual dodging of the road which made haste to plunge again into the covert, we had a fine sense of woods, and springtime, and the open air.

Our driver gave me a lecture by the way on Californian trees—a thing I was much in need of, having fallen among painters who know the name of nothing, and Mexicans who know the name of nothing in English. He taught me the madrona, the manzanita, the buckeye, the maple; he showed me the crested mountain quail; he showed me where some young redwoods were already spiring heavenwards from the ruins of the old; for in this district all had already perished: redwoods and redskins, the two noblest indigenous living things, alike condemned.

At length, in a lonely dell, we came on a huge wooden gate with a sign upon it like an inn. "The Petrified Forest. Proprietor: C. Evans," ran the legend. Within, on a knoll of sward, was the house of the proprietor and another smaller house hard by to serve as a museum, where photographs and petrifactions were retailed. It was a pure little isle of touristry among the solitary hills.

The proprietor was a brave old white-faced Swede. He had wandered this way, heaven knows how, and taken up his acres—I forget how many years ago—all alone, bent double with sciatica, and with six bits in his pocket and an ax upon his shoulder. Long, useless years of seafaring had thus discharged him at the end, penniless and sick. Without doubt he had tried his luck at the diggings, and got no good from that; without doubt he had loved the bottle, and lived the life of Jack ashore. But at the end of these adventures, here he came; and, the place hitting his fancy, down he sat to make a new life of it, far from crimps and the salt sea. And the very sight of his ranch had done him good. It was "the handsomest spot in the Californy mountains." "Isn't it handsome, now?" he said. Every penny he makes goes into that ranch to make it handsomer. Then the climate, with the sea breeze every afternoon in the hottest summer weather, had gradually cured the sciatica; and his sister and niece were now domesticated with him for company—or, rather, the niece came only once in the two days, teaching music the meanwhile in the valley. And then, for a last piece of luck, "the handsomest spot in the Californy mountains" had produced a petrified forest, which Mr. Evans now shows at the modest figure of half a dollar a head, or two-thirds of his capital when he first came there with an ax and a sciatica.

This tardy favorite of fortune—hobbling a little, I think, as if in memory of the sciatica, but with not a trace that I can remember of the sea—thoroughly ruralized from head to foot, proceeded to escort us up the hill behind his house.

"Who first found the forest?" asked my wife.

"The first? I was that man," said he. "I was cleaning up the pasture for my beasts, when I found this"—kicking a great redwood, seven feet in diameter, that lay there on its side, hollow heart, clinging lumps of bark, all changed into gray stone, with veins of quartz between what had been the layers of the wood.

"Were you surprised?"

"Surprised? No! What would I be surprised about? What did I know about petrifactions—following the sea? Petrifaction! There was no such word in my language! I knew about putrefaction, though! I thought it was a stone; and so would you, if you was cleaning up pasture."

And now he had a theory of his own, which I did not quite grasp, except that the trees had not "grewed" there. But he mentioned, with evident pride, that he differed from all the scientific people who had visited the spot; and he flung about such words as "tufa" and "silica" with careless freedom.

When I mentioned I was from Scotland, "My old country," he said; "my old country"—with a smiling look and a tone of real affection in his voice. I was mightily surprised, for he was obviously Scandinavian, and begged him to explain. It seemed he had learned his English and done nearly all his sailing in Scotch ships. "Out of Glasgow," said he, "or Greenock; but that's all the same—they all hail from Glasgow." And he was so pleased with me for being a Scotsman, and his adopted compatriot, that he made me a present of a very beautiful piece of petrifaction—I believe the most beautiful and portable he had.

Here was a man, at least, who was a Swede, a Scot, and an American, acknowledging some kind of allegiance to three lands. Mr. Wallace's Scoto-Circassian will not fail to come before the reader. I have myself met and spoke with a Fifeshire German, whose combination of abominable accents struck me dumb. But, indeed, I think we all belong to many countries. And perhaps this habit of much travel, and the engendering of scattered friendships, may prepare the euthanasia of ancient nations.

And the forest itself? Well, on a tangled, briery hillside—for the pasture would bear a little further cleaning up, to my eyes—there lie scattered thickly various lengths of petrified trunk, such as the one already mentioned. It is very curious, of course, and ancient enough, if that were all. Doubtless, the heart of the geologist beats quicker at the sight; but, for my part, I was mightily unmoved. Sight-seeing is the art of disappointment.

There's nothing under heaven so blue
That's fairly worth the traveling to.

But, fortunately, heaven rewards us with many agreeable prospects and adventures by the way; and sometimes, when we go out to see a petrified forest, prepares a far more delightful curiosity in the form of Mr. Evans, whom may all prosperity attend throughout a long and green old age.

ERNEST PEIXOTTO

from ROMANTIC CALIFORNIA

In this selection from Romantic California, *Ernest Peixotto (1869–1940), artist, illustrator, author, and coeditor of the bohemian San Francisco literary magazine* The Lark, *describes an encampment around 1910 at Bohemian Grove, on the Russian River near Santa Rosa.*

The Bohemian Club began as a retreat from the all-encompassing worship of wealth that overtook San Francisco during and after the gold rush. Jack London, Ambrose Bierce, Mark Twain, and John Muir were among the early members, and the wealthy were excluded from membership. Before long, though, to pay the bills, the club began to offer memberships to businessmen with bohemian leanings. By the time Peixotto wrote this piece, the club and Bohemian Grove had become gathering sites for the rich and famous.

On a bend of the Russian River about eighty miles to the north of San Francisco there stands a forest of redwood trees, never touched by the woodman's ax, a grove whose mighty tree trunks, massive as the clustered columns of a Gothic cathedral, lift their heads skyward in stately and imposing order, devoid of branches to a great height. In distant perspectives of these dim-lit forest aisles, the boughs of far-off treetops interlace in flowing traceries, framing peeps of sky into mullioned windows of strange and beautiful design. Sunbeams filter through the shimmering leaves and play in brilliant spots upon the ground, but the light falls sparingly, as in the rich gloom of some church interior.

Did you ever rest in the nave of a cathedral? Did you ever follow the lift of its mighty piers, the arch of its soaring vaults, the far perspectives of aisle and transept and chapel, the broad sweep of the pavement? So in these forest aisles. The shafts, nerved with bark, the interlacing feathery boughs, the colored sky windows, the floor carpeted with pine needles—droppings of ages, softer underfoot than the priceless weaves of the "Savonnerie." No sound breaks the eternal solitude except at times the tap of a woodpecker, the chirp of a squirrel, or the wind sighing through the pine boughs high upon the summit of the trees, radiant in the sunshine.

Once and once only each year these woods wake to life and echo to the voice of man. Annually at the full of the harvest moon people gather in this solitude; for the grove belongs to the Bohemian Club of San Francisco, which here celebrates its Midsummer Jinks in full consciousness that the night will be clear and the air balmy, the California summer being without rain.

Two weeks before the date set for the Jinks, the Sire and his assistants and a corps of workmen and club servants go up to the grove and make camp. The winter's brushwood is cleared away; the electric fittings, the stage, the platform, prepared for the big night. Tents are pitched in a portion of the grove where the shade is less dense, where the sweet-smelling bay, the oak, and the California laurel sweep their feathery branches in fairy arches. The tents are arranged with comfort and shaded with redwood boughs; the artist members busy themselves in the "studio," painting caricatures, signs, and quaint devices to decorate the camp streets. And what an appetite the men develop in this outdoor life, and how good to have it catered to by a well-regulated cuisine!

Each afternoon the train brings up a fresh quota of members and the days take on a merrier tone. In the evening all gather round the campfire, whose spluttering blaze lights up a unique circle of seats made of a single tree, cut in sections of such immense size that seat and back at once have been made by the removal of a quadrant. Here the night passes in song, jest, and story. The company grows larger and larger as the great day approaches, until on the Saturday of the Jinks a special train brings the main bulk of the club membership to the grove just in time for dinner—a dinner of six hundred covers, prepared, cooked, and served with the same care and precision as in the town clubhouse. And a merry dinner it is, the members sitting at concentric circular tables so that all may be as close together as possible, the millionaire elbowing the artist, the judge the actor—all brother Bohemians at this festal board.

The High Jinks is not, as its name might imply, an effervescence of hilarity. It is a dignified proceeding, elaborately planned, and most painstakingly carried out.

For the last thirty years the Midsummer Jinks has been a feature of the club's life. At first of a simpler form, consisting mainly of papers, music, and poems read in the fitful blaze of the campfire, with succeeding years it has taken on a more ambitious tone, until now it has become an entertainment as elaborate as any theatre could produce, but with a setting and an opportunity for surprise such as no theatre in the world can boast, for there is no stage, properly speaking—the characters at times appearing most unexpectedly in bursts of light on hillsides, the processions weaving half a mile through glooms of woodland solitudes.

Each time, the Jinks varies in theme. There have been Indian Jinks and Shakespeare Jinks, Gypsy Jinks and Aztec Jinks, and of late years, "Grove Plays" more intimately connected with the wood-land spirit, the pagan conception of the forest.

Of the older type of play, two of the most remarkable that I have witnessed were the so-called Buddha Jinks and the Druid Jinks.

For the first-named, a white statue was erected against the redwood background—a copy of the famous Daibutsu of Kakamura, sixty feet in height, in whose folded hands six men might stand. Before it a circle was enclosed by walls three hundred feet in circumference, and at its feet seven altars were erected and trimmed with boughs. After dinner the members, donning white kimonos, marched in procession toward this woodland temple, where they ranged themselves round the circle to greet the seven High Priests as they entered, robed in rich vestments specially sent from Japan for the occasion. The ceremonies that followed were conducted with the most imposing dignity. A church organ, sunk into the ground and played by means of an electric attachment, supplied a weird and unearthly accompaniment to the chants of many voices, and to the priests as each intoned a sonnet—the Voice of the Grove, the Murmuring Waters, the Voices of the Trees: the Redwood, the Madroño, the Bay Tree. Before each priest blue wreaths of smoke ascended from cressets of incense and sandal-wood and mingled with the play of tinted lights from calciums hidden in the surrounding foliage.

For the Druid Jinks the *mise-en-scène* was far less elaborate: a pile of logs for seats, a rough sort of altar, and a rude gateway built of giant stones. The Jinks had begun in the usual way, by an address from the Sire and a musical number by the great chorus massed on the left, when a horn was heard far off in the woods. A second unlooked-for blast, and the Sire despatched a messenger to find out who could thus break the silence of the forest meeting at this hour. The messenger, returning in a moment, reported that a strange company was without and demanded admittance. Upon the Sire's

BENEATH THE REDWOODS

O trees! so vast, so calm!
Softly ye lay
On heart and mind today
The unpurchaseable balm.

Ere yet the wind can cease,
Your mighty sigh
Is spirit of the sky—
Half sorrow and half peace.

Mourn ye your brothers slain,
That now afar
From hush and dews and star
Man barters for his gain?

Mourn them with all your boughs,
For I must mourn,
In seasons yet unborn,
The cares that they will house.

GEORGE STERLING

consent, a weird and fantastic procession entered the enclosure through the rude gateway: six tall priests in white, with long, white beards that hung below their waists, bearing upon their shoulders a coffin decorated with twisting snakes and the skulls of oxen; following them more priests, and then a double file of prisoners of sad and dejected mien, bound hand and foot to a chain; next a lumbering wagon with solid wooden wheels, drawn by a pair of cream white oxen and bearing the High Priest, a pale and venerable patriarch, in reality a man of eighty years.

Upon arriving before the Sire's stand, the High Priest, perched upon his creaking cart, demanded by what right men had invaded this Druid Temple, where from time immemorial his people had offered up their yearly sacrifices. He further demanded that the Sire vacate the altar. The Sire consented, provided his men be permitted to remain and witness the sacrificial rites. The High Priest, acquiescing, then explained that each year his clan gathered to sacrifice their prisoners, barbarians all, unless one of these could adduce sufficient reason for sparing his life. If one of them could show good reason, then not only his life but the lives of all his companions would be spared. So, one by one these Northmen, robed in skins, were led forth, each to plead for his life: one in a song for his sweetheart's sake; another in pantomime, urging his love of nature, of the trees, the rivers, and the mountains; and yet another his family ties and the love he bore his aged parents. But all these reasons were judged insufficient, as being common to the lot of all human beings—all until the last, a Bohemian, first of his kind, made his plea.

This role was taken by one of California's leading lawyers, and never will anyone who heard him forget his pleading, for never did he defend a prisoner with more warmth or eloquence. The burden of his entreaty was the Brotherhood of Man. He asserted that, carrying no sword and no spear, he held in his belt a weapon more potent far than any yet devised by man, and that though the priests might kill him, they never could kill the principle for which he stood. And he drew from his belt a loving cup and held it on high.

The High Priest was visibly moved by this appeal—a new plea indeed—and he said: "I will give you a chance for your life. Over your head hangs the Great Golden Egg. Touch it, and if your hand comes away stained with blood it is a sign from the gods that you and your companions must be sacrificed. If, on the other hand, your fingers remain unpolluted, your lives shall be spared."

The Bohemian raised his hand to the Great Golden Egg suspended in midair, and as he touched it, it broke and a white dove flew forth far into the woods—surely a peace sign from the gods. So into the coffin Care was put in place of the pagans, and was carried off to be cremated upon the funeral pyre. This ceremonial of the Cremation of Care terminates each High Jinks. All human troubles are supposed to be put into the casket and placed upon a funeral pyre. When the fire is ignited, in a blaze of glory and a shower of rockets and colored balls, they go up in smoke, so that the remainder of the night may be given over to supper, the Low Jinks, and fun and jollity. Few are the eyes that close till morning.

The more recent "Grove Plays" have been held upon the hillside stage. No theatre can boast such a setting. The mighty shafts of two forest giants form the proscenium colums. The hill behind, grown with other groups of redwoods, slopes rapidly upward, zigzagged with half-hidden paths and capable of infinite transformations. Shrubs, ferns, saplings lend their traceries to its scenic effects, which, under the mystery of night and the strange effects of chiaroscuro made possible by modern devices of electric lighting, form pictures of indescribable beauty.

Will Irwin's "Hamadryads" has, to the present writing, been perhaps the most beautiful of these "Grove Plays." George Sterling's "Triumph of Bohemia," however, made an unusually perfect performance, poetic in treatment and beautifully staged, telling the story of the trees that, threatened first by the Four Winds, then by their terrible enemy, Fire, defy them all. Then comes Man, tempted by Mammon, their worst foe, who is about to destroy them, when Bohemia intervenes and saves them—a singularly appropriate theme, indeed, for this play was given just after the club had acquired the grove by purchase to save it from the woodman's ax.

On the morning following the Jinks, always a Sunday, the symphony orchestra gives a concert, one of the most delightful features of this midsummer outing. The peace and quiet of the grove, the sunshine as it filters through the shimmering branches, the men lounging about on benches or on the soft pine needles, the sweet strains of the music, the swish of the violins, the soft breathings of the reeds, the more blatant notes of the brass, all take on a new sonority in the seclusion of this perfect forest hall and make one believe in an earthly Eden, in a veritable Forest of Arden, far removed from the cares and tribulations of this world.

JACK LONDON

from THE VALLEY OF THE MOON

"I am planning a serial, the motif is back to the land," Jack London (1876–1916) wrote to Cosmopolitan *editor Roland Phillips in 1911. "I take a man and a woman, young, who belong to the working class in a large city....The woman gets the vision. She is the guiding force. They start wandering over the country of California....After many hints and snatches of vision, always looking for the spot, they do find the real, one-and-only spot and settle down to successful, small-scale farming." This is* Valley of the Moon, *with characters Saxon and Billy loosely based on Charmian and Jack London, serialized in* Cosmopolitan *in 1913.*

In the real-life Valley of the Moon, just north of Sonoma, the Londons had Wolf House built of redwood trees, locally quarried boulders, volcanic rock, and blue slate. A few days before they were to move in, most of the house burned to the ground; only the walls were left standing. Eight hundred acres of London's ranch, including the site of the house, are now Jack London State Historic Park.

Crossing a bridge and rounding a sharp turn, they were suddenly enveloped in a mysterious coolness and gloom. All about them arose stately trunks of redwood. The forest floor was a rosy carpet of autumn fronds. Occasional shafts of sunlight, penetrating the deep shade, warmed the somberness of the grove. Alluring paths led off among the trees and into cozy nooks made by circles of red columns growing around the dust of vanished ancestors—witnessing the titanic dimensions of those ancestors by the girth of the circles in which they stood.

Out of the grove they pulled to the steep divide, which was no more than a buttress of Sonoma Mountain. The way led on through rolling uplands and across small dips and canyons, all well wooded and a-drip with water. In places the road was muddy from wayside springs.

"The mountain's a sponge," said Billy. "Here it is, the tail end of dry summer, an' the ground's just leakin' everywhere."

"I know I've never been here before," Saxon communed aloud. "But it's all so familiar! So I must have dreamed it. And there's madroños!—a whole grove! And manzanita! Why, I feel just as if I was coming home—Oh, Billy, if it should turn out to be our valley."

"Plastered against the side of a mountain?" he queried, with a skeptical laugh.

"No; I don't mean that. I mean on the way to our valley. Because the way—all ways—to our valley must be beautiful. And this; I've seen it all before, dreamed it."

"It's great," he said sympathetically. "I wouldn't trade a square mile of this kind of country for the whole Sacramento Valley, with the river islands thrown in and Middle River for good measure. If they ain't deer up there, I miss my guess. An' where they's springs they's streams, an' streams means trout."

They passed a large and comfortable farmhouse, surrounded by wandering barns and cow sheds, went on under forest arches, and emerged beside a field with which Saxon was instantly enchanted. It flowed in a gentle concave from the road up the mountain, its farther boundary an unbroken line of timber. The field glowed like rough gold in the approaching sunset, and near the middle of it stood a solitary great redwood, with blasted top suggesting a nesting aerie for eagles. The timber beyond clothed the mountain in solid green to what they took to be the top. But, as they drove on, Saxon, looking back upon what she called her field, saw the real summit of Sonoma towering beyond, the mountain behind her field a mere spur upon the side of the larger mass.

Ahead and toward the right, across sheer ridges of the mountains, separated by deep green canyons and broadening lower down into rolling orchards and vineyards, they caught their first sight of Sonoma Valley and the wild mountains that rimmed its eastern side. To the left they gazed across a golden land of small hills and valleys. Beyond, to the north, they glimpsed another portion of the valley, and, still beyond, the opposing wall of the valley—a range of mountains, the highest of which reared its red and battered ancient crater against a rosy and mellowing sky. From north to southeast, the mountain rim curved in the brightness of the sun, while Saxon and Billy were already in the shadow of evening. He looked at Saxon, noted the ravished ecstasy of her face, and stopped the horses. All the eastern sky was blushing to rose, which descended upon the mountains, touching them with wine and ruby. Sonoma Valley began to fill with a purple flood, laving the mountain bases, rising, inundating, drowning them in its purple. Saxon pointed in silence, indicating that the purple flood was the sunset shadow of Sonoma Mountain. Billy nodded, then chirruped to the mares, and the descent began through a warm and colorful twilight.

On the elevated sections of the road they felt the cool, delicious breeze from the Pacific forty miles away; while from each little dip and hollow came warm breaths of autumn earth, spicy with sunburnt grass and fallen leaves and passing flowers.

They came to the rim of a deep canyon that seemed to penetrate to the heart of Sonoma Mountain. Again, with no word spoken, merely from watching Saxon, Billy stopped the wagon. The canyon was wildly beautiful. Tall redwoods lined its entire length. On its farther rim stood three rugged knolls covered with dense woods of spruce and oak. From between the knolls, a feeder to the main canyon and likewise fringed with redwoods, emerged a smaller canyon. Billy pointed to a stubble field that lay at the feet of the knolls.

"It's in fields like that I've seen my mares a-pasturing," he said.

They dropped down into the canyon, the road following a stream that sang under maples and alders. The sunset fires, refracted from the cloud driftage of the autumn sky, bathed the canyon with crimson, in which ruddy-limbed madroños and wine-wooded manzanitas burned and smoldered. The air was aromatic with laurel. Wild grapevines bridged the stream from tree to tree. Oaks of many sorts were veiled in lacy Spanish moss. Ferns and brakes grew lush beside the stream. From somewhere came the plaint of a mourning dove. Fifty feet above the ground, almost over their heads, a Douglas squirrel crossed the road—a flash of gray between two trees; and they marked the continuance of its aerial passage by the bending of the boughs.

"I've got a hunch," said Billy.

"Let me say it first," Saxon begged.

He waited, his eyes on her face its she gazed about her in rapture.

"We've found our valley," she whispered. "Was that it?"

He nodded, but checked speech at sight of a small boy driving a cow up the road, a preposterously big shotgun in one hand, in the other as preposterously big a jackrabbit.

"How far to Glen Ellen?" Billy asked.

"Mile an' a half," was the answer.

"What creek is this?" inquired Saxon.

"Wild Water. It empties into Sonoma Creek half a mile down."

"Trout?"—this from Billy.

"If you know how to catch 'em," grinned the boy.

"Deer up the mountain?"

"It ain't open season," the boy evaded.

"I guess you never shot a deer," Billy slyly baited, and was rewarded with, "I got the horns to show."

"Deer shed their horns," Billy teased on. "Anybody can find 'em."

"I got the meat on mine. It ain't dry yet—" The boy broke off, gazing with shocked eyes into the pit Billy had dug for him.

"It's all right, sonny," Billy laughed, as he drove on. "I ain't the game warden. I'm buyin' horses."

More leaping tree squirrels, more ruddy madroños and majestic oaks, more fairy circles of redwoods, and, still beside the singing stream, they passed a gate by the roadside. Before it stood a rural mailbox, on which was lettered "Edmund Hale." Standing under the rustic arch, leaning upon the gate, a man and woman composed a picture so arresting and beautiful that Saxon caught her breath. They were side by side, the delicate hand of the woman curled in the hand of the man, which looked as if made to confer benedictions. His face bore out this impression—a beautiful-browed countenance, with large, benevolent gray eyes under a wealth of white hair that shone like spun glass. He was fair and large; the little woman beside him was daintily wrought. She was saffron brown, as a woman of the white race can well be, with smiling eyes of bluest blue. In quaint sage green draperies, she seemed a flower, with her small vivid face irresistibly reminding Saxon of a spring-time wake-robin.

Perhaps the picture made by Saxon and Billy was equally arresting and beautiful, as they drove down through the golden end of day. The two couples had eyes only for each other. The little woman beamed joyously. The man's face glowed into the benediction that had trembled there. To Saxon, like the field up the mountain, like the mountain itself, it seemed that she had always known this adorable pair. She knew that she loved them.

"How d'ye do," said Billy.

"You blessed children," said the man. "I wonder if you know how dear you look sitting there."

That was all. The wagon had passed by, rustling down the road, which was carpeted with fallen leaves of maple, oak, and alder. Then they came to the meeting of the two creeks.

"Oh, what a place for a home," Saxon cried, pointing across Wild Water. "See, Billy, on that bench there above the meadow."

"It's a rich bottom, Saxon; and so is the bench rich. Look at the big trees on it. An' they's sure to be springs."

"Drive over," she said.

Forsaking the main road, they crossed Wild Water on a narrow bridge and continued along an ancient, rutted road that ran beside an equally ancient worm fence of split redwood rails. They came to a gate, open and off its hinges, through which the road led out on the bench.

"This is it—I know it," Saxon said with conviction. "Drive in, Billy."

A small, whitewashed farmhouse with broken windows showed through the trees.

THE LOGGING CAMPS

FRANÇOIS LEYDET

from THE LAST REDWOODS

In this selection from The Last Redwoods *(1969), François Leydet describes the changes in north coast logging from the days when it was necessarily limited by the strength and endurance of the men who did the work to the modern inventions and increased mechanization that brought the industry to a new level of excess.*

These were the heroic days of lumbering, when the sheer brawn of men and beasts was pitted against the great trees. Swedes, Finns, and Norwegians; Frenchmen and Germans; Englishmen, Scotsmen, and Irishmen; graduates of the Maine woods and "bluenoses" from lower Canada made up the population of the redwood logging camps, and although they might have had trouble at times understanding each other, they all shared the same pride in the depth and cleanness of their ax cuts.

The chopping boss, or bull buck, planned the strips to be cut, and a set of choppers might work from a month to three months on one strip. A staging was built around the trunk of a tree above the butt swell and on this the pair of choppers stood. Their equipment included two axes, two eight-foot saws, one twelve-foot saw, two dozen plates, one dozen shims, ten wedges, two sledges, one pair of gun stocks, one plumb bob. This last item was all-important, for with it the choppers determined whether the tree was straight or a leaner, and if the latter, they adjusted their cut so as to make it fall in the right direction (usually uphill), where a bedding of smaller trees and branches had been prepared to fill in the low spots and to cushion its fall. It was bad luck to the crew that made the slightest miscalculation, for they could bring hundreds of tons of wood crashing down on their heads. Or the tree could fall afoul of its lay-out and shatter into fragments; hundreds of dollars' worth of wood would be abandoned on the ground and the loggers would move on to the next tree, all their sweat and toil having gone for naught. Felling a giant redwood up to twelve feet in diameter with hand ax and crosscut saw often took as much as three days.

Once felled, the trunk was cut into lengths suitable to the market, and the barkers pried off the bark with long poles. Then it was up to the jackscrewers to roll the logs within reach of the bull team crew—a dangerous job as the log would sometimes take an unexpected roll. Teams of bulls or oxen (or sometimes horses) hauled the logs down the skid road to the riverside dump. A string of logs was joined by chains and dog hooks, with the heaviest butt, weighing up to twenty tons, in the lead. On this the chain tender rode, keeping a sharp eye on the water carrier, often Chinese, whose duty it was to go between the head log and the rear oxen and wet the skids in the road so the logs would slide more easily. "The six to eight yoke of bulls tugging at the long line of bumping logs is one of the most animated scenes in a lumber camp," an eyewitness wrote. "These brutes are of enormous size, stolidly obedient to the 'Whoa haws' and 'Gees' of the teamsters, and surprisingly quick to get out of the way of a flying log. In a hard pull the faithful creatures fairly get down upon their knees to make it."

At the dump, or landing, the jackscrewers took over once more, rolling the logs into the river. (Another common method of bringing the logs to the river was to send them in a box flume—an exciting sight as each naked bole came smoking down at terrific speed, making a huge splash as it struck the water.) Once in the river the logs remained on the spot until the rainy season, when freshets could move them. When the rains came, whether it was midnight or daytime, the log drivers were routed out to rush the log jam down the swollen river. Sluice dams were sometimes built to gather a head of water. When enough water had backed up behind the dams they were "tripped" or broken, and the logs were shot down to the mill in the ensuing flash flood.

This system of floating the logs down streams lasted in Humboldt County until about 1880, when logging railroads generally superseded it. In Mendocino County the log drives lasted much longer. In 1928, twenty million board feet of redwood were successfully flushed down Big River, and the last dam was tripped as late as 1936. The Mendocino stream banks still show the scouring effect of the log drives. It was in Mendocino, too, that the most picturesque methods were used to ship out the lumber. The rugged coast has few natural harbors, but the lumber schooners worked their way into the small coves, or dog holes, mooring under the high sheer cliffs with the aid of their own anchors or of a makeshift buoy. An apron chute extended from the top of the cliff to the ship's pitching deck, and down this the lumber slid. Or it was lowered on swaying slings suspended from a wire cable, one end of which was anchored to the cliff and the other in the cove or ocean. Sometimes whole logs weighing many tons were swung aboard by this method.

At about the time when steam locomotives, dragging long strings of log-carrying flatcars across vertiginous trestles, became a common sight in the redwood region, another type of steam engine could be heard chugging in the woods. "In 1881," writes [Donald C.] Peattie, "John Dolbeer, a pioneer operator among the

Eureka redwoods, brought out of his blacksmith shop an invention that made the bullwhackers guffaw. It was a sort of donkey engine with a vertical boiler, a horizontal one-cylinder engine, and a big drum on which to wind up the tentacles of steel cable. He made these fast to a gigantic log, then opened up his engine wide. The log came thrashing down the skid road faster than the bullwhackers could cuss an ox, and the smirks died from their faces, for their jobs were gone."

The transition was actually not quite that sudden—the last straining bull team was used in 1914—but the "Dolbeer Donkey" and its more powerful offspring quickly revolutionized logging. More efficient than the slow, plodding oxen, they were also far more destructive. The hauling of logs no longer was confined to skid roads; the butts came crashing through the forest from every direction, ploughing up the ground, crushing the undergrowth, bulldozing young trees in their path. Even more devastating were the fires set by the loggers. "This Big Basin country is an example, and I can speak on this matter from personal observation," wrote a resident of the Santa Cruz mountains in 1900. "How often, in the hottest of the summer, have I not wished bad luck to the suffocating smoke that covers our beautiful scenery as with a black pall, day after day, hiding the face of Ben Lomond with an unsightly veil, and increasing the temperature by at least ten degrees. If you ask, 'Where is the fire?—it must be doing a great deal of damage,' the aborigine of the mountains will answer with the utmost indifference, 'Oh, no; they are only burning brush in the Big Basin.' Sounds quite harmless, does it not?

"But the burning away of the underbrush means this: a certain section has been designated, or rather doomed, by the owner, to be cleared; that is, the big trees (redwoods) are to be felled and made ready for the sawmill. When the mighty monarchs of the forest lie prone at last, the entire bark is stripped from off their

trunks....Then the torch is applied some fine dark night, and everything in that section, the birds in their nests, the merry little tree
squirrel, the swift deer and the spotted fawn, the giant ferns and the
rare orchids—everything is burned to death. The enormous trunks
of the redwoods, green and full of sap, alone resist the fire fiend;
tops, branches, bark, are all burned to ashes, and madroños, oaks,
firs, and young redwood trees are reduced to cinders and pitiful
looking black stumps."

Such protests were of little avail against an industry that by
the turn of the century had become the most important in the
state. As the population grew so did its demand for wood—in all of
its uses. And such was the versatility of redwood that its applica-
tions were practically unlimited. Dr. W. L. Jepson gave a striking
summary of them in his *The Silva of California* (1923): "The writer
of these lines is a Californian. He was rocked by a pioneer mother
in a cradle made of redwood. The house in which he lived was
largely made of redwood. His clothing, the books of his juvenile
library, the saddle for his riding pony were brought in railway cars
chiefly made of redwood, running on rails laid on redwood ties,
their course controlled by wires strung on redwood poles. He
went to school in a redwood schoolhouse, sat at a desk made of
redwood and wore shoes the leather of which was tanned in redwood vats. Everywhere he touched redwood. Boxes, bins, bats,
barns, bridges, bungalows were made of redwood. Posts, porches,
piles, pails, pencils, pillars, paving-blocks, pipe lines...were made of
redwood....

"One of the most emphatic tributes to the economic value of
redwood is that new uses are constantly being discovered for it. We
ship our choicest grapes to distant lands packed in redwood sawdust. We replace steel water conduits with redwood. We supply
redwood doors to the Central American market because the white
ant does not eat redwood."

And so, being too good to live, the redwoods continued to fall by the thousands every year. The twentieth century brought increasing mechanization to logging operations. Both in the woods and the mills, methods became more and more efficient and less backbreaking to the men. The gasoline-powered chain saw replaced the old handsaws and lopped off the trees like a guillotine. In 1935, crawler tractors began to drag the logs to the landings, rendering the donkey engine obsolete. Except where the ground is too steep and high-lead logging—cable-hauling the logs up abrupt slopes—is necessary, the cats are used almost exclusively today. Huge off-highway trucks generally supplanted the logging railroads in the task of bringing the logs from landing to mill, and dusty logging roads everywhere penetrated the forest, making accessible even the most remote stands.

For the first thirty years of the century, the annual cut averaged five hundred million board feet of redwood. During the depression years of the thirties this dropped to three hundred million. But in World War II the drain on the forests accelerated. Immense quantities of redwood timber were rushed to the Pacific theater. Wartime restrictions on home construction and other consumer uses of wood limited the cut. But the demand was there, accumulating like water behind a dam. And with V-J Day the dam burst. The tempo of cutting speeded up and by the early fifties reached one billion board feet of redwood a year.

ERNEST INGERSOLL

from "IN A REDWOOD LOGGING CAMP"

As a naturalist and writer, Ernest Ingersoll (1852–1946) cre-
ated a large body of work intended for a general audience and
drawn from an abiding love for landscape. His numerous
magazine articles and books include an account of travel in
the Rockies, works on birds, and a collection of dragon lore.
"In a Redwood Logging Camp" was published in Overland
Monthly *1883.*

Tradition says that credit for the very first attempt to make lumber
with a saw in this region (for the Russians hewed all their beams
and planks) belongs to John Dawson, of Bodega. Dawson was one
of three sailors who abandoned their ship at San Francisco as early
as 1830, preferring the free and easy life of the Californians. In two
or three years they became citizens under the Mexican government
and took up granted ranches hereaway, Dawson marrying the
daughter of a Spanish dragoon officer. She was only fourteen when
she went to live as mistress of the Cañada de Pogolome, and only
seventeen when she found herself the richest widow in Northern
California. Dawson's lumber was cut over pits by means of a ripsaw,

which he handled without help. Not half a century later steam mills in this district are turning out two hundred thousand feet of lumber daily.

The center, or at least one center, of this lumbering is here at Duncan's, where the Russian River receives a tributary named Austin's Creek. A wonderful railway follows its banks half a dozen miles back into the hills to supply the mill with logs....

The track is rudely built and rickety, the rails being heavy strap iron bolted upon stringpieces. It runs shakily through tunnels of infinitely varied verdure, curves along ledges blasted out of the brown and fern-hung rocks of the creek shore, traverses low ground upon causeways of ties and stringers, each as big as a hogshead, ventures out upon some precarious bracket trestle whence it might plunge directly into the stream. Almost from the first we have entered the old forest, where (now that the choppers have passed on) we revel in the beauty of unhindered plant luxuriance: in the lofty spires of kingly redwoods, and of pines and spruces ambitious to equal them; in the glossy masses of erect pepperwoods, whose leaves look like oleander, smell of bay rum, and tingle upon the tongue like curry; in the awkward form of the half-flayed madroña; and in the grace of the light-toned masses of maple, alder, and small shrubbery along the waterside. Enjoying this green wilderness, and with interest freshened by the sight of huge pedestals that once bore trees, and by increasing of the choppers, we reach the logging camp. Here, however, no cutting is being done today, so we walk across the ridge to the next gulch....

We presently learn our proximity to the scene of the chopping by the roaring profanity coming up from sources invisible as yet....Following two men who, ax in hand, were making their way up toward one of the larger-sized redwoods upon the steep hillside, we watched their attack.

"The first question, sir," said the leading axman, politely, "when we are going to fall a big tree, is where she'll lay; because unless a man cares (i.e., is careful) to fall her right, she'll break all up, and the bigger the trunk the more liable she is to break. You can see down across the creek there how that one snapped."

We looked where he pointed, and saw that a bole fully six feet in diameter had broken squarely across; the brittleness of this timber, nevertheless, is not excessive, compared with other soft woods. Meanwhile the chopper was holding his ax in front of his upturned face, letting it hang head down between his thumb and finger, like a plummet, while he squinted past it at the top of the tree, upon whose perfect shaft no branches grew below the upper quarter.

"I can tell by this whether she leans out of the perpendic'lar. If she does, you've got to allow for it; but this one don't, and I guess, Joe, we'll drop her right along that knoll just to the east'ard o' that oak stump—see it? But we'll have to roll that there log out of the way a little, or she'll break her back acrost it, sure."

Having made this simple preparation (sometimes hours are spent in dragging logs to fill gullies, or in leveling knolls and getting stumps out of the way), the men returned and began chopping out some mortise holes in the trunk about four feet above the ground. These were intended for the insertion of their iron-shod spring-boards—pieces of flexible planking about four feet long and six inches wide, upon which they were to stand while chopping at a height too great to reach from the ground.

The undercut was made first, and it was a fine sight to watch these stalwart men perched upon their strips of springy board, hurling their ax heads deep into the gaping wound, and never missing the precise point at which they aimed. I do not know any attitudes more manly or motions more muscularly graceful than those of the chopper; but perhaps the noble surroundings may count more largely than we think in this estimate.

In about an hour the undercut had approached the heart of the tree, and the men desisted from their work, which must now proceed on a scientific basis.

"As I said afore," the chopper explained, "we must fall a tree straight and true where we've fixed for it, or else she'll go to pieces. In order to do this we've got to measure it this way."

As he speaks he picks up, from near where his coat and saw and water caddy are lying, two sticks about four feet in length—one a square stiff lath, the other switchlike. Going to the tree he lays one end of the lath upon the partially exposed stump in the under-cut, its extremity resting against the heart of the wood at the exact center of the bole. Then stooping and sighting along it, he moves the outer end of the lath until it points exactly along the line where the trunk is intended to be thrown.

"Joe, go out there about a hundred feet or so and set a stake; I want to show these gentlemen how nicely we can drive it in with this big sledge we're goin' to let loose directly."

"Do you mean to say you will drop your tree as accurately as that?"

"You bet—hit that stake plumb; 'n' it'll take more mumble-te-peg'n you're worth, I reckon, to pull it out afterward!"

Meanwhile he went on with his mathematics. Having aimed the lath, he measured with his switch from its outer end to the "corner" at each side of the undercut, and finding one side a little shorter than the other, chopped in until he had equalized the hypotenuses of the two right-angled triangles, whose straight sides were back to back in the line of the lath. The object and importance of this was to make sure that the limit of the undercut, where the strain and breakage controlling the fall of the tree (and marked by the line of upright slivers in it stump) would finally come, should be at right angles to the intended direction of that fall.

"How tall do you think this tree is ?" I ask.

"Well, I should say pretty nigh on two hundred feet; but it is easy enough to find out exactly."

Taking his ax, the chopper cut a straight stake, sharpened its end, and placed it before him while he stood very erect. Then with his knife he cut a notch just four inches above the point on the stake which came squarely opposite his eyes—this extra four inches being in allowance for planting the stake in the ground. Walking away to a point on the hillside level with the base of the tree, and about the right distance, as he guessed at it, he planted the stake and lay down on his back behind it, with his heels against its foot, and his eye trying to bring the notch on the stake in range with the topmost plumelet of the redwood. One or two slight shiftings of position enabled him to get this range, and thereby to construct an equal-sided triangle. It only remained to measure with his five-foot rule the distance from his eyes to the base of the tree to learn the height of the tree, representing the other side of the triangle. The fact in this case was one hundred and eighty feet.

This practical triangulation finished, the axes were laid aside, and the springboards inserted in new mortises behind the tree, and a big two-handed saw set at work to make the overcut. Soon the crevice begins to open a little, and then a little more, until the cautious woodmen begin to cast their eyes aloft, watching carefully the signal that the next stroke would be the last, cutting the one remaining tendon that holds the mighty column up, for already there are sudden strange shivering motions in the densely bushy thickets of foliage that adorn its lofty crown, and dead twigs rattle down, snapped off by thrills of approaching destruction....

I think I hear the ominous crackings of tense fiber, the partings of well-knit rind, and the hushed commotion of shocked branches and crowded leafage overhead. Then comes the final stroke of the ax, severing the last slender stay, and, with a mingled roar and scream of frightened despair, the huge mast, carrying all its lofty spars and well-set rigging, slowly leans to its fate, gathers headway, spurns with giant heel the faithless stump which hitherto has borne it proudly against every gale and torrent, and so, stately to the last, "rustling, crackling, crashing, thunders down."

Picking our way through the settling dust and debris of crushed branches which lie in a thousand splinters of red and green around the head of the prostrate chief, we look for the stake with which Joe challenged our credulity but fail to find it, for it has been driven "plumb through to China," as Joe avers.

"Accidents must happen pretty often in this business," we remark.

"Yes, right often, both to men and animals. Sometimes a tree is weak, and topples over before you're ready for it; or, instead of lying still when it strikes, it sort o' picks itself up and takes a long jump forward, which is unexpected and liable to hurt somebody. Then the worst of all is where the butt breaks off and shoots back behind the stump like one o' them darned big battering rams you read about, and worked by sheet lightnin' at that. Yes, a heap of men gets killed in the woods every year. We never had none killed dead right here, but a mighty curious thing happened last September was a year. One of the men went to work in the mornin' 'long with the rest—good, solid man he was, too, with heaps of sand in him. He didn't come in to dinner, nor when night come. Then we begun to question round, and found none of the boys had saw him since mornin'. We found his coat and tools, but nary hide nor hair of him then nor no time afterward. We rather looked for a sheriff to be comin' round the next day or two, thinkin' the fellow might have got wind he was onto his trail (though we knew nothin' agin him—but you can't 'most always tell, you know) but none came."

"What was your conclusion as to this strange disappearance?"

"Well, we just allowed that one of these big trees had got the drop on that fellow as it were, and druv him clean into the ground. Cigar? No, thank ye, I'll stick to my pipe."

The wastefulness of this lumbering is one of the striking features of the scene. Only the largest trees are cut, those measuring less than two feet in diameter rarely being touched, and the ax is laid not to the roots (though they are not thick and widely divergent, considering the height and weight they support), but some distance above, so that in very large specimens the massive stump, upon whose flat top you might build a comfortable house, stands ten or twelve feet above the ground and contains hundreds of feet of sound lumber, which must be left to rot or burn. Then, many trees are broken by their fall, so that large parts of them are useless; other parts may be knotty, or crooked, or inconvenient to drag out, and so only half of a great trunk will be utilized. Huge logs are consumed, also, in road-making and bridge-building in the hills, and dozens of small trees are crushed by the fall of their greater companions. Then, when a district is pretty well cleared of its best timber, fire is set in the brush and prostrate trunks. Feeding eagerly upon the resinous wood, half dried and broken, it gathers so much heat that the saplings are nearly all killed, and the flaky, tinderlike bark of the larger trees is singed in a way which must greatly injure and often destroy them. Moreover, these fires, fanned by the gusty breezes rushing in every afternoon from the ocean, often get beyond control, and sweeping through the oily tops and brittle trunks, spread blackened ruin over miles and miles of precious forest....

The tree having been felled, men proceeded to trim away its top and to split off its thick coat of bark. This can often be pried away almost without breaking it, except on top, so that a great cast, as it were, of the trunk is left in the bark, which lies there, after the logs are removed, like a huge ruined canoe. I have seen masses of redwood bark fifteen inches in thickness; the tree which it clothed, if straight and sound, would be worth a thousand dollars. It does not follow, however, that the biggest trunks are the most valuable, since it often happens that very large trees prove unsound or completely hollowed.

The stripping of top branches and bark having been effected, the trunk is sawed into logs fifteen or twenty feet in length. A path is now cleared to them from the nearest road sufficiently good to take in six or eight yoke of oxen. This does not require to be a very good path either—though in some cases much labor and rough engineering is required for these wood roads—since the agility of the little oxen is quite wonderful, when one notes what barriers of fallen trunks and what almost vertical slopes of hillside are surmounted. Near the lower end of the log an iron hook, called a "dog," is driven in, where the drag chain is attached. Then, under a shower of such "good mouth-filling oaths" as would have satisfied Falstaff, under resounding thwacks and proddings of an iron-tipped goad, the slipping and stumbling cattle snake the log endwise down the hill. But a single log must be of extraordinary size to content the driver. Having arranged the oxen in line at the head of the little gully, which previous draggings have smoothed out, he chains together two, three, even five or six logs, and starts up the slow-moving cattle with a train behind them four or five rods long. Though the pitches the cattle scramble down are too smooth and steep for us to follow, surefooted they stay upon their legs, and keep out of the way of the logs; thus all goes well, yet the shouts and imprecations of the bullwhacker never cease. He curses the logs, which are trailing along without a fault; he hurls vile but vivid epithets at the exemplary oxen collectively and individually; he swears at the meek Chinaman who travels ahead diligently wetting the ground to make it slippery; he damns everything all the time, yet is suave and polite and mild-mannered to us as we scramble alongside, for his profanity is purely professional, and his objurgations to be taken wholly in a Pickwickian sense.

The snaking out of these logs is another source of casualty to the lumberman, arising not so often from the logs, however, as from the big round butts which in many cases are sawed off from the original trunk. These are like huge, solid cartwheels and of great weight: if one of them gets loose upon the steep hillside, whatever stops it must stand stiff and high. We were taking break-fast with Charlie Nolan, the wide-awake foreman at the camp, one day, Nolan sitting where he could look out of the open door and up the mountain. Suddenly he dropped his knife, grabbed up a small boy in each hand, and shouting, "Get out of this!" made for the door. Nobody waited to inquire what was the matter, but followed the injunction, turning, when the open air was gained, just in time to see the stoppage, by a firm stump, of an immense butt, which had come thundering down through the thinned woods, aiming directly at our cottage, whose frail walls would have offered no obstacle whatever to its progress. Breakfast tasted much better after this escape from losing it altogether.

The railway having been reached by the bull team and their train, the logs are laid lengthwise upon a sloping platform or bank strengthened by buried skids, where a white foreman and two or three Chinese laborers easily roll them down upon the cars, aiding themselves with cant hooks, jackscrews, and consonantal expressions in two languages designed to relieve the feelings.

Having been placed upon the cars, the logs are secured by ropes and "dogs" so that they cannot fall, and then are taken at a breakneck pace down to the mill, and tumbled over upon a slanting platform, whence they can easily be rolled upon the small car which carries them up into the mill by stationary engine power....

The men had gathered in the long wooden shed for supper, eating on wooden tables, but with an abundance of furniture and a plentiful bill of fare. Supper was hurried through this evening, for the men had on hand a frolic which had also the serious purpose of ridding the camp of an obnoxious old boar that had acquired a troublesome taste for the blood of Mongolian shanks, whose shrunken lines could ill spare the commodity. Reinforced with great heartiness by the Chinese contingent, the whole camp therefore turned out on a boar hunt, assisted by several dogs even more diverse in breed than their masters. The approved weapons for this sort of chase, I understand, are rifles, spears, and knives; but here were to be seen only a club or two and some ropes looped with lassos, except that a valiant wielder of the brush brought up the rear with a six-shooter tightly clutched in his red right hand. The advance was not incautious. That pig had long made himself respected to the extent that when he appeared, every man not only gave him the right of the road, but hastened to climb upon a stump, so as to run no risk of incommoding his swineship in the least by his presence.

It was not long, however, before a series of energetic grunts was heard ahead and the army stopped, the artist mounting a very high stump. He said he thought they had stumbled on a bear, and he wanted to be where he could fire over the heads of all the men. Though only a black and bristling pig, a bear of the biggest kind could not have held the army at bay more thoroughly. If he had charged, I tremble to think what might have happened; but he rushed away into the bushes and ran into a corner, where he became the victim of strategy, and was presently bound and led forth in degrading captivity, followed by a procession of one artist, a score of grinning lumbermen, and a mob of chattering and dancing Chinese, for the intention was not to kill him, but only to eradicate his pugnacious propensities.

This done, the painter put up his pistol, and we all adjourned to the big shanty, where some of the men pulled off their boots and stretched themselves in restful ease upon their bunks, while others shuffled the cards for "a little game" or did odd jobs of tinkering.

It was a strange and interesting picture the interior of the big shanty made, as the darkness of the outside withdrew all the light from within, and left the walls and the faces illumined only by a great fire of resinous redwood chunks built upon a raised earthen hearth that occupied the whole center of the cabin, and the smoke of which escaped up a big bell-hooded flue in the ceiling.

The talk fell upon the enemy ignobly conquered; upon their work and the probable plans of "the old man," meaning their employer; upon some men who had just departed, which carried it away to Frisco, and drifted it upon the familiar ground of reminiscences of the dance house, the poker table, and the men who were always waiting to "get the drop" on somebody, or watching that somebody didn't get the drop on them: stirring stories some of them, but as unreportable as the vigorous metaphors in which they were portrayed.

ANNA M. LIND

from "WOMEN IN EARLY LOGGING CAMPS"

In "Women in Early Logging Camps," Anna Lind recalls her days waiting tables at a Humboldt County logging camp not long after World War I. Published in 1975 in the Journal of Forest History, *the article is a welcome look at the social details of logging camps from a woman's point of view, with some insight regarding the changes that took place as modern roads made the camps less remote.*

One Sunday evening in early April 1926, I stepped aboard a cabooselike railroad car at Korbel, California, a small mill town. I was on the way to my first logging camp job to work for the Northern Redwood Lumber Company. Young, naive, inclined to be bookish, I watched with interest as men of varying ages, clad in waist overalls and hickory shirts, crowded into the car. These men were loggers returning to camp after a Sunday off in Eureka. There were a few young choker-setters and rigging slingers, but most were middle-aged with weather-beaten, outdoor faces. These were the donkey punchers, firemen, hooktenders, fallers, and buckers, and even a powder monkey was aboard.

Because this was my first camp job in the woods, I was curious about everything. I'd never seen hickory shirts or caulk boots before—or real loggers, for that matter!

The men settled back for a two-hour ride as the train jerked and slowly began picking up speed. We sat facing each other on two long benches against the walls of the car, and as the only young woman in a car full of rugged loggers, I was soon the object of good-natured banter. Noticing that I was too shy to respond, an older man responded to the teasing. I learned later he was the woods boss.

It was dark as we pulled into the cluster of wooden camp buildings, but the cookhouse and rows of bunkhouses were brightly lit by the camp generator. I followed the men into the kitchen where Christina, the head cook, had a bountiful smorgasbord of cold cuts, pastries, bread, and coffee for the returning loggers. Loggers, I soon found, were always hungry and had cast-iron stomachs besides. The next day I was to learn they could lay away a big meal in eight minutes or less.

Morgan, a flunky, was serving the men thick slabs of bread and meat. "Hi," she smiled and asked my name. "Anna," I replied, liking her at once. She was a slender young woman nicknamed Two-Speed because she was a very fast worker but very slow in speaking. Ida, the dishwasher, was helping serve the men. A plump and motherly older woman, she handed me a logger-sized sandwich and a thick china cup of fragrant coffee.

Finding a seat by the wood box, I began looking around the clean, compact kitchen where I would be working. The long wood-burning range with its large firebox and two big ovens caught my eye. On its 24-by-36 inch cast-iron griddle, hotcakes, steaks, chops, fish, and eggs were cooked. The pine floor was clean from scrubbing. Strong shelves on the bare walls were stacked with deeps (oval bowls about three inches deep) and platters. Gray graniteware tea and coffeepots were lined up neatly on one large shelf. The cookhouse was rugged and primitive, but I liked what I saw. The feeling of belonging in the woods was already putting its claim on me.

So far as I know, women first began working in the logging camps of the Pacific Northwest during the World War I years of 1917 and 1918. By their own endeavor and efficiency they proved themselves capable of good work under the hard conditions of camp life. Looking at the impassive cook, Christina, and the elderly Ida, I wondered if they had been among these pioneering women.

Christina walked over to where I was sitting. "Can you cook?" she asked abruptly.

"Yes, I can cook," I replied.

"In large quantities?"

"Yes."

"Humph, where did a young thing like you learn how?"

"I happen to have had a very strict and disciplined bringing-up," I answered.

The flat face seemed to soften. "Well, all right. I just wanted to make sure. You will leave with the men after breakfast in the morning to cook dinner for them in the dinner shed."

"Dinner shed?" I had never heard of a dinner shed.

"It's a small shed at the top of the incline where log cars are loaded before they are sent down to the logging lokey below. You'll be cooking for twenty-five men." She smiled grimly and pointed to a room off the kitchen. "You will also flunky for thirty-five men in that dining room."

I knew I could cook, but waiting table was entirely new to me, and my first attempt proved very embarrassing. At breakfast the following morning I loaded up with as many plates of hotcakes as my inexperienced hands allowed. Entering the dining room, I was confronted with a roomful of seated men, their eyes turned toward me, and overcome by nervousness I stumbled over my own feet and fell, plates and hotcakes flying. I wanted to sink through the floor and disappear.

No one laughed. Loggers are said to be rough men, but they can also be gentle. An old windfall bucker helped me to my feet while others gathered up the plates and spilled hotcakes. "There, hon," the old bucker said kindly. "Just go back to the kitchen and get us some more hotcakes." His common sense eased my embarrassment, and somehow I managed to keep the food coming through breakfast.

It was Two-Speed who taught me the simple trick of balancing six deeps or platters on my left arm while carrying one in my right hand. To keep our arms from getting burned, we used a side towel laid over our left arm and shoulder.

Cooking dinner in the dinner shed was easy, but walking up the steep hill to it made my young legs ache. Later, whenever the woods boss wasn't around, the men and I would ride up the steep slope on an empty logging car towed by a steam donkey.

Everything was new and fascinating to me. I watched the big redwood logs come in from the landing on cars shunted to the tracks at the top of the incline by a puffing steam locomotive, or "lokey" as we called it. There, the loaded cars, one at a time, were hooked onto a cable and lowered down the steep hillside to the tracks below. Sometimes a loaded car would jump the track, and I would watch in awe as Red, the donkey puncher, would snatch off his hat, throw it on the ground, and systematically stomp it to pieces with his caulked boots, swearing continuously. Even more amazing was Red's uncanny skill at getting the load back on the track again.

The dinners I cooked in the dinner shed were big meals with meat, potatoes, gravy, salad, vegetables, and always pie. Loggers love pie, and I would have to hurry to get them baked by dinnertime. There would also be a large pan of freshly made doughnuts, still warm, waiting for the men. After dinner there was always washing up, tables to reset, and the hike back to camp, where I would help Christina with the evening meal.

Since Christina was a good cook, and I was willing to work hard, we made a good team. We really loaded down the tables with wholesome food. Christina, ever ready to surprise the men with something new, questioned me for new recipes and new ways of preparing food.

◇————————◇

Between work periods, Two-Speed and I enjoyed hiking among the tall beautiful redwoods. Besides the new logging grades cut in the virgin timber, there were game trails to follow. Ida with her caring, motherly way would caution us. "You two girls should be taking a nap in the afternoons instead of gallivanting around the woods. You need your rest!" Once we almost became lost. When Peter, the woods boss, heard of it, he only cautioned us.

"If you girls ever get lost, just stay put. Don't panic and wander around. Sit down and wait, and you'll be found a damned sight quicker."…

Perhaps because the camp girls themselves felt the call of the brooding timber and belonged there, we got along very well together. We lived close, sharing what was commonly called the flunky shack. The real name was women's quarters, but no one ever referred to it by that name.

Sitting cozily together on powder boxes, busily plying peeler and knife, was a time to chatter and exchange confidences. Perhaps there was going to be a Saturday night dance in some nearby town, and the logging company was furnishing transportation. Naturally we wanted to go because we'd be the most popular girls there. The loggers from camp would want to dance with their little waitresses. Most of our dresses were Sears and Roebuck or Montgomery

Ward. We'd plan on which one to wear and what we needed to borrow from each other. I had yet to meet my young logging brakeman with his laughing gray eyes, his hickory shirt opened at the neck. He was still in the future, and I was young and liked to dance....

The flunky shack, like the men's bunkhouses, was spare in furnishings. Just as the girls had no business in the men's bunkhouses, the flunky shack was off limits to the men. We slept on narrow iron cots with rough bedding. The shack was kept warm with a wood-burning heater, the wood cut and brought in by the bull cook. A bull cook was usually a worn-out logger whose job was to keep the kitchen and bunkhouse supplied with firewood, plus other odd chores around camp. For cupboards, there was an orange case or an egg case nailed to the wall. Other egg cases were upended and used for stands, covered with clean flour sacking. Our pretty dresses that we ironed with such care were hung on coat hangers, then on nails driven into the bare walls. There were no chairs, so we used the beds to sit on. This way of life was rugged, but we accepted it as part of our job, for the woods had laid its claim on the girls who worked in camps....

As in any line of work where men and women are thrown together, a certain amount of hanky-panky went on. But not as much as one would think. In a camp full of men, set far back in the woods, with only three to five women, it just wouldn't work. Most of the camp girls realized what they did in one camp would follow them to another, and they wanted to keep their names clean of gossip. Yet romance often blossomed....

As better roads made the camps more accessible and more families began living in, family houses were furnished by the company....Men stayed longer in camp and were steadier, not quitting because of trivial incidents or because of rumors floating around of better-paying jobs elsewhere.

The women had a hand in this. It was nice to come home to a smiling face. The good smells of supper cooking and kids scrubbed clean and stretching out their hands for something left over from daddy's lunch made a welcome change in a logger's life. As the saying went in the camps, when a woman kissed her logger husband good-bye in the morning, she was never sure he'd be coming home that night. Logging has always been a dangerous occupation. They were sturdy women, those loggers' wives who gave up a soft living in town to rough it over wood stoves, sometimes with outside privies. There were no movies out there, no amusements but battery-set radios. They had to make their own amusements. Pinochle was a favorite card game on evenings when several families gathered. We also used to have pinochle games in the afternoons while our husbands were at work in the woods.

Our logger husbands needed us. On cold rainy days when the men came home at night drenched to the skin, wives helped to peel off the wet, clinging clothes that stuck to their cold bodies like glue, every stitch wringing wet. There would be a warm fire in the kitchen range, a pot of steaming coffee, or if anywhere near payday, a hot drink or two. I'll put it in simple words. I, who had been warm and dry all day, could not do enough for my young husband.

Like their men who lived dangerously every minute of the day while working in the woods, the women in camp were a sturdy lot. Our doors were never locked, nor was anything ever stolen....

It seems that women in the logging camps, whether working in the cookhouse or living in family houses, exerted a good influence over the men. I've worked in a number of logging camps and can truthfully say I was always treated courteously and like a lady. I've read or heard somewhere that Stewart Holbrook said "Loggers are nature's gentlemen." And it's true.

VERNON PATTERSON

from WISE AS A GOOSE

A teacher of language and literature in Orange County, California, a poet and journalist, Vernon Patterson also authored two novels: All Giants Wear Yellow Breaches *(1935), a chronicle of boyhood in turn-of-the-century Missouri, and* Wise as a Goose, *(1939), a novel of the California redwood country.* Wise as a Goose *details the state of the logging industry just before World War II and expands on the labor issues that underlie so much of what has been written about the redwoods.*

In the fall of 1923 Muller and Schmidt, the largest laborer's employment agency in San Francisco, occupied one large rectangular room, walled with blackboards and with rows of plain wooden benches along the sides. There were no doors and the room was open in front its full width, like the stall of a stable. Due to the lowness of the ceiling, the place was always a little dark and retained a dampish smell. For a distance of some six feet around each of the sand spittoons scattered about in the room, the floor was befouled with orange peel, wads of tobacco, and other filth.

It was late afternoon. On the benches along the walls a dozen or more men sat waiting. Several of them had been there since early morning. Those few who could afford them read newspapers, concentrating on the HELP WANTED, MALE columns. Others merely sat, staring at nothing.

At the far end of a bench one man, a cap over his eyes, was stretched his length, asleep, his feet turned sidewise so that the holes in the soles of his shoes were plainly visible.

Several times a day the boss, a huge ambulant stomach spanned by an equatorial belt, emerged from a boarded enclosure at the back of the room, propelled his globose forefront to the blackboard and chalked up a notice of a job. At such times there was always a stir among the waiting men; necks would crane, every eye follow the chubby, slow-writing fingers. There were now a dozen jobs listed on the board:

Fender and Body Metal Finisher, Color Dinger;
2 Solder Wipers. Must be fast. $3.50;
Cook, Country Hotel. $50 and Found;
7 Hardrock Miners, Nevada. Strike Conditions.

Occasionally the boss would come out and with an ostentatious flourish erase one of the notices, thus indicating that the job had been filled.

The man who had been asleep on the bench wakened, stretched his legs, yawned, sleepily ran his fingers through his hair. He was a young man, perhaps twenty-six, obviously well set up; but his clothes—he wore corduroys faded from many washings and the soiled collars of two shirts protruded above his coat—together with the fact that his thin cheeks were covered with a week's growth of beard, gave him the appearance of a man much older. The only unusual aspect of his features was that of his eyes; they were very brown, like his curly hair, and almost oriental in their almond-shaped length. After scanning the late entries on the blackboard, he fumbled in his pocket for Durham and papers. "Do any decent jobs ever come into this slave market?" he inquired, abruptly addressing an older man who sat beside him reading a paper.

"I dunno," was the reply, spoken with a slight German accent. "I been here every day for a week, an' they ain't had but two calls for carpenters so far. An' one o' them was up in Oregon. What's your trade?"

"Anything. I'll do anything—except scab."

The older man looked over his spectacles with the sniffy condescension of the skilled craftsman regarding the muck-stick laborer. "No trade man iss oud o' luck these days," he advised, turned the pages of his paper, and went on reading.

"Say, lad," a bald, freckled fellow with the long scraggy neck of a picked chicken, who sat on the opposite side of the carpenter, leaned forward and drawled, "Did you say you wanted anything?"

"Yeah."

"Married?"

"No."

"Ever do any loggin'?"

"Loggin'? No, but I would."

"Well, tell ya, there was a guy boarded at my place got a job out o' here yesterday up the redwood country. He said the boss told him in there when he got the job that the mills was runnin' full blast now—some of 'em even puttin' on night shifts. But they ain't gettin' any men through the agencies down here 'ceptin' for special jobs. Like this here guy, he was a fireman. They sent him up to work on one o' them bull donkeys."

"Yeah? Where is this place?"

"Wyola."

"Where's that?"

"It's up the northern part o' the state."

"How long's it take to get there from here?"

"We-el now, there you got me. Lemme see, on the train—you get the Pacific Coast Railway over Sausalito—Oh, I reckon it'd take you about—"

"How many miles is it?"

"Well, by George now, I couldn't tell you that either. At a guess—just a guess, mind you—I'd say it was all o' three hundred miles or thereabouts."

"Three hundred." The young man looked thoughtful. He sighed and got to his feet. "Well, thanks for the tip. I just might take a jaunt up there."

"Where'd you come from, lad?" the other went on curiously. "Live here in town?"

"No—I—come from down Texas way."

"That so? Got a second cousin lives in San Antonio myself. How's things down there?"

"Rotten."

The long-necked man shook his head. "Guess they're pretty bad ever'where."

The boy grunted and, shoving his hand into his pocket, fingered the two silver half-dollars he found there. "I know I've got to get something pretty damn soon," he mumbled. "And there don't seem to be much around this burg." He moved to the door. "Yeh, might take a trip up into that redwood country. So long."

But the long-necked man rose and followed him. "So long, lad. An' say, here's my card," he whispered. "Ever you come to town an' want a good workin' man's boardin' place, you can't beat my wife's cookin'. Chicken dinner ever' Sunday. Twenty-five to thirty-five a month up."...

◇――――◇

Dan was awakened the following morning by a voice yelling down at him, "Hey, jungle buzzard! Git t' hell out o' there!"

He pulled himself up out of the hatch, and while the shack, armed with a long oak club, stood silently watching, swung down the grabirons.

The train had stopped in a long cut. On one side a rocky bluff rose up somewhat higher than the cars, and on the other, an incline strewn with rubble led down to a broad gently flowing river walled on the farther bank by a dense growth of trees, behind which rose blackly wooded mountains. There was no sign of human habitation.

Once safely on the ground he called up to the brakeman, "Where's the nearest town, Jack?"

The shack merely pointed with his club toward the front of the train.

Walking on down the curving track in the direction indicated, after some two hundred yards he came to a flimsy wooden stairway leading up the face of the bluff, and mounting the steps he was surprised to see unfolded fanlike before him a small mountain town.

Through the very center of the town and proceeding toward a background of hills stump-dotted and guttered with rain runnels ran a narrow street lined with shabby unpainted cottages, and on a quarter-mile slope extending up from the river at the right, a gigantic brick smokestack rose from an aggregation of buildings and yards—a lumber mill. Near the mill, twigged by a spur to the main line of the railroad, lay a pond half-covered with floating logs. From his perch on the bluff he watched a man armed with a pike pole guiding a log across the open water. When the log had been jockeyed into position and just before it was caught by the jack chains to be dragged up into the mill maw, the man leaped gracefully to another log where, birling the log with his feet, arms uplifted, he balanced himself like a bird on a swaying branch.

Over the river, which curved broadly around the town, and among the trees on the opposite bank, shreds of fog drifted. The humid air bore a smell of resin and wet leafage. From the distant mill buildings came a continuous rumble of machinery.

He was hungry, and making his way down the street, he accosted the first passerby and inquired where he could find a restaurant.

"There ain't no restaurants in Bridgeport," was the answer. "There's a hotel across the river in Wop Flat where they serve meals, but that's three miles from here."

"Where do all the people in this town garbage?"

"Home, or in the comp'ny mess hall."

"That's the mill there?"

"Yep."

"Where's the superintendent's office?"

"Lookin' fer job o' work?"

"Yeah."

"Go straight on down the street here till you come to a big buildin' with a red porch in front—that's the hirin' office."

"Thanks."

He found the "hirin' office" without difficulty and there was curtly directed to "see Mr. Treadwell in the personnel department."

Outside Mr. Treadwell's door hung a sign, NO HELP WANTED. Nothing daunted, however, he pushed open the door. You couldn't be shot for trying.

A cadaverous looking man, prematurely bald, in his eyes a vague, preoccupied stare, rose from behind a desk littered with papers.

"Mr. Treadwell?"

The man forced a vacant smile as he acknowledged his name, but when Dan continued, "I'm looking for a job," his bony features relaxed into an expression of weak irascibility. "Doggone it," he began in a querulous tone, "didn't you see that sign outside? I can't understand why you fellows—"

But he never finished his complaint, for at that moment the door behind Dan burst open and a burly gray-haired old man wearing a red cruiser coat stormed into the room and, confronting Mr. Treadwell, who shot to his feet as if he had been sprung from his chair, bellowed, "What the God damn hell do you mean, Treadwell, sendin' a Portagee piler down to tend dog for Cronin! What do you want t' do, kill the saw crew? 'Zat some more o' your damned college-bred efficiency? See here, Treadwell," the old man lowered his voice to a growl and, reaching across the desk, slapped the personnel manager's vest emphatically with the back of his hand, "I want a man on that carriage that can talk American, by Christ, and I want 'im right away! Is that clear?"

Mr. Treadwell stood erect, almost leaning backward, his chin lifted and face pale as whey. "Yes, Mr. Cadogan. Yes, sir." And hastily searching among the papers on his desk he found a notebook and began to thumb the pages. "I think I have in mind here just the man you want, sir. Let me see—yes." He reached for the telephone and shouted a number.

Mr. Cadogan waited, head held tensely forward, glaring. He took a cigar from the pocket of his coat, jabbed a quarter length of it into his mouth and glowered about the room as if he were searching for someone on whom he could release his still unspent fury. His eyes were keen, thick-lidded, heavily thatched with gray. Perceiving Dan, he snapped, "Who the hell are you?"

"My name's Dan Ashton."

The other grunted, fumbled in his pocket for a match, with quick puffs lit his cigar. "Lookin' for a job?"

"Yeah," he said carelessly.

"Where'd you come from?"

"'Frisco."

"Ever worked in a mill before?"

"No."

"Do you want a job where you have to work like hell?"

"Lead me to it."

The old man gave him one sharp, appraising glance before he swung around and flung over his shoulder, "Come with me."

Outside on the porch he pointed with a hairy forefinger to a barnlike building up the street. "That's the mess hall an' bunkhouse. Go there an' tell Sorenson I said t' fix you up with a meal check an' a bed. Then get over t' the mill and report t' Cronin on Saw no. 2. Make it fast!" he added.

"Okay."

Sorenson proved to be a filthy, snaggle-toothed old crumboss. Dan found him, a gunnysack suspended from his shoulder, sprinkling sawdust on the bunkhouse floor preparatory to sweeping out. His chin and the flaccid dewlap beneath it were discolored, the front of his vest scaly with droppings of tobacco juice. After grumpily providing Dan with a room—a narrow smelly cubicle giving onto a corridor—he led the way across an intersecting runway into the mess hall, where he took from a rack a brass check stamped with the number 477.

"That's your meal check. Don't lose it or you'll have to pay twenty-five cents for another one."

"All right, son. Gracias."

"An' don't call me 'son'!" the crumboss cackled wrathfully.

Dan grinned and left.

◆————————◆

He had no difficulty finding Saw no. 2, where he presented himself to Cronin, the sawyer, a half-pint Englishman with squirrel eyes, who without asking any questions called over to him a gangling, red-headed boy named Pink.

"Show this man how to handle the dogs."

Dan followed Pink around the sawyer's box to a flat-topped car about twenty feet in length, built close to the ground and mounted on trucks which ran on a three-wheeled track.

"This here's the carriage," Pink explained. "You'll notice it runs parallel to the line of the saw cut. The logs move up here from the pond to the transfer"—pointing to a trough beside the carriage over which ran a number of flat-link chains studded with prongs—"an' then they're rolled over here onto the log deck with the kicker. Sometimes they—"

"Not so fast. What's the kicker?"

"That dingus with the steel shovin' arms. But you don't have to worry about that; it's operated by the sawyer. Your job is when the logs are rolled onto the platform ready for the saw, to take care o' these two sets o' levers an' that headblock with the extension hook on it. Now this lower lever controls the knees that adjust the logs when they have bottle-butts, the sinkers—but I'll show you more about that later. This top lever is the one that controls the dogs. The dogs are those steel hooks that clinch the log an' hold it in place on the platform. Now you watch me while I do it. Okay, Mr. Cronin!" he called.

Dan stood by watching as the automatic loader moved a log into place on the side of the carriage facing the saw, before which Cronin stood peering out of his little box, his eyes glittering, and Pink with an easy movement threw his weight backward and downward on the various sets of levers.

"Brace yourself now!" he shouted. "The carriage is goin' to start!" And almost at the same instant the carriage, bearing log, Pink, and Dan, began to move along the rails. Steam driven, it rolled smoothly and with increasing speed down the track until the length of the log had passed the saw; then it stopped and glided swiftly back again. This movement was repeated several times while Dan stood with difficulty, balancing himself on the moving platform. Suddenly he heard a low humming that increased to a steely scream as the band saw, gathering speed, nipped the end of the log, ate into it, and, proceeding down its length, sliced off the first salmon-colored slab. Then the carriage stopped, the dogs were released, and the three electrically driven shoving arms—the center one equipped with a cant hook—rose like human members and turned it over. Once more the saw was flung screaming into the soft wood, after which the log was turned over on its flat side and another slice taken off. Presently when all four sides had thus been squared the beam was ready, and thereafter, back and forth without pause and with amazing rapidity and precision, the carriage bore the log against the swift blur of the saw. Slab after slab fell onto the live rollers and was whisked away to the edgers and trimmers. The noise was indescribably shrill; it seemed to shatter the air and quiver over the body like gooseflesh.

"See that now!" Pink shouted, when the great log had been entirely reduced to boards. "It's not hard to learn. On the next log you take these two sets o' dogs. Watch me how I do it on mine. An' remember to set the levers down as hard as you can! If you don't set 'em down tight an' the log shifts a little it might snap off the saw, which wouldn't be healthy because that saw is travelin' better than ten thousand linear feet a minute, Okay. No, wait! Take the peavey there an' help me shift this new log over a little before we start."

The new log in place on the platform, Dan set his levers as carefully as he could. He found that it was not so simple as it appeared: under Pink's supervision he was forced to reset the levers three times before the sawyer, in answer to Pink's nod, finally pulled the carriage throttle and the car began to move.

"The taper levers are hard to learn at first," Pink explained as they were adjusting the next log. "Butt wood is tricky. Some of it's conky an' soft, an' some of it, like on the trees that have goose pens, is burly an' hard."

"What's a goose pen?"

"It's a tree with the inside o' the butt rotted out or burned out by fire. The heat penetrates an' dries out the wood around the cavity an' makes it brittle. It looks okay, but when you put the levers into it, it's liable to split or crumble under the pressure. Then too, especially on butt logs, you have to clamp the lever teeth in deep because the sapwood is gummy an' thick around the lower part o' the tree."

◇————————◇

As the morning passed Dan grew a little more adept. Fortunately the logs were for the most part small in thickness, and on the few misshapen butt logs, known as sinkers, Pink, who was obviously a kindly lad, assisted him with the taper levers, adding helpful though sometimes irrelevant information about logging in general. But the job was not essentially complicated, and he soon caught on. While one log was being sawed, sometimes another had to be loosened from some obstruction on the log deck and placed in readiness. This was by far the most difficult part of the work; it was done by hand with peaveys, and as the morning advanced and the logs coming in from the pond increased in thickness, it became doubly hard to shift them. Dan's clothes soon grew wet with sweat.

"Take off your shirt!" Pink shouted in one of their infrequent moments of respite when the new log was in readiness on the turner and the saw was screeching through a dry, brittle butt.

He took the advice and threw off his shirt. Thereafter he felt cooler, but his body was soon black and itchy with sawdust. Then his hands began to trouble him. Contact with the metal lever handles first reddened and then blistered the tender skin. Perceiving him in the act of blowing on his hands, Pink took off his gloves and threw them across the platform. "Put 'em on!"

He took them shamelessly. They were stiff and sopped with perspiration and grime, but they did serve to protect a little the angry blisters forming on his palms.

So deafening was the shrill of the saw and the general clamor of the mill that Dan did not hear the twelve o'clock "wissel," and did not realize that it was noon until the saw died down and from a shimmering comet became a toothed blue ribbon on the wheels.

Pink approached him with a grinning, "C'mon, let's garbage." And as they made their way through the now incongruously silent length of the mill toward the mess hall, "Well, how do you like it as far as you've gone?"

Dan's most acute reactions to the morning's labor were a ringing in the ears and a shivery feeling of nausea at the pit of his stomach. His hands hung at his sides like two weighted, throbbing clubs.

"It's tough, but I think I can make out all right once I get used to it," he answered honestly, his voice trembling. "How do you think I did?"

"Oh hell, you did fine!" Pink replied quickly. "I could tell Cronin liked the way you caught on. But if you don't mind my telling you a few things, you're makin' it too hard on yourself. Tendin' dog can be the toughest job in the whole damn mill, an' if you don't learn how to take it easy you're likely to strain a gut or something. You have to use the weight of your body on the levers. The peaveys, too. You're relyin' too much on the strength o' your arms. How's your mitts feel now?"

"Not so bad, thanks to your gloves."

"Let's see 'em."

Dan held out his hands.

Pink glanced at the galled palms in which were several broken blisters and grunted. "By tonight they'll probably be swelled up like poisoned pups. After you garbage I'd advise you to go over buy yourself some soft leather gloves."

"Yeah, I reckon I'll do that; I hate like hell to take yours."

"Oh, that's all right; I didn't mean that. But my gloves are stiff pig an' they'll hurt your hands almost as much as not havin' any at all. What you need is a soft sheep glove until your hands get toughened up."

He and Pink crowded into the mess hall with several thousand other grimy employees. The long rows of oilcloth-covered tables were spread with great platters of sliced beef and steaming vegetables. Male flunkies patrolled the aisles, replenishing the dishes as fast as they were emptied.

He had not realized how hungry he was until he began to eat. But even though he wolfed enormous quantities of beef, soggy boiled potatoes, and artillery, it was little to what he saw some of the men around him eating. Their heads bobbing low over their plates, they ate silently and rapidly, paying no attention to anything until their hunger was satisfied, when they immediately rose from their places. At the door each man paused to receive back the metal check he had surrendered when he came in and take a dirty toothpick from a greasy bowl before going outside for a smoke. Half an hour after the hall was opened, the last man was gone and the flunkies and bull cooks were gathered in one corner of the room setting a table for their own meal.

On the porch outside Dan found Pink seated on the steps in conversation with a lanky Finn tallyman whom he introduced as Axel Rostler. The Finn smiled and extended his hand. It was a small twisted smile, the wrinkles pinching around a jagged puckery sear at the left side of his mouth. Speaking quietly and in perfect English, his lips hardly moving, he said, "Very glad to know you. Sit down."

"Well," Pink inquired, "how do you feel now?"

"Better."

"Fine." Pink nodded, indicating a wooden building directly across the street. "If you want to go over and get yourself some gloves, the store's right over there."

Dan thought of the few coins in his pocket and reflected that a pair of gloves would cost at least a dollar. "Oh, I think my hands'll be all right," he said. "They feel better already."

Pink gave him a shrewd glance and growled amiably, "What the hell. Here, take this book." And he took from his pocket a book of coupons, monkey money, redeemable at the company store. "Go over an' get yourself pair gloves."

"But—hell—"

"Don't be a fool! Go on, take it."

Still he hesitated.

Pink was nettled. "Say, listen here, Jack—"

"Dan."

"Well, anyway, listen to me. There's been exactly three guys wranglin' those dogs in the last ten days, an' the third one couldn't even talk English. Get me right. I'm no tin Jesus; I'm merely savin' up a good dogger."

Amused, Dan glanced at the Finn. "What's all this?"

The Finn was cleaning his nails with his pocket knife. Without looking up he said, "Better take the book, son."

"Okay. Gracias." And taking the book, Dan crossed the street and purchased a pair of fine sheepskin gloves. When the store-keeper, on seeing his hands, gratuitously sprinkled the inside of the gloves with borax powder he appreciated the courtesy. He felt that he was going to like this job. In the face of all the friendly assistance he had received from him, he especially felt that he was going to like the freckle-faced Pink. From long experience he knew that workingmen ordinarily live much to themselves, their feelings being evidenced chiefly in terse acrid complaints and explosive boastings. Pink was obviously an exception....

His first payday came the following Saturday night and his check—deducting a dollar and a quarter a day for board and a seventy-five-cent hospital fee—left him exactly seventy-two dollars.

After he cashed his check his first move was to search for new quarters. He had come to detest the vermin-ridden bunkhouse with its deficient sanitation and tiny rooms smelling of dirty socks and disinfectant. And the steel bed covered with a hard and extremely bumpy mattress reminded him of the overseas sleeping accommodations in the army.

He was not able to locate a room anywhere in town, though he gave over several evenings to the search. He found that all the buildings in Bridgeport, from the unpainted, weatherbeaten structure that housed the motion picture theatre to the board cottages of the mill workers, were owned by the company. The cottages were rented to the workers for a nominal sum, and in return for this privilege the company exercised the strictest dictatorial rights over its tenants. The arrangement was almost feudal. He discovered, for example, that no building could be rented for a period longer than one month, that no renter was permitted to sublease all or any part of a store or dwelling, and that no buildings could be acquired for the purpose of engaging in any business that would compete with the company store. There was even a rule that householders were not permitted to raise vegetables or produce in their yards. The latter rule was designed to force all employees to trade at the company store, where prices for foodstuffs were a little higher than in any other town south of Wyola.

The company supplied electricity but no gas, and fuel was largely restricted to refuse mill wood purchased from the company. Scrip books of coupons redeemable at the store were issued on demand, and their use was encouraged since they served to keep all workers more or less in a state of peonage. Outside the mill all initiative was paralyzed. Houses were run down, yards flowerless and choked with weeds—even the children were, many of them, malnourished and rickety.

The chief topic of conversation in town was the company. Indeed the very word "company" had for most of the washed-out citizenry of Bridgeport some of the awful implications of the word Jehovah. The company existed for them as an impersonalized power, and its dictates, in the form of typewritten onionskin notices tacked on the mill door, had many of the attributes of divine law. There remained for the workers but one sovereign privilege, that of choice: they could either obey the company-made regulations and keep their mouths shut; or they could protest, which meant the automatic loss of their jobs and prompt eviction from their homes.

To be sure, there were some, chiefly among the unmarried men, who nursed a savage though necessarily secret resentment against the company. They were for the most part cynical belly-pinched pariahs, but their souls were their own. To them the company was simply a group of capitalist mugwumps engaged in the predatory business of getting all they could for as little as they could. Cadogan they dubbed "Wolf"; and Treadwell, at whose office they got their jobs, was contemptuously referred to as "Petunia." The company infirmary was "the morgue," the medical attendants "croakers" or "tonsil snatchers"; the company store was a "simp trap"; the food served in the mess was "slum not fit for hogs"—everything, in short, was "rotten," "crummy," or "dehorn."

These men were in some cases Wobblies, "card men," and chiefly as a result of the aggressive activities of their organization for the betterment of mill and camp conditions prior to and during the war, there was a standing order to all foremen and bosses to root them out wherever found. The mere fact that a man was discovered in possession of a red card was sufficient to cause his immediate dismissal.

One evening a few days previously Dan had been invited by Axel Rostler, the Finn tallyman, to attend a private meeting of the Wobblies. The meeting was held at the home of one of the mill workers, and though Dan had found most of the Wobblies he had encountered on skid row glib with belly philosophy, suspicious of any causal searching beyond the ends of their noses, he was persuaded to go. His sympathies lay naturally with the workers—they were the creators, the builders; and he was not without a decided, though not very militant, sense of class consciousness. At the same time it often seemed to him that there was little to choose between labor and capital. Equally self-centered, they had a common morality; neither cared a damn for the rights of the other, and both used the same repressive means to achieve their ends....

Axel, Dan soon discovered, was not a bad sort. He was friendly and by no means lacking in sense. He rarely spoke of himself and it was from Pink, who knew him slightly, that Dan learned something of his history.

A flinty, hard-bitten boomer, flat receding forehead and pale blue eyes, his blond hair growing a little higher over the left temple, during the war Axel had been a rigging packer, an I.W.W. organizer, working chiefly in the Oregon and Washington lumber camps. The ugly scar at the left side of his mouth had been inflicted by a pair of brass knucks in the hands of a Portland scab herder. In conversation he had a detached, half-humorous, ironic manner, with none of the explosive, oversimplifying characteristics of the typical Wobbly. He talked easily, in a sort of deadpan way, only one side of his lips moving; and though obviously self-educated, could cite an amazing number of facts on almost any economic subject. In common with many fundamentally matter-of-fact people, he also had a penchant for myth and abstraction, and one night at Tony's, long-tongued with wine, he and Dan sat until dawn arguing the possibility of an afterlife.

When speaking of the I.W.W., however, his manner was habitually careful, guarded. He never once admitted his membership in the organization, but in answer to Dan's questions he did explain with apparent frankness the hierarchy of its structure and the favorite kinds of strikes employed.

"Strikes. In the 'intermittent strike,'" he said, "the wage slaves usually go out, say, for two or three days. When scabs are brought in, they go back to work. When the scabs leave, they go out again. Sometimes they call this the 'irritation strike.' In 1917 fifty thousand lumber slaves went out and tied up the Northwest lumber industry for two months. They were striking for an eight-hour day, using 'irritation' tactics. They'd go into the woods, work eight hours, pull the whistle and quit. When boss'd fire 'em, they'd move on to another camp, do the same thing there.

"The 'lazy strike' is another kind of strike on the job. There's no violence; the slaves simply stay at work and ca'-canny—slow down. Production decreases. Maybe they pretend they're inexperienced. They fumble, ask so many questions the boss gets grayheaded. Nothing can be pinned on anybody. If the boss says, 'I thought you were an experienced logger,' for instance, the slave says, 'I am—but not in redwood; I'm a pine logger!'

"The 'protest strike' is usually a one-day strike. A demonstration of solidarity or an expression of mass opinion. They had one for Mooney two years ago."

"How about sabotage, Axel?"

"Depends upon what you mean by sabotage. For a wage slave to pretend he's inexperienced is a form of sabotage. Sabotage can be committed by obeying the laws. If the streetcars and all the public conveyances in a city strictly obeyed the laws, the whole traffic system would be slowed up. Or if all the clerks in the bake shops let the public know exactly what ingredients go into the making of bread, and especially pastry, telling nothing but the strict truth to the customers, the baking industry would go bankrupt in a week. As for violence, the Wobblies don't advocate it."

"No?"

"No."

PETER E. PALMQUIST

PHOTOGRAPHING THE
HUMBOLDT COUNTY REDWOODS

◆──◆

My first encounter with redwood trees has remained deeply etched in my memory. I was seven years old, World War II still raged, and my parents were in the midst of an early back-to-the-land experience. My father decided that he and I would take a trip to rural Humboldt County in search of a new home. My parents wished to be isolated and self-sufficient.

In June 1944, as soon as I finished the second grade, we boarded the northbound Northwestern Pacific train. Most of the trip was at night, and I slept soundly until our predawn arrival at South Fork, a railroad siding only a short distance from today's Founders Tree Grove. It was still pitch black as we left the train and began a mile-long walk to the tiny town of Dyerville (now extinct). Almost immediately, we were enveloped in an ominous maze of gigantic redwood trees that seemed to squeeze my breath away. The road was only a primitive track winding through the still forest, and time itself seemed frozen. Unable to obtain breakfast in Dyerville, we turned westward towards Bull Creek, the site of an active logging operation.

As the dawn broke, we found ourselves entering a scene of unbelievable devastation. Even the road was littered with newly felled trees. The trunks of these fallen giants were so immense that we were frequently forced to walk great distances just to get around them. At the same time, the air was becoming increasingly choked with smoke from the round-the-clock backfires. These fires were used to burn the waste branches and underbrush and to make it easier for the bucking crews to dismantle the downed trees. The loggers were just beginning their long day's labor, and soon the shouts of "timber!" were followed by thunderous, earthshaking crashes.

It was as though I had walked onto a raging battlefield or perhaps a scene from Dante's *Inferno*. I found myself wondering if it would ever be possible to fully explain the beauty and the destruction that I had just witnessed.

When I was ten or eleven, I began taking my first photographs with my mother's box camera. Since film and commercial processing were expensive, I had to content myself with only limited access to picture taking. Following my twelfth birthday, however, my interest increased and I decided to try processing film myself. Soon, I had established a darkroom in our attic (the only dark place in the house), and I began to pursue my new hobby with a vengeance. Remembering my early experiences with the Bull Creek redwoods, I decided that the mysterious and daunting Humboldt County redwood forests would be a priority on my long list of photographic challenges.

During the late 1940s, when I first tried my hand at photographing redwood trees, I soon found that capturing effective images of the deep forest was not an easy matter. The groves were excessively dark and gloomy, and film sensitivity was quite low, necessitating the use of a tripod and prolonged time exposures. Today's color films, for instance, have a normal sensitivity range as high as 800 ASA by comparison to an ASA of only 12 for Kodachrome color slide film in 1950. Also, it was nearly impossible to get far enough away to see an entire tree, and if you tipped your camera upward, the trees looked as though they were going to topple over backwards, an optical phenomenon referred to as keystoning.

Bright sunny days were a special nightmare for the redwood forest photographer. If you exposed your film for the sunlight, the shadows became inky black and without detail. Likewise, exposing for the shadows caused the highlights to become badly overexposed, creating an unpleasant chalky effect on your finished prints. Eventually, I learned to balance my film, exposure, and processing techniques and began to have some creditable technical results. Another overriding concern involved the pictorial aesthetics of the photograph: composition, tonality, depth of focus, and a host of other elements had to be carefully balanced before the image could be truly considered an artistic success.

Twenty years later, I designed a class called "Natural Resources Photography," which I taught at Humboldt State University beginning in 1968 and through the 1970s. One of my class sessions was specifically designed to examine the potential truthfulness or reality of a photograph as an effective document of nature. My principal prop was an enlarged black-and-white photograph of a Humboldt County redwood grove. My leading question to the class was "Does this photograph clearly and accurately represent a real redwood forest?" Invariably, everyone agreed that it did. This response provided me ample opportunity to point out a number of ways in which the photograph was in fact a failure in terms of capturing reality: 1) it was not in color; 2) the viewer was limited to the particular standpoint and point of view of the camera; 3) the photograph did not smell or sound like a forest; and 4) it failed to communicate the many kinesthetic responses, such as changes in temperature, dampness, or wind, normally associated with an actual visit to a redwood forest. The students—training to become natural resource professionals— were quite astonished to think that they had mentally filled in so many of these missing elements. Without exception, each of the students had previously experienced a redwood forest, and the black-and-white photograph had merely triggered an awareness based on these past experiences. "Imagine," I continued, "your response to this same photograph if you had spent your entire life living in a desert and had never before visited a forest of any kind."

What does it take to create an outstanding photograph of redwoods? A striking viewpoint, dramatic lighting effects, and appropriate tonal values or full color are all important elements for an effective photograph. Adding a child or other human form to the composition helps a viewer better comprehend the immense scale inherent in an old-growth forest. Close-up details of the forest floor, bark, or foliage also enable the creative photographer to portray the forest environment effectively. The use of a wide-angle lens can force perspective, creating space and making the forest seem larger, while a telephoto lens has the opposite effect. Technical considerations aside, the most successful photographs of the Humboldt County redwoods are those that effectively serve the needs of their intended audience.

Portfolio

This portfolio of forty-eight photographs represents the work of eleven photographers. The images were all taken in Humboldt County, California, and range in date from about 1870 through about 1970, or roughly one hundred years of visual documentation. Since the redwood lumbering industry has long been a mainstay of Humboldt County's economy, it should come as no surprise that many of the photographs concentrate on timber harvesting and milling.

During the nineteenth century, outdoor photography was difficult at best. Photographic equipment was cumbersome, and sensitizing and processing photographic plates in the field was a serious challenge, in some instances even dangerous. Daguerreotype plates, for instance, were developed in mercury vapor at 160 degrees Fahrenheit, and consequently many early photographers suffered from the effects of mercury poisoning. The wet-collodion process sometimes employed potassium cyanide, a compound that was quickly fatal if ingested or absorbed through an open scratch in the skin. Early lenses lacked anti-reflection coatings and were generally uncorrected for most of the optical aberrations that are absent from modern lenses.

Early film emulsions were primarily sensitive to blue light. This meant that skies—primarily reflecting blue light—were easily overexposed, while reds, browns, greens, all colors consistent with the color palette of a redwood forest, were rendered severely underexposed. Wind was also a major factor. Because of the long time exposures, an errant breeze could cause a blurring of foliage and spoil the photograph. Most photographers tried to avoid the wind by working only in the morning and on windless days. Carleton E. Watkins, one of California's most illustrious landscape photographers, often began his work at dawn in order to circumvent the wind and was known to make exposures as long as one hour to compensate for the low light levels at this early time of day. Handling and transporting fragile glass-plate negatives was yet another problem that bedeviled early landscape photographers.

Between 1860 and about 1890, most photographers used the wet-collodion process to make their glass-plate negatives. The procedure required a careful cleaning of the glass plate followed by a coating of collodion (a thick, syrupy liquid that was poured onto the plate as an emulsion) followed by dipping the plate in silver nitrate sensitizing solution. This process had to be accomplished on site— usually with the aid of a portable dark tent—and the negative quickly exposed and processed while still damp. Wet-collodion photographer William Bell, who did survey photography in Colorado for the United States government in 1872, described his typical workday:

> I arise at 4 A.M.; feed the mule; shiver down my breakfast; mercury at 30 [degrees], candle dim, cup and plate tin; my seat the ground. After breakfast I roll up my bedding, carry it up to be loaded on the pack mule, water and saddle my riding mule, and by that time it is broad daylight. If negatives are to be taken on the march, the photographic mule is packed with dark-tent, camera, etc. The temperature has risen from 30

*[degrees] to 65 [degrees]. One finds difficulty in flowing a 10 x
12 plate with thick enough collodion to make a sufficiently
strong negative without redevelopment, and to have a plate
ready for development that has not dried on account of the
distance the plate has been carried and [the] time intervening
between sensitizing and development...these troubles are constant.* [Philadelphia Photographer *10, no. 109 (January
1873): 101]*

By the 1890s, the widespread availability of factory-prepared dry-
plate negatives was a big help for the outdoor photographer. No
longer did the photographic plate need to be prepared and
processed under field conditions. Instead, photographers could
carry their exposed but unprocessed plates back to their base dark-
rooms to develop at their leisure. Other huge technical changes
were also under way, the most notable being the photography
industry's interest in servicing the burgeoning amateur market
with the mass production of smaller, roll-film cameras. Eastman
Kodak Company, of course, became a leader in this industry.
While it was easier for increasing numbers of individuals to take
nature photographs, there were two persistent technical problems: the new film was still not sensitive to the full spectrum of
nature's colors, and there was no anti-halation backing. Modern
films have anti-halation coatings on the back side of the film to
prevent or inhibit unwanted light from penetrating the film, hitting the back of the plate holder, and bouncing back into the film.
This problem was most noticeable in strong highlights, in which
the margins of the highlights were significantly degraded by this
errant re-exposure.

The first full-color film, called autochrome, was invented
about 1908. This short-lived system used dyed starch crystals to produce a one-of-a-kind transparent positive. The ever popular
Kodachrome, the next transparent positive film, did not make its
debut until about 1937. Full-spectrum black-and-white film

(panchromatic) did not make its appearance until well into the twentieth century.

While the portfolio does not include any works in color, there is a sampling of wet-plate, dry-plate, sheet-film and roll-film photographs. Some were taken on negatives as large as 11 x 14 inches and others as tiny as 35-mm roll film. As would be expected, commercial examples are dominant.

Notes on the Photographers

Plates 1–4: Amasa Plummer Flaglor (1848–1918) was born in Canada and began his photographic career at age fourteen when he apprenticed to a San Francisco portrait photographer. He moved to Humboldt County in March 1871. During the 1870s, Flaglor was the region's most dominant photographer. He was primarily a portrait photographer; his surviving outdoor views are few but serve as excellent historical examples. Plate 1, for instance, is a veritable memorial to the high romance—man against nature—of the redwood logging of yesteryear: the choppers have already completed their undercut, while the assembled visitors provide us with a marvelous sense of scale. If we assume that the average shoulder width of each visitor was approximately two feet, then the diameter of the tree was at least twenty feet. Because of the lack of sharpness at the photograph's perimeter, it is likely that it was made with a lens intended for portraiture. Note also the practical logging details, such as the springboard platforms that the choppers stood on while they worked (compare with Plate 12, which shows a number of "misery whips" [saws] and a better look at the springboards in action). Redwood trees were commonly cut well above the base in order to minimize the amount of extra work caused by the swelling near the butt and the general toughness of the wood near the ground. Plates 2 through 4 picture successive steps in the harvesting process. Plate 2 shows the bucking process, in which the tree is cut into saw-log lengths. The ox team was used to skid these sections to a landing for later transport by train to the mill. In Plate 3 we see a trainload of de-barked logs arriving at the mill. In the foreground are stacks of drying lumber, while Plate 4 provides an early glimpse of a logging pond. Storing logs in water helped prevent "checking" (cracking) and kept the log in a green condition, thus making it easier to mill. The water also washed away rocks and other objects that might dull the saws. Flaglor's photographs are completely documentary in nature and were usually taken from an elevated standpoint.

Plate 5: Robert Frederick Blum (1857–1880) became an apprentice to A. P. Flaglor by age nineteen and later managed Flaglor's branch gallery in Ferndale. Seeking to gain additional photographic experience, Blum worked for a major gallery in San Francisco, where he contracted typhoid fever and died at age twenty-three. About 1878, Blum made a small series of town views including Plate 5, which shows a large redwood log being transported on Main Street, Rohnerville. The log is held on a "truck" with iron-rimmed wheels. At least two teams of oxen are shown. A log of this size could easily weigh as much as fifteen tons.

Plate 6: Martin Howe Grant (1831–1889), another Canadian, arrived in Humboldt County around 1876. Primarily a portrait photographer, Grant did a number of 11 x 14-inch photographs of local celebrations, primarily Fourth of July events, fire department festivals, and various fraternal gatherings. Plate 6 is one of the most interesting—and one of my favorites—of all redwood logging images taken in the region at this early time. The single train carries a total of sixteen saw logs containing almost ninety thousand board feet of soon-to-be-milled lumber. The waving American flags, together with the "Sunday-dressed" crowd, provide eloquent testimony to the pride of the moment.

Plates 7–10: Edgar Cherry (born c. 1845) was a traveling landscape photographer who visited Humboldt County on several occasions

between 1882 and 1884. In 1884, Cherry published a photographi-
cally illustrated book called *Redwood and Lumbering in California
Forests.* Each book was illustrated with twenty-four original photographs tipped onto special pages located between text pages. No
two copies of the book are precisely alike in terms of image selection. To compound the extreme rarity of these photographs, none
of these images were ever reproduced in any other form.
Approximately thirty copies of *Redwood and Lumbering in California
Forests* are known today. It is these images that provide the clearest
and best visual compendium of the surging growth of redwood
logging in Northern California during the early 1880s. Plate 7, for
example, is a wonderfully graphic view of a mill-man posing with
redwood "cants" (large timbers intended for resawing into boards).
Plate 8 records a logging train transporting a load of milled lumber
across the Mad River trestle. Each of Cherry's images is intended to
reveal the various steps of redwood harvesting, including the
remarkable "Evans Third Saw" shown in Plate 9. This elaborate set
of four saws was driven by steam, and judging by the height of the
workman, was capable of cutting boards six feet wide. Saws no. 1
and no. 2 were the primary cutting saws. Meanwhile, saw no. 3
began the next cut, with saw no. 4 trimming off the upper edge of
each board.

Plates 11–21: Augustus William Ericson (1848–1927), a Swedish
immigrant, served Humboldt County as its major commercial photographer for nearly forty years. In 1866, at age eighteen, he traveled to Chicago before finding work in the logging industry in
Michigan. By 1869 he had reached Humboldt County, where he
worked for the Trinidad Mill Company, first as a manual laborer
and then as the company bookkeeper. In the spring of 1877, Ericson
moved to Arcata, where he became a telegrapher and tried his hand
at several businesses, among them a partnership in a local drugstore
and "job printing" local billheads and handbills. His first experience
with outdoor photography probably coincided with the production

of Edgar Cherry's book *Redwood and Lumbering in California Forests* during the early 1880s. In the meantime, Ericson married and began a family that would eventually total eight children. Gregarious and popular, Ericson took an interest in all aspects of his community, and it is not surprising that he found photography appealing. Using a camera that made 8 x 10-inch glass negatives, Ericson took it upon himself to document virtually every facet of life on California's North Coast. In 1893, his photographs were used to illustrate a picture book entitled *In the Redwood's Realm*. The same year, his photographs represented Humboldt County at the Chicago World's Columbian Exposition. Although Ericson photographed every aspect of his community, he was particularly adept at documenting the redwood products industry. Plates 12, 13, 14, 16, and 18 illustrate various steps in the transformation of redwood trees into redwood lumber. Plates 15 and 17 reveal the immense size of redwood logs. Plate 15, of course, is a quintessential example of the David-and-Goliath aspect of redwood harvesting. Plate 17 pictures a workman hewing a single board, measuring four inches by sixteen feet, that was intended for display at the Chicago World's Columbian Exposition of 1893. The immense redwood stump shown in Plate 19 served as a unique prop for a succession of school and fraternal groupings. Today, Ericson's photographs continue to be published as the strongest symbols of pioneer Humboldt County and of the halcyon years of redwood logging in Northern California prior to environmental controls.

Plates 22–24: Ray Jerome Baker (1880–1972) was born in Rockford, Illinois, but spent his early years in Minnesota. Baker came to Eureka during a summer trip in 1904. He liked the area enough to purchase a photographic studio, where he produced thousands of outdoor views and studio portraits until his departure in 1908. Like Ericson, Baker photographed commercial enterprises, including shipping and the early automotive industry. Unlike Ericson, however, Baker was considered outspoken and radical, especially because of his membership in the local Socialist Party. Also, his hearing was impaired, and this often created problems of communication and contributed to his reputation as a scrappy radical. Plate 24, with its reference to "Sunlight in the Redwoods," is an excellent example of Baker's pictorial awareness. Even his starkly industrial images display a well-ordered sense of composition and close attention to foreground detail (Plates 22 and 23). Baker later moved to Hawaii, where he became a prominent fixture and was deservedly referred to as "the most famous photographer in Hawaiian history." When he retired in 1959 he was quoted as saying, "I've been the most fortunate of men. My hobby is my occupation."

Plates 25–28: Jesse A. Meiser (1870–1939) began life in the Midwest but lived many years in the northern part of Washington State. He moved to Eureka in 1901 but apparently did not enter the local photography field until 1905. Primarily interested in scenic work, he made a considerable number of pictorial landscapes which he sold to the newly developing tourist trade (see Plate 28). Meiser also proved especially adept at capturing local maritime disasters, of which there were many. First on the scene with his camera and first to offer shipwreck images for sale, he was soon dubbed the "Photographic Minute Man" for this Johnny-on-the-spot photojournalism. Unlike Baker, Meiser did not actually attempt to make a living from the redwood industry but preferred, instead, to concentrate on elements which would appeal to visitors. Plates 25, 26, and 27 are strong examples of his dramatic approach to making redwoods appear as awesome as possible. Meiser, considered an aggressive businessman, spent his spare time teaching at the local College of Photography, which he founded. He is also credited with several photographic patents, including one for an innovative camera shutter. He left Humboldt County in 1912 but continued to work as a photographer in other parts of California until his death.

Plates 29–34: The Art-Ray Company specialized in the production of scenic postcards, many of them scenes along the Redwood Highway. In 1946, two brothers, Charles Arthur Payne (1888–1953) and Leslie Raymond Payne (1893–1962), settled in Crescent City, California, some seventy miles north of Eureka. The name of the company was derived by combining the brothers' middle names. Art-Ray postcards were produced until about 1956, and tens of thousands were sold at five cents each. Although it seems incomprehensible that the brothers could operate profitably on a handmade product that yielded at best no more than three cents each, they seemed perfectly content in their work. During a portion of each year, one or both brothers would set out on a picture-taking journey to gather new views. They traveled in a car that towed a small travel trailer and along the way sold stock from their previous year's production. The photographs were taken on 5 x 7-inch sheet film. After processing, the negative was scribed to show the cropping of the 3½ x 5-inch postcard and a caption was added in India ink (see examples). The Art-Ray postcards featured "points of interest" along Highway 101. Drive-thru trees (Plate 29), oddities of nature (Plate 30), and humor (Plate 33) were emphasized as much as possible. Although most of the photographs are documentary, examples such as Plate 31 show that the brothers had an eye for dramatizing the ordinary. Today, surviving Art-Ray postcards are important historical resources, inasmuch as many of the structures and sites they photographed have been significantly altered over the past fifty years.

Plates 35–40: David Harper Swanlund (1926–1984) was a native of Eureka and a member of a photographic dynasty: his father, uncle, and brothers were also photographers. David was trained at the Fred Archer School of Photography in Los Angeles. He was drafted into the service during World War II and served three years in the Army Air Corps Intelligence Service. After his discharge, he returned to Eureka to work in the family studio. In 1955, he left the family business and opened a commercial photography laboratory, specializing in photo finishing. David also worked as an aerial and industrial photographer, with many of his assignments connected with the forest products industry. Most of his work was done with a 4 x 5-inch press camera, sheet film and/or film packs, a far cry from the clumsy glass-plate negatives of his predecessors. Redwood logging and lumbering techniques had also changed radically, with powerful tractors and trucks replacing the animal and steam powered machinery of earlier times. Plate 38, an aerial view of the Pacific Lumber Company at Scotia, serves as a case in point. Not only do we see a mass system of lumbering at work—Pacific Lumber was the largest producer of redwood lumber in the world—but David Swanlund's ability to photograph from above was a remarkable improvement on the concept of the "best general view." In many ways, David Swanlund was a photographer's photographer, dedicated and hardworking. This statement is even more meaningful when you discover that he had only one working eye; the other was made of glass.

Plates 41–48: Peter Eric Palmquist (b. 1936). The photographs in this section were all taken during the 1960s. Not only do they show pronounced changes in the logging industry, but they represent huge advances in photography as well. Plates 41–44 and 47, for example, were all taken with a handheld 35mm camera; the remainder on 2¼-inch roll film. In either case, my equipment fit comfortably in a small carrying bag, a far cry from the equipment used by my predecessors. Plate 41 shows a faller using a sighting device to determine the placement of the undercut. These men became so practiced in the art of felling giant trees that they often placed a target stick upright in the ground several dozen yards away; they seldom missed driving the stick into the ground. Plates 42 and 43 show innovative "off-road" trucks in action. These special trucks were far too heavy to operate on public highways and many logging companies built private roads directly between forest and mill. Other dramatic changes include the utilization of sawdust and milling waste by converting them to paper. Plate 46 shows another emblem of change: system for dumping an entire truckload of sawdust at once, a task activated by the truck driver himself, literally with the "push of a button." Plate 44 shows the dedication of the Avenue of the Giants, symbolizing ongoing changes in public policy towards redwood forest management. Plate 45 pictures logging competitions in an annual event called the Lumberjack's Jubilee; declining logging and industry mechanization have cut deeply into events of this kind, and such events are rarely seen today. Likewise, with the utilization of milling waste, the once ubiquitous teepee burner (Plate 47) has also drifted into oblivion. A more personal symbol of change is seen in a newly constructed (in 1961) section of the Redwood Highway (Plate 48). This scene is only a short distance from the spot where I first entered the Humboldt County redwoods in 1944!

PLATE I: Big tree, on Mr. Richard Allard's claim, North Fork Elk River, 18 feet in diameter, April 1872. Photograph by Amasa Plummer Flaglor

PLATE 2: Bucking crew with oxen, c. 1872. Photograph by Amasa
Plummer Flaglor

JOHN VANCE'S MILL

Railroad and Logging Works,
Mad River, Humboldt County,
California.
1875

PLATE 3: John Vance's mill, Mad River, Humboldt County, 1875. Photograph by
Amasa Plummer Flaglor

PLATE 4: Lumber mill, Humboldt County, c. 1875. Photograph by Amasa
          Plummer Flaglor

PLATE 5: Large log with oxen, Rohnerville, c. 1878. Photograph by Robert Frederick Blum

PLATE 6: Trainload of 16 logs measuring 88,568 [hoard] feet, from the logging woods of John Vance, Mad River, Humboldt County, c. 1885. Photograph by Martin Howe Grant

PLATE 7: Lumberman with redwood cants, c. 1883–1884. Photograph by Edgar Cherry

PLATE 8: Logging train on Mad River trestle, c. 1883–1884. Photograph by
Edgar Cherry

PLATE 9: Evans Third Saw (actually four saws cutting simultaneously),
c. 1883–1884. Photograph by Edgar Cherry

PLATE 10: Fourth of July excursion to the logging woods, c. 1883–1884.
Photograph by Edgar Cherry

PLATE II: Old-growth redwood grove, c. 1893. Photograph by Augustus William Ericson

PLATE 12: Felling crew with axes and misery whips, c. 1893. Photograph by Augustus William Ericson

PLATE 13: Cutting shingle bolts, c. 1893. Photograph by Augustus William Ericson

PLATE 14: Woods crew using tackle and steam donkey to move saw log, c. 1896.
Photograph by Augustus William Ericson

PLATE 15: Sections of a single tree cut into saw logs, c. 1896. Photograph by Augustus William Ericson

PLATE 16: Logging locomotive with gypsy winch attachment, c. 1896.
Photograph by Augustus William Ericson

PLATE 17: Redwood plank 4 inches thick, 16 feet wide, Elk River, Humboldt County, c. 1893. Photograph by Augustus William Ericson

PLATE 18: Lumber mill with milled lumber, c. 1896. Photograph by Augustus William Ericson

PLATE 19: School group on redwood stump, near Fieldbrook, c. 1896. Photograph by Augustus William Ericson

PLATE 20: Native Americans with redwood slab house, near Hoopa, c. 1896.
Photograph by Augustus William Ericson

PLATE 21: Hotel Sequoia c. 1898. Photograph by Augustus William Ericson

PLATE 22: Dolbeer Steam Donkey in operation, c. 1908. Photograph by Ray Jerome Baker

PLATE 23: Skidding logs with the aid of a Dolbeer steam donkey, c. 1908.
Photograph by Ray Jerome Baker

Sunlight in the Redwood. Baker Photo. No. 8.

PLATE 24: Sunlight in the redwoods c. 1908. Photograph by Ray Jerome Baker

PLATE 25: Clear redwood plank, Dolbeer & Carson, Eureka, California c. 1910.
Photograph by Jesse A. Meiser

PLATE 26: Demonstrating the size of the butt cut, c. 1910. Photograph by Jesse A. Meiser

PLATE 27: Fallen tree with void large enough to hold a mounted rider, c. 1910.
Photograph by Jesse A. Meiser

PLATE 28: Old-growth grove near Dyerville, c. 1910. Photograph by Jesse A. Meiser

PLATE 29: "The Chandalier [sic] Tree" at Underwood Park c. 1940s. Photograph by the Art-Ray Company

"Adoption or Return of Life" In Skeleton Park, 7½ Miles North of Crescent City, On Redwood Highway #101. 630—ART-RAY.

PLATE 30: "Adoption or Return of Life." In Skeleton Park, on Redwood Highway c. 1940s. Photograph by the Art-Ray Company

Looking heavenwards up "The Black Bears' Den", On Path of the Woods.

582-CART. RAY.

At Big Tree Park, On Redwood Hgw.

Within the image:
"Photo Stump"
Original height 275 feet,
and Volume 60,000 board feet.
In Skeleton Park on US Highway #101.
7 miles north of Crescent City, Calif.

475-ART-RAY

Photo Stump

PLATE 32: "Photo Stump" on U.S. Highway 101 c. 1940s. Photograph by the
Art-Ray Company

PLATE 33: "He and She," Redwood Highway c. 1940s. Photograph by the Art-
Ray Company

In-image handwritten text:
Fallen Tree Stump at
Richardson Grove State Park
(Original Height 320 Feet. Age 1250 Years. Diameter 13 Feet.)

1504 ART-RAY

PLATE 34: Fallen tree stump at Richardson Grove State Park (original height 320 feet, age 1250 years, diameter 13 feet) c. 1940s. Photograph by the Art-Ray Company

PLATE 35: Caterpillar tractor skidding redwood logs, c. 1950s. Photograph by David Harper Swanlund

PLATE 36: Giant log deck of redwood awaiting transport to the mill, c. 1950s.
Photograph by David Harper Swanlund

PLATE 37: Loading redwood logs at landing, c. 1950s. Photograph by David Harper Swanlund

PLATE 38: Pacific Lumber Mill, Scotia, c. 1950s. Photograph by David Harper
Swanlund

PLATE 39: Milling redwood lumber, c. 1950s. Photograph by David Harper
Swanlund

PLATE 40: Stacking redwood lumber to be air-dried, c. 1950s. Photograph by David Harper Swanlund

PLATE 41: Sighting the undercut, Simpson Timber Company logging show, 1962. Photograph by Peter Eric Palmquist

PLATE 42: Loading an off-highway logging truck, Simpson Timber Company, 1962. Photograph by Peter Eric Palmquist

PLATE 43: Truck driver and second loader cinching log binders, Simpson
Timber Company, 1962. Photograph by Peter Eric Palmquist

PLATE 44: Governor Edmund G. "Pat" Brown at the dedication of the Avenue of the Giants, July 1960. Photograph by Peter Eric Palmquist

PLATE 45: Contestants, Lumberjack's Jubilee, Arcata, c. 1963. Photograph by Peter Eric Palmquist

PLATE 46: Unloading sawdust, Samoa, c. 1965. Photograph by Peter Eric
Palmquist

PLATE 47: Interior, abandoned teepee burner, c. 1970. Photograph by Peter
Eric Palmquist

PLATE 48: U.S. 101, the Redwood Highway, c. 1961. Photograph by Peter Eric Palmquist

INTO THE MYSTIC

MARY AUSTIN

from THE LANDS OF THE SUN

Mary Austin (1868–1934) migrated from Illinois to California's San Joaquin Valley with her family at the age of twenty. For the next four years, and then for seven more in Lone Pine, on the eastern side of the Sierra Nevada, she studied the landscape in sumptuous detail; she said that learning the rhythms of the country around Lone Pine—"the running of quail, the creaking of the twenty-mule team, the beating of the medicine drum"—taught her how to write, but she was almost entirely isolated from the literary world. This ended when she moved to Los Angeles in 1899 and later Carmel, where she helped establish the Carmel Writers' Colony and associated with such writers as Jack London, George Sterling, Ambrose Bierce, and Charles Warren Stoddard. The great virtue of her work is that it is an expression of her awareness, unconventional in her own lifetime, of how deeply our understanding of nature affects our own well-being. The Lands of the Sun *was published in 1927.*

The whole Sierra along the line of faultage has the contour of a wave about to break. It swings up in long water-shaped lines from the valley of the San Joaquin and rears its jagged crest above the abrupt desert shore. Seen from close under, some of these two- and three-thousand-foot precipices have the pitch of toppling waters. As they rose new-riven from the earth their proportions must have been more than terrifying.

Later the Ice Age bore downward from the north and through immeasurable years carved the fractured granite into shapes of enduring beauty. It rounded the great jutting fronts, it insured them against the tooth of time with the keen icy polish with which they shine still against the morning. It gouged narrow wall-sided canyons, cut the course of rivers, and, sinking like a graver's tool into the heart of the range, scooped out deep wells of pleasantness. Afterward, when the ice was old, it must have moved more slowly, for the lines it left, retreating northward, were more flowing, the hill crowns rounder. And then the mountain was besieged with trees. They stormed it, scaled its free precipices—you can see by the thick mold of the valleys what ranks and ranks of them went down, and along the snow line how, by the persistence of assault, they are bent and contorted.

This is the whole effect of the somber swathes of pine that mask the Sierra slopes. They march—along the watercourses they climb—up sheer precipices in staggering files, trooping in the passes; across the smooth meadow spaces they lock arms, they await the word of command. By a very little observation they are seen to be ranged in orderly companies. Here a warm current of air traveling steadily from the superheated valleys carries the life zone higher, there a defiant bony ridge drops it a few thousand feet, but the relative arrangement of species does not greatly vary. The broad oaks, like reverend grandsires, from the foothills see the procession go by; they follow it as far as the gates of the mountain, crutched and bowed. All the lower canyons are full of a rabble of deciduous trees, chinquapins, scrub oak, madroño; full of gay camp followers, lilac, dogwood, azaleas, strumpet penstemons, flaunting lupines, monkshood, columbine.

The gray nut pine, wide branched, unwarlike but serviceable, opens the ranks of conifers. Then the long-leaved pines begin, *ponderosa, coulteri,* and the slender, arrowy, fire-resisting *attenuata.* On the western slope, increasing as it goes northward, the redwood holds all the open country, but it is no climber like *monticola,* the largest of all true pines, the captain of the Sierra forests. The firs assume the water borders and low moraines; clannish, incommunicable, they seem not to find it worthwhile to grow unless they grow statelily. Above all these rise the thin-barked pines, the lodgepole, Douglas spruce, *Libocedrus,* and the hardy junipers in windy passes. About the meadows and lake borders the quaking aspens push like children between the knees along the line, and highest, most persistent, is the creeping-limbed, wind-depressed, white-barked pine, under whose matted boughs the wild sheep bed.

The trees have each its own voice—a degree of flexibility or length of needles upon which the wind harps to produce its characteristic note. The traveler in the dark of mountain nights knows his way among them as by the street cries of his own city. The creaking of the firs, the sough of the long-leaved pines, the whispering whistle of the lodgepole pine, the delicate *frou-frou* of the redwoods in a wind—these come out for him in the darkness with the night scent of moth-haunted flowers. But there is one tree that for the footer of the mountain trails is voiceless; it speaks, no doubt, but it speaks only to the austere mountain heads, to the mindful wind and the watching stars. It speaks as men speak to one another and are not heard by the little ants crawling over their boots. This is the "big tree," the sequoia. In something less than a score of forest patches, about the rim of the Twin Valleys, the sequoia abides, out of some possible preglacial period, out of some past of which nothing is left to us but the fading memory of the "giants in those days." The age of individual big trees can be computed in terms of human history. There are evidences written in the rings of these that they endured the drought which made the famine in the days of Ahab the king, against which Elijah prayed. These are growing trees whose seeds are fertile.

One might make a very dramatic collocation of the rise and fall of empires against the life period of a single sequoia, and that would be easier than to transcribe by mere phrases the impression of one of these green towers of silence on the sense. Single and deeply corrugated as a Corinthian column, with only a lightly branched crown for a capital, they spire for five thousand years or so, and then the leaf crown becomes rounded to a dome in which the winds breed. Warm days of spring, their young nestling zephyrs come fluttering down the deep wells of shade to shake the saplings of a hundred years. In summer the fine-leafed foliage catches the sun like spray, diffusing vaporous blueness. But the majesty of their gigantic trunks is incommunicable; after a while the stifling sense of awe breaks before it, and you go on with your small affairs as children will go on playing even in the royal presence.

HERMANN KEYSERLING

from THE TRAVEL DIARY OF A PHILOSOPHER

The Travel Diary of a Philosopher is the two-volume product of Count Hermann Keyserling's (1880–1946) journey around the world in 1911, in which he studied cultures from Egypt to Sri Lanka and India, China, Japan, Hawaii, and the Americas, seeking culture and spirituality that transcended nationalism and ethnocentrism: "When I shall have perceived all the co-ordinates," he wrote, "I ought also to have determined their center. I ought then to have passed beyond all accidents of time and space. If anything at all will lead me to myself, a digression round the world will do so." The School of Wisdom that Keyserling founded in Darmstadt, Germany, in 1920 became a key forum for spiritual thinkers of the day, including Carl Jung, Herman Hesse, and Rabindranath Tagore.

The air of California must possess an immense formative power. I observe what is going on in me: it is a real metamorphosis. The consciousness of being recedes; that of "becoming" increases; and those imperatives which reflect the objective tendencies of nature everywhere in the subjective sphere are already stepping into the foreground: one should grow, should increase, should advance...

Here stand the mightiest trees in the world. About six hundred specimens of *Sequoia gigantea,* two to three hundred feet high, fifteen to thirty feet thick, form a holy grove, commanding reverence to a greater degree than romantic fancy could have conceived. It is dusky in there and cool, in spite of the August sun, which stands at its zenith. Its rays hardly find their way through the bushy crowns; the red of the trunks glows through the twilight as if the evening light were eternal. The giants stand there, upright and fresh, just as if thousands of years had not passed since the day of their creation. They are not lonely, for young people throng below them; they are not dead to the present, for year upon year their seed falls down to the distant earth; they are not old, for they are not threatened by natural death.

I am overwhelmed by a wave of the profoundest feeling of happiness. The earth is not as yet feeble from age! It is still capable of preserving and creating mighty things! For the first time I look up to grandeur without melancholy. Never before have I contemplated in paleontological collections the remains of prehistoric magnificence without bitterness, nor have I ever thought without pain of the giants which our era produces every now and again from atavism or accident: for to me it seemed only too certain that the creative power of our planet is dying out, that soon only dwarfs and cripples will be able to continue upon it. Now I see that the youngest of the continents still possesses the primordial power of primitive days. I gratefully greet it therefore as the refuge of our future.

Humanity has never been so dependent upon physical conditions as are the white men of today; that is because they have set themselves a problem as no one else before them: they want to continue to change themselves *ad indefinitum.* Instead of setting themselves limits in given circumstances, they strive to get beyond them all so that no successful effort means an ultimate end to them. But only the youthful body is capable of changing and adapting itself, and that only to a certain point; for this reason all grown-ups become crystallized sooner or later, all civilized nations have ceased their development at some point, leaving further innovations to younger blood. For us no such boundary is visible in idea; the peculiarly fluid character of our civilization makes every fixed aim and all stagnation seem inconceivable, it demands a new attitude every moment, and exacts that everyone who wishes to join in must remain adaptable. This, however, means that he must remain completely young for the whole of his life. Thus, our problem is primarily a physical one. Many suspect this: the physical is idealized today as it has never been before. Gospels are preached in which health occupies the central position, just as love does in the Christian gospels. But what these apostles generally forget is that man as a physical being is profoundly interwoven in his connection with nature and can do little without it. Even rejuvenation succeeds rarely except through transplantation into younger soil: eternal youth is only conceivable in a world which remains eternally young itself. In order to find bodies such as we need today, of boundless power of tension, of unfailing plasticity, an endlessly vitalizing outer world would be needed, young as creation was upon the fifth day. This seems to exist here; American nature possesses the creative power of the beginning of time in an unweakened state. Just as it has succeeded in fusing diverse races and making Americans of types chosen at random in the shortest period—not merely a variety of human beings, but a real type—so it may be expected of American nature that it can create the body which is a match for the constantly increasing mental tension, and which would be capable of perpetual change.

In America, if anywhere, we will complete our evolution. Europe will soon have spoken its last word of historical importance.

Tradition in itself is a fetter, which becomes more binding from generation to generation, and ultimately suffocating, and the history of Europe is already so long that a radical liberation and innovation will hardly be successful upon its soil, not even if its inhabitants become ever so rejuvenated and attempt to evade the catastrophe, even through the most violent revolutions. This time too the old truth will be proved, that new cultures only flourish upon new soil; in this latest historical crisis too the problem of new forms will be solved, not by the most mature but by those who are the crudest. And that it must be so is quite obvious in this case: when we Westerners undertook, unlike all previous cultures who conducted life subject to the realm of ideas, to impress this realm upon the domain of the earth, we were really beginning a new epoch of creation; we begin as beings of spirit and soul precisely where physical nature started in the Triadic epoch. For this reason, the man of the New World fits into the sequoia grove, this oasis of prehistoric days, better than into the ruins of Rome....

ARTHUR CONAN DOYLE

from OUR SECOND AMERICAN ADVENTURE

In one of countless tributes written in the twentieth century to the majesty and power of the redwood forest, Arthur Conan Doyle here recounts his visit to Marin County's Muir Woods in the twenties.

Arthur Conan Doyle (1859–1930) worked as a ship's surgeon on voyages to the Arctic and to Africa before settling in London in 1891 as an ophthalmologist. Almost immediately, his writing career took off and he was able to abandon his medical practice; by the 1920s, he was the most highly paid writer in the world. Later in life, in his fifties, he became interested in spiritualism and lectured on the subject in Europe, Australia, the United States, and Canada. Our Second American Adventure *is a memoir of his second U.S. lecture tour.*

It is a nice question whether San Francisco does not stand first in natural beauty of all cities in the world. I speak of natural advantages only and not of historical glamour, which would make many European cities preeminent. But taking Nature alone, here is a harbor which is second only to that of Sydney; here is beautiful hill scenery in the very city itself; and finally there is Mount Tamalpais, the one and only Tamalpais, which should be ascended by the traveler if he has only a single clear day in the city of the Golden Gate. Our whole party went up it on the day after our arrival, and we were agreed that in all our wanderings we had never had a more glorious experience.

You cross the harbor in a ferry, the trip taking you twenty minutes, and find yourself in a small town called Sausalito—there is a welcome dignity in these Spanish names. There the railroad begins, and after a short journey you change into a mountain train and begin your ascent. The line is curved so skillfully that at no place is the rise more than one in seven, and no cogs are needed. It would charm a botanist—would that I were one!—to note how you start from subtropical palms and cacti and yuccas, mounting up through the various flora, the tanbark oaks, the bay trees with their delicious scents, the eucalypti of various orders, and the maples, until you emerge into rhododendrons and firs and heaths and ferns with wild lupine and kingcups, and much to remind us of the dear uplands of Sussex. One is faced here with the eternal problem as to how on earth this high altitude vegetation ever got there, whether blown by the winds or brought by the birds, or how. In isolated mountains in the heart of Africa you will find, as I understand, all our upland English shrubs and flowers. It is one more mystery of Nature.

Finally, after an hour of slow, clanking progress, we were at the inn on the top of the mountain, twenty-six hundred feet above the bay, which lay in its glory, with many convolutions and gulfs and extensions, more like some motionless model of the world than the world itself. There were wonderful gradations of color there, the deep blue of the sea, the olive green of the dried-up plains and foothills, the deep green of the fir groves on the mountainside, and the drabs and yellows of the sands. Seven counties were visible, and a mountain a hundred miles away stood up as a white cone upon a clear day. The great city lay below us on its promontory, and we saw Oakland across the bay, and all the outlying towns in which the businessmen have their homes. It was a truly majestic sight, the powers of Nature and of man, each admirable in its own domain.

We walked round the crest of the mountain, and then descended in a car which ran by its own gravity, a delightful mode of progression when it continues for nearly an hour. The end of this wonderful toboggan course was the Muir Woods, where in a cleft of the hill the great sequoias lie. All words are futile to describe the tremendous majesty of the great redwoods, and mere figures such as three hundred feet as their height, or the fact that a hollow trunk can contain thirty-six people, leave the imagination cold. One has to be alone or with some single, very intimate companion to get the true impression, the deep silence of the grove, the shadowy religious light, the tremendous majesty of the red columns, the vistas between them, the solemn subconscious effect produced by their two thousand years of age. There are no insects in their bark, and nothing, not even fire, can destroy them. We saw scars of old brushfires upon their flanks, and noted that considerable oaks nearby had no such scars, which gave an idea of how many years had elapsed since that mark was branded on them. We wandered for two hours along the borders of the clear trout stream which runs through the redwood grove.

The whole mountain has been most reverently and excellently developed by a private company, the representative of which, Mr. Whitmore, acted as our guide. It could not have been better done, for it has been made accessible and yet tenderly guarded from all vulgarity. One is not allowed to pick a flower in the redwood grove. The latter place has been taken over by the government, and one feels that it should all be national property. The only place which I can recall resembling Tamalpais is the famous Tibidabo Hill above Barcelona; but the Californian effect is on a far grander scale.

ROBINSON JEFFERS

THE BEAKS OF EAGLES

The poetic legacy of Robinson Jeffers (1887–1962), and the image of the isolated pacifist struggling with a pessimism verging on misanthropy and at the same time reveling in the powerful beauty of the central California coast, are an essential part of California letters. "The Beaks of Eagles" was written in 1936.

An eagle's nest on the head of an old redwood on one of the
    precipice-footed ridges
Above Ventana Creek, that jagged country which nothing but a
    falling meteor will ever plow; no horseman
Will ever ride there, no hunter cross this ridge but the winged
    ones, no one will steal the eggs from this fortress.
The she-eagle is old, her mate was shot long ago, she is now
    mated with a son of hers.
When lightning blasted her nest she built it again on the same
    tree, in the splinters of the thunderbolt.
The she-eagle is older than I; she was here when the fires of
    eighty-five raged on these ridges,

She was lately fledged and dared not hunt ahead of them but ate
    scorched meat. The world has changed in her time;
Humanity has multiplied, but not here; men's hopes and thoughts
    and customs have changed, their powers are enlarged,
Their powers and their follies have become fantastic,
The unstable animal never has been changed so rapidly. The
    motor and the plane and the great war have gone over him,
And Lenin has lived and Jehovah died: while the mother-eagle
Hunts her same hills, crying the same beautiful and lonely cry and
    is never tired; dreams the same dreams,
And hears at night the rock-slides rattle and thunder in the throats
    of these living mountains.
                        It is good for man
To try all changes, progress and corruption, powers, peace and
    anguish, not to go down the dinosaur's way
Until all his capacities have been explored: and it is good for him
To know that his needs and nature are no more changed in fact in
    ten thousand years than the beaks of eagles.

JUDY VAN DER VEER

from NOVEMBER GRASS

Judy Van der Veer (1912–1982) was born in Pennsylvania but spent most of her life as a ranchwoman in the backcountry of San Diego County. She wrote regularly for the Christian Science Monitor. *Besides* November Grass (1940), *her novels include* The River Pasture, A Few Happy Ones, Hold the Rein Free, *and* Higher than the Arrow.

Sometimes there was such a quietness on the land that each small sound stood distinct and alone. If a bird chirped, it was as if the only bird in the world made the only sound that it could. Before night came on, the stillness was breathless and the hills grew intensely bright.

Everybody was wishing for rain; this long dry fall was getting on people's nerves. If the girl kept on, following the cows further every day, all the roadside grass would be grazed off. But she didn't worry. It seemed as if the unchanging days, the ever clear sky, the yellowing leaves, and the dry grass had made her feel so quiet and contented that it was no use to fret about anything.

Morning after morning she saw the mountains clear with color, and she didn't tire of watching them. In the intense heat and dryness of midmorning she sat in cold shade and looked and listened to small happenings around her. Birds and ground squirrels and insects in the grass held her attention. The laws of design entranced her. The gods had taken such care and pains over the decoration of a small insect wing that the girl could feel that nothing was too trifling to be overlooked.

When she thought about how each small life feels itself the center of the universe—how sunshine, rain, or food is good or bad, depending on each individual need, how certain times and conditions cause different meanings for each thing that lives—she was overwhelmed with wonder and despair at the way the world ends a thousand times a minute. If she crushed an insect the sun was blotted out, the stars fallen, the earth shattered—forever and ever the universe ceased to be for one atom of living.

Then she thought, for every time a particle of life broke out of an egg, crept from a cocoon, or pushed out of a womb, the pageantry of earth and sun, moon and stars, color and sound, and scent and feeling was created again.

People were forever inquiring about the purpose of life and speaking of the great riddle of creation. As far as the girl could see, life was its own excuse for being. Life was given to be lived. The tiniest insect served its purpose if it grew to its utmost in its hour in the sunlight. It seemed that everything was busy growing, and, barring accident, a thing didn't start dying until it had stopped growing. That might be the secret of the redwood trees up north. It is said that no one of those trees ever died a natural death. For thousands of years they had been growing, and they must keep growing to keep living.

Humans stopped growing too soon. They became adults and settled into a dull way of living and thinking, and minds and bodies began decaying together. The girl thought that for herself this was good growing weather. No pasture grass was growing these November days, but while she was waiting for the time of grass she could be growing inwardly....

JACK KEROUAC

from THE DHARMA BUMS

Born Jean Louis Lebris de Kerouac in Massachusetts to parents from Quebec, Jack Kerouac (1922–1969) became the most celebrated novelist and prose stylist of the Beat movement. He saw his work not as radical prophecy, but as the continuation of the traditions of Proust and Thomas Wolfe. He was deeply religious (Catholic and a serious student of Buddhism) and felt a deep affinity with poet Gary Snyder, here fictionalized as the character Japhy. Their friendship reflected a common passion for scholarly and ecstatic spiritual practice drawing on the full span of world religion, in a kind of new, Pacific Coast transcendentalism. They climbed Mount Tamalpais together in 1956. Kerouac died in alcoholic retreat from unwanted celebrity in 1969.

The party went on for days; the morning of the third day people were still sprawled about the grounds when Japhy and I sneaked our rucksacks out, with a few choice groceries, and started down the road in the orange early-morning sun of California golden days. It was going to be a great day, we were back in our element: trails.

Japhy was in high spirits. "Goddammit it feels good to get away from dissipation and go in the woods. When I get back from

Japan, Ray, when the weather gets really cold we'll put on our long underwear and hitchhike through the land. Think if you can of ocean to mountain Alaska to Klamath a solid forest of fir to bhikku in, a lake of a million wild geese. Woo! You know what woo means in Chinese?"

"What?"

"Fog. These woods are great here in Marin, I'll show you Muir Woods today, but up north is all that real old Pacific Coast mountain and ocean land, the future home of the Dharma-body. Know what I'm gonna do? I'll do a new long poem called 'Rivers and Mountains Without End' and just write it on and on on a scroll and unfold on and on with new surprises and always what went before forgotten, see, like a river, or like one of them real long Chinese silk paintings that show two little men hiking in an endless landscape of gnarled old trees and mountains so high they merge with the fog in the upper silk void. I'll spend three thousand years writing it, it'll be packed full of information on soil conservation, the Tennessee Valley Authority, astronomy, geology, Hsuan Tsung's travels, Chinese painting theory, reforestation, Oceanic ecology and food chains."

"Go to it, boy." As ever I strode on behind him and when we began to climb, with our packs feeling good on our backs as though we were pack animals and didn't feel right without a burden, it was that same old lonesome old good old thwap thwap up the trail, slowly, a mile an hour. We came to the end of the steep road where we had to go through a few houses built near steep bushy cliffs with waterfalls trickling down, then up to a high steep meadow, full of butterflies and hay and a little seven a.m. dew, and down to a dirt road, then to the end of the dirt road, which rose higher and higher till we could see vistas of Corte Madera and Mill Valley far away and even the red top of Golden Gate Bridge.

"Tomorrow afternoon on our run to Stinson Beach," said Japhy, "you'll see the whole white city of San Francisco miles away in the blue bay. Ray, by God, later on in our future life we can have a fine free-wheeling tribe in these California hills, get girls and have dozens of radiant enlightened brats, live like Indians in hogans and eat berries and buds."

"No beans?"

"We'll write poems, we'll get a printing press and print our own poems, the Dharma Press, we'll poetize the lot and make a fat book of icy bombs for the booby public."

"Ah the public ain't so bad, they suffer too. You always read about some tarpaper shack burning somewhere in the Middlewest with three little children perishing and you see a picture of the parents crying. Even the kitty was burned. Japhy, do you think God made the world to amuse himself because he was bored? Because if so he would have to be mean."

"Ho, who would you mean by God?"

"Just Tathagata, if you will."

"Well it says in the sutra that God, or Tathagata, doesn't himself emanate a world from his womb but it just appears due to the ignorance of sentient beings."

"But he emanated the sentient beings and their ignorance too. It's all too pitiful. I ain't gonna rest till I find out *why*, Japhy, *why*."

"Ah don't trouble your mind essence. Remember that in pure Tathagata mind essence there is no asking of the question why and not even any significance attached to it."

"Well, then nothing's really happening, then."

He threw a stick at me and hit me on the foot.

"Well, that didn't happen," I said.

"I really don't know, Ray, but I appreciate your sadness about the world. 'Tis indeed. Look at that party the other night. Everybody wanted to have a good time and tried real hard but we all woke up the next day feeling sorta sad and separate. What do you think about death, Ray?"

"I think death is our reward. When we die we go straight to nirvana Heaven and that's that."

"But supposing you're reborn in the lower hells and have hot redhot balls of iron shoved down your throat by devils."

"Life's already shoved an iron foot down *my* mouth. But I don't think that's anything but a dream cooked up by some hysterical monks who didn't understand Buddha's peace under the Bo Tree or for that matter Christ's peace looking down on the heads of his tormentors and forgiving them."

"You really like Christ, don't you?"

"Of course I do. And after all, a lot of people say he is Maitreya, the Buddha prophesied to appear after Sakyamuni, you know, Maitreya means 'Love' in Sanskrit and that's all Christ talked about was love."

"Oh, don't start preaching Christianity to me, I can just see you on your deathbed kissing the cross like some old Karamazov or like our old friend Dwight Goddard who spent his life as a Buddhist and suddenly returned to Christianity in his last days. Ah that's not for me, I want to spend hours every day in a lonely temple meditating in front of a sealed statue of Kwannon which no one is ever allowed to see because it's too powerful. Strike hard, old diamond!"

"It'll all come out in the wash."

"You remember Rol Sturlason my buddy who went to Japan to study those rocks of Ryoanji. He went over on a freighter named *Sea Serpent* so he painted a big mural of a sea serpent and mermaids on a bulkhead in the mess hall to the delight of the crew who dug him like crazy and all wanted to become Dharma Bums right there. Now he's climbing up holy Mount Hiei in Kyoto through a foot of snow probably, straight up where there are no trails, steep steep, through bamboo thickets and twisty pine like in brush drawings. Feet wet and lunch forgot, that's the way to climb."

"What are you going to wear in the monastery, anyway?"

"Oh man, the works, old T'ang Dynasty style things long black floppy with huge droopy sleeves and funny pleats, make you feel real Oriental."

"Alvah says that while guys like us are all excited about being real Orientals and wearing robes, actual Orientals over there are reading surrealism and Charles Darwin and mad about Western business suits."

"East'll meet West anyway. Think what a great world revolution will take place when East meets West finally, and it'll be guys like us that can start the thing. Think of millions of guys all over the world with rucksacks on their backs tramping around the back country and hitchhiking and bringing the word down to everybody."

"That's a lot like the early days of the Crusades, Walter the Penniless and Peter the Hermit leading ragged bands of believers to the Holy Land."

"Yeah but that was all such European gloom and crap, I want my Dharma Bums to have springtime in their hearts when the blooms are girling and the birds are dropping little fresh turds surprising cats who wanted to eat them a moment ago."

"What are you thinking about?"

"Just makin up poems in my head as I climb toward Mount Tamalpais. See up there ahead, as beautiful a mountain as you'll see anywhere in the world, a beautiful shape to it, I really love Tamalpais. We'll sleep tonight way around the back of it. Take us till late afternoon to get there."

The Marin country was much more rustic and kindly than the rough Sierra country we'd climbed last fall: it was all flowers, flowers, trees, bushes, but also a great deal of poison oak by the side of the trail. When we got to the end of the high dirt road we suddenly plunged into the dense redwood forest and went along following a pipeline through glades that were so deep the fresh morning sun barely penetrated and it was cold and damp. But the odor was pure deep rich pine and wet logs. Japhy was all talk this morning. He was like a little kid again now that he was out on the trail. "The only thing wrong with that monastery shot in Japan for me, is, though for all their intelligence and good intentions, the Americans out there, they have so little real sense of America and who the people are who really dig Buddhism here, and they don't have any use for poetry."

"Who?"

"Well, the people who are sending me out there and finance things. They spend their good money fixing elegant scenes of gardens and books and Japanese architecture and all that crap which nobody will like or be able to use anyway but rich American divorcees on Japanese cruises and all they really should do is just build or buy an old Jap house and vegetable garden and have a place there for cats to hang out in and be Buddhists, I mean have a real flower of something and not just the usual American middleclass fuggup with appearances. Anyway I'm looking forward to it, oh boy I can just see myself in the morning sitting on the mats with a low table at my side, typing on my portable, and my hibachi nearby with a pot of hot water on it keeping hot and all my papers and maps and pipe and flashlight neatly packed away and outside plum trees and pines with snow on the boughs and up on Mount Hieizan the snow getting deep and sugi and hinoki all around, them's redwoods, boy, and cedars. Little tucked away temples down the rocky trails, cold mossy ancient places where frogs croak, and inside small statues and hanging buttery lamps and gold lotuses and paintings and ancient incense-soaked smells and lacquer chests with statues." His boat was leaving in two days. "But I'm sad too about leaving California...s'why I wanted to take one last long look at it today with ya, Ray."

We came up out of the gladey redwood forest onto a road, where there was a mountain lodge, then crossed the road and dipped down again through bushes to a trail that probably nobody even knew was there except a few hikers, and we were in Muir Woods. It extended, a vast valley, for miles before us. An old logger road led us for two miles then Japhy got off and scrambled up the slope and got onto another trail nobody dreamed was there. We hiked on this one, up and down along a tumbling creek, with fallen logs again where you crossed the creek, and sometimes bridges that had been built Japhy said by the Boy Scouts, trees sawed in half the flat surface for walking. Then we climbed up a steep pine slope and came out to the highway and went up the side of a hill of grass and came out in some outdoor theater, done up Greek style with stone seats all around a bare stone arrangement for four-dimensional presentations of Aeschylus and Sophocles. We drank water and sat down and took our shoes off and watched the silent play from the upper stone seats. Far away you could see the Golden Gate Bridge and the whiteness of San Francisco.

Japhy began to shriek and hoot and whistle and sing, full of pure gladness. Nobody around to hear him. "This is the way you'll be on top of Mount Desolation, this summer, Ray."

"I'll sing at the top of my voice for the first time in my life."

"If anybody hears ya it'll just be the conies, or maybe a critic bear. Ray that Skagit country where you're going is the greatest place in America, that snaky river running back through gorges and into its own unpeopled watershed, wet snowy mountains fading into dry pine mountains and deep valleys like Big Beaver and Little Beaver with some of the best virgin stands of red cedar left in the world. I keep thinking of my abandoned Crater Mountain Lookout house sitting up there with nobody but the conies in the howling winds, getting old, the conies down in their furry nests deep under boulders, and warm, eating seeds or whatever they eat. The closer you get to real matter, rock air fire and wood, boy, the more spiritual the world is. All these people thinking they're hardheaded materialistic practical types, they don't know shit about matter, their heads are full of dreamy ideas and notions." He raised his hand. "Listen to that quail calling."

"I wonder what everybody's doing back at Sean's."

"Well they're all up now and starting on that sour old red wine again and sitting around talking nothing. They should have all come with us and learnt something." He picked up his pack and started off. In a half-hour we were in a beautiful meadow following a dusty little trail over shallow creeks and finally we were at Potrero Meadows camp. It was a National Forest camp with a stone fireplace and picnic tables and everything but no one would be there till the weekend. A few miles away, the lookout shack on top of Tamalpais looked right down on us. We undid our packs and spent a quiet late afternoon dozing in the sun or Japhy ran around looking at butterflies and birds and making notes in his notebook and I hiked alone down the other side, north, where a desolate rocky country much like the Sierras stretched out toward the sea.

At dusk Japhy lit a good big fire and started supper. We were very tired and happy. He made a soup that night that I shall never forget and was really the best soup I'd eaten since I was a lionized young author in New York eating lunch at the Chambord or in Henri Cru's kitchen. This was nothing but a couple of envelopes of dried pea soup thrown into a pot of water with fried bacon, fat and all, and stirred till boiling. It was rich, real pea taste, with that smoky bacon and bacon fat, just the thing to drink in the cold gathering darkness by a sparkling fire. Also while pooking about he'd found puffballs, natural mushrooms, not the umbrella type, just round grapefruit-size puffs of white firm meat, and these he sliced and fried in bacon fat and we had them on the side with fried rice. It was a great supper. We washed the dishes in the gurgling creek. The roaring bonfire kept the mosquitoes away. A new moon peeked down through the pine boughs. We rolled out our sleeping bags in the meadow grass and went to bed early, bone weary.

"Well Ray," said Japhy, "pretty soon I'll be far out to sea and you'll be hitchhiking up the coast to Seattle and on through the Skagit country. I wonder what'll happen to all of us."

We went to sleep on this dreamy theme. During the night I had a vivid dream, one of the most distinct dreams I ever had, I clearly saw a crowded dirty smoky Chinese market with beggars and vendors and pack horses and mud and smokepots and piles of rubbish and vegetables for sale in dirty clay pans on the ground and suddenly from the mountains a ragged hobo, a little seamed brown unimaginable Chinese hobo, had come down and was just standing at the end of the market, surveying it with an expressionless humor. He was short, wiry, his face leathered hard and dark red by the sun of the desert and the mountains; his clothes were nothing but gathered rags; he had a pack of leather on his back; he was bare-footed. I had seen guys like that only seldom, and only in Mexico, maybe coming into Monterrey out of those stark rock mountains, beggars who probably live in caves. But this one was a Chinese twice-as-poor, twice-as-tough and infinitely mysterious tramp and it was Japhy for sure. It was the same broad mouth, merry twin-kling eyes, bony face (a face like Dostoevsky's death mask, with prominent eyebrow bones and square head); and he was short and compact like Japhy. I woke up at dawn, thinking "Wow, is *that* what'll happen to Japhy? Maybe he'll leave that monastery and just disappear and we'll never see him again, and he'll be the Han Shan ghost of the Orient Mountains and even the Chinese'll be afraid of him he'll be so raggedy and beat."

I told Japhy about it. He was already up stoking the fire and whistling. "Well don't just lay there in your sleeping bag pullin your puddin, get up and fetch some water. Yodelayhee hoo! Ray, I will bring you incense sticks from the coldwater temple of Kiyomizu and set them one by one in a big brass incense bowl and do the proper bows, how's about that. That was some dream you had. If that's me, then it's me. Ever weeping, ever youthful, hoo!" He got out the hand-ax from the rucksack and hammered at boughs and got a crackling fire going. There was still mist in the trees and fog on the ground. "Let's pack up and take off and dig Laurel Dell camp. Then we'll hike over the trails down to the sea and swim."

"Great." On this trip Japhy had brought along a delicious combination for hiking energy: Ry-Krisp crackers, good sharp Cheddar cheese a wedge of that, and a roll of salami. We had this for breakfast with hot fresh tea and felt great. Two grown men could live two days on that concentrated bread and that salami (concentrated meat) and cheese and the whole thing only weighed about a pound and a half. Japhy was full of great ideas like that. What hope, what human energy, what truly American optimism was packed in that neat little frame of his! There he was clomping along in front of me on the trail and shouting back "Try the meditation of the trail, just walk along looking at the trail at your feet and don't look about and just fall into a trance as the ground zips by."

We arrived at Laurel Dell camp at about ten, it was also supplied with stone fireplaces with grates, and picnic tables, but the surroundings were infinitely more beautiful than Potrero Meadows. Here were the real meadows: dreamy beauties with soft grass sloping all around, fringed by heavy deep green timber, the whole scene of waving grass and brooks and nothing in sight.

"By God, I'm gonna come back here and bring nothing but food and gasoline and a primus and cook my suppers smokeless and the Forest Service won't even know the difference."

"Yeah, but if they ever catch you cooking away from these stone places they put you out, Smith."

"But what would I do on weekends, join the merry picnickers? I'd just hide up there beyond that beautiful meadow. I'd stay there forever."

"And you'd only have two miles of trail down to Stinson

Beach and your grocery store down there." At noon we started for the beach. It was a tremendously grinding trip. We climbed way up high on meadows, where again we could see San Francisco far away, then dipped down into a steep trail that seemed to fall directly down to sea level; you had sometimes to run down the trail or slide on your back, one. A torrent of water fell down at the side of the trail. I went ahead of Japhy and began swinging down the trail so fast, singing happily, I left him behind about a mile and had to wait for him at the bottom. He was taking his time enjoying the ferns and flowers. We stashed our rucksacks in the fallen leaves under bushes and hiked freely down the sea meadows and past seaside farm-houses with cows browsing, to the beach community, where we bought wine in a grocery store and stomped on out into the sand and the waves. It was a chill day with only occasional flashes of sun. But we were making it. We jumped into the ocean in our shorts and swam swiftly around then came out and spread out some of our salami and Ry-Krisp and cheese on a piece of paper in the sand and drank wine and talked. At one point I even took a nap. Japhy was feeling very good. "Goddammit, Ray, you'll never know how happy I am we decided to have these last two days hiking. I feel good all over again. I know somethin good's gonna come out of all this!"

"All what?"

"I dunno—out of the way we feel about life. You and I ain't out to bust anybody's skull, or cut someone's throat in an economic way, we've dedicated ourselves to prayer for all sentient beings and when we're strong enough we'll really be able to do it, too, like the old saints. Who knows, the world might wake up and burst out into a beautiful flower of Dharma everywhere."

After dozing awhile he woke up and looked and said, "Look at all that water out there stretching all the way to Japan." He was getting sadder and sadder about leaving.

GARY SNYDER

from MOUNTAINS AND RIVERS WITHOUT END

*Born in San Francisco in 1930, Gary Snyder studied anthro-
pology, Asian languages, and literature in college. An intimate
of Jack Kerouac, Allen Ginsberg, and other Beat writers, he is
now considered a seminal influence on postwar environmen-
talism and American Buddhist thought and practice. He continues to live, teach, and write in Northern California.*

The Circumambulation of Mt. Tamalpais

Walking up and around the long ridge of Tamalpais, "Bay Mountain," circling and climbing—chanting—to show respect and to clar-
ify the mind. Philip Whalen, Allen Ginsberg, and I learned this practice in Asia. So we opened a route around Tam. It takes a day.

Stage One
Muir Woods: the bed of Redwood Creek just where the Dipsea
Trail crosses it. Even in the dryest season of this year some running
water. Mountains make springs.

Prajñāpāramitā-hridaya-sūtra
Dhāranī for Removing Disasters
Four Vows

Splash across the creek and head up the Dipsea Trail, the steep wooded slope and into meadows. Gold dry grass. Cows—a huge pissing, her ears out, looking around with large eyes and mottled nose. As we laugh. "—Excuse us for laughing at you." Hazy day, butterflies tan as grass that sit on silver-weathered fenceposts, a gang of crows. "I can smell fried chicken" Allen says—only the simmering California laurel leaves. The trail winds crossed and intertwining with a dirt jeep road.

Two
A small twisted ancient interior live oak splitting a rock outcrop an hour up the trail.

Dhāranī for Removing Disasters
The Heat Mantra

A tiny chörten before this tree.

Into the woods. Maze fence gate. Young Douglas fir, redwood, a new state of being. Sun on madrone: to the bare meadow knoll. (Last spring a bed of wild iris about here and this time too, a lazuli bunting.)

Three
A ring of outcropped rocks. A natural little dolmen-circle right where the Dipsea crests on the ridge. Looking down a canyon to the ocean—not so far.

Dhāranī for Removing Disasters
Hari Om Namo Shiva

And on to Pan Toll, across the road, and up the Old Mine Trail. A doe and a fawn, silvery gray. More crows.

Four
Rock springs. A trickle even now—

The Sarasvatī Mantra
Dhāranī for Removing Disasters

—in the shade of a big oak spreading out the map on a picnic table. Then up the Benstein Trail to Rifle Camp, old food-cache boxes hanging from wires. A bit north, in the oak woods and rocks, a neat little saddhu hut built of dry natural bits of wood and parts of old crates; roofed with shakes and black plastic. A book called *Harmony* left there. Lunch by the stream, too tiny a trickle, we drink water from our bota. The food offerings are swiss cheese sandwiches, swede bread with liverwurst, salami, jack cheese, olives, gomoku-no-moto from a can, grapes, panettone with apple-currant jelly and sweet butter, oranges, and soujouki—greek walnuts in grape-juice paste. All in the shade, at Rifle Camp.

Five
A notable serpentine outcropping, not far after Rifle Camp.

Om Shri Maitreya
Dhāranī for Removing Disasters

Six
Collier Spring—in a redwood grove—water trickling out a pipe.

> Dhāranī of the Great Compassionate One

California nutmeg, golden chinquapin the fruit with burrs, the chaparral. Following the North Side Trail.

Seven
Inspiration Point.

> Dhāranī for Removing Disasters
> Mantra for Tārā

Looking down on Lagunitas. The gleam of water storage in the brushy hills. All that smog—and Mt. St. Helena faintly in the north. The houses of San Anselmo and San Rafael, once large estates... "Peacock Gap Country Club"—Rocky brush climb up the North Ridge Trail.

Eight
Summit of Mt. Tamalpais. A ring of rock pinnacles around the lookout.

> Prajñāpāramitā-hridaya-sūtra
> Dhāranī for Removing Disasters
> Dhāranī of the Great Compassionate One

> Hari Krishna Mantra
> Om Shri Maitreya
> Hari Om Namo Shiva

All about the bay, such smog and sense of heat. May the whole planet not get like this.
Start the descent down the Throckmorton Hogback Trail. (Fern Canyon an alternative.)

Nine
Parking lot of Mountain Home. Cars whiz by, sun glare from the west.

> Dhāranī for Removing Disasters
> Gopala Mantra.

Then, across from the California Alpine Club, the Ocean View Trail goes down. Some yellow broom flowers still out. The long descending trail into shadowy giant redwood trees.

Ten
The bed of Redwood Creek again.

> Prajñāpāramitā-hridaya-sūtra
> Dhāranī for Removing Disasters
> Hari Om Namo Shiva
> Hari Krishna Mantra
> Four Vows

—standing in our little circle, blowing the conch, shaking the staff rings, right in the parking lot.

TOM WOLFE

from THE ELECTRIC KOOL-AID ACID TEST

Tom Wolfe (b. 1931) was born in Richmond, Virginia, studied at Washington and Lee University and Yale, and then worked as a journalist for the Springfield Union, *the* Washington Post, *and the* New York Herald Tribune. *His* Kandy-Kolored Tangerine-Flake Streamline Baby *(1965) intro-duced "new journalism," which, according to Wolfe, gives a full objective description, plus something previously only found in fiction: the subjective or emotional life of the charac-ters.* The Electric Kool-Aid Acid Test *(1968) is a colorful, even Day-Glo, evocation of the early sixties experiences of Ken Kesey and the Merry Pranksters.*

A very Christmas card,
        Kesey's new place near La Honda.
        A log house, a mountain creek, a little wooden bridge
        Fifteen miles from Palo Alto beyond
        Cahill Ridge where Route 84
        Cuts through a redwood forest gorge—

A redwood forest for a yard!
A very Christmas card.

And—
Strategic privacy.
    Not a neighbor for a mile.
    La Honda lived it Western style.
One work-a-daddy hive,
    A housing tract,
    But it was back behind the redwoods.
    The work-a-daddy faces could
    Not be seen from scenic old Route 84,
    Just a couple Wilde Weste roadside places, Baw's
        General Store,
    The Hilltom Motel, in the Wilde Weste Touriste mode.
    With brown wood signs sawed jagged at the ends,
    But sawed neat, you know,
As if to suggest:
    Wilde West Roughing It, motoring friends,
    But Sanitized jake seats
    Ammonia pucks in every urinal
    We aim to keep your Wilde West Sani-pure—
Who won the West?
Antisepsis did, I guess.

    La Honda's Wilde Weste lode
    Seems to be owed to the gunslinging Younger Brothers.
    They holed up in town
    And dad-blame but they found a neighborly way
    To pay for their stay.
    They built a whole wooden store, these notorious
        mothers.

But them was the Younger Brothers,
Mere gunslingers.
Now this Kesey
And his Merry Humdingers down the road—...

◆————————◆

Carl asked Kesey to take Sandy out west with him, to La Honda, to get him out of the whole New York morass. And if there was any place for curing the New York thing, this was it, out back of Kesey's in the lime :::::: light :::::: bower :::::: up the path out back of the house, up the hill into the redwood forest, Sandy suddenly came upon a fabulous bower, like a great domed enclosure, like what people mean when they talk about a "cathedral in the pines," only the redwoods were even more majestic. The way the sun came down through the redwood leaves—trunks and leaves seemed to stretch up for hundreds of feet above your head. It was always sunny and cool at the same time, like a perfect fall day all year around. The sun came down through miles of leaves and got broken up like a pointillist painting, deep green and dapple shadows but brilliant light in a soaring deep green super-bower, a perpetual lime-green light, green-and-gold afternoon, stillness, perpendicular peace, wood-scented, with the cars going by on Route 84 just adding pneumatic sound effects, *sheee-oooooooooo,* like a gentle wind. All peace here; very reassuring!

ARMISTEAD MAUPIN

from SIGNIFICANT OTHERS

Armistead Maupin (b. 1944) is the author of Tales of the City, *an entertaining and gripping novel of contemporary San Francisco with a groundbreaking emphasis on all the aspects and issues of gender.* Tales *was followed by* More Tales of the City, Further Tales of the City, *and several other titles in the series. Most of* Significant Others, *published in 1987, takes place at the Bohemian Grove encampment for rich and powerful men (see also Ernest Peixotto's "A Midsummer Night's Entertainment") and at the adjoining, fictitious Wimminwood gathering.*

Like Booter, most Bohemians arrived at the Grove by car from the city. The press in its endless fascination with money and power grossly exaggerated the number of Lear and Lockheed jets that landed at the Santa Rosa airport during the July encampment. Many of the members—well, some of them, anyway—were uncomplicated fellows with ordinary, workaday jobs in the city.

They came to the Grove for release from their lives, not to plan mergers, plot takeovers, or wage war. So what if the A-bomb had been brainstormed there back in 1942? That, Booter knew for a fact, had been in mid-September, almost two months after the encampment had shut down.

The real function of the Grove was escape, pure and simple. It provided a secret haven where captains of industry and pillars of government could let down their guard and indulge in the luxury of first-name-only camaraderie.

Escape was certainly what Booter had in mind as he sped north on the freeway, away from Frannie and the city and the cruel vagaries of a career in aluminum honeycomb.

◆————————◆

After an hour's drive, he left the freeway and headed west on the road to Guerneville, where sunlit vineyards and gnarly orchards alternated abruptly with tunnels of green gloom. When the river appeared, glinting cool and golden through the trees, so too did the ragtag resort cabins, the rusting trailers, the neon cocktail glasses beckoning luridly from the roadside.

He drove straight through Guerneville, doing his best to ignore the pimply teenagers and blatant homosexuals who prowled the tawdry main street. He had liked this town better in the fifties, before its resurgence, when it was still essentially a ruin from the thirties.

In Monte Rio he turned left, crossing the river on the old steel bridge. Another left took him along a winding road past junked cars and blackberry thickets and poison oak pushing to the very edge of the asphalt.

At the end of this road lay the big wooden gates to the Grove and the vine-entangled sign that invariably caused his heart to beat faster:

PRIVATE PROPERTY. MEMBERS AND GUESTS ONLY.

TRESPASSERS WILL BE PROSECUTED.

He drove through the gates and past the gray-frame commissary buildings, coming to a stop in front of the luggage dock and check-in station. Climbing out of the car, he adjusted his tie, brushed the wrinkles out of his suit, and inhaled the resinous incense of the great woodland cathedral that awaited him.

The familiar cast of characters was already assembled: the jubilant new arrivals, the blue-jeaned college boys who did the valet parking, the leathery rent-a-cops with their cowboy hats and huge bellies and belt buckles the size of license plates.

Sweating a little, he opened the trunk and hauled his two suit-cases to the luggage dock marked "River Road." He was filled with inexplicable glee as he grabbed a stubby golf pencil and inscribed two old-fashioned steamer trunk labels with the words *Manigault* and *Hillbillies*. Why did this feel so much like coming home?

After relinquishing his BMW to a valet parker, he spotted Farley Stuart and Jimmy Chappell and sauntered up behind them. "Damn," he said, "we're in trouble now!"

Both men hooted jovially, clapping him on the back. Jimmy looked a little withered after his bypass operation, but his spirit seemed as spunky as ever. Farley, heading for the shuttle bus, turned and aimed a finger at Booter. "Come for fizzes tomorrow morning. Up at Aviary."

Aviary was the chorus camp. Farley was a valued baritone, an "associate" member whose talent alone had qualified him for a bunk in Bohemia. He wasn't an aristocrat by any stretch of the imagination, but he was a nice fellow just the same.

Booter pointed back at him and said, "You got a deal."

He knew already that he wouldn't go (he expected an invita-tion to fizzes up at Mandalay), but his burgeoning spirit of brother-hood made saying no a virtual impossibility.

He was amused, as always, when the guard at the check-in sta-tion punched him in, using a conventional industrial time clock. This, he'd been told, had largely to do with billing for food, as mem-bers were charged for any meals that occurred during their time at the Grove, regardless of whether or not they chose to eat.

The guard was one he liked, which comforted him, since this was the fellow who would know the most about his comings and goings.

When he was done, he found Jimmy and Farley holding the shuttle bus for him. He decided to walk, flagging them on—a joint decision, really, between a vain old man proud of his endurance and a wide-eyed boy ready to explore.

Somewhere up ahead, someone was playing a banjo.

◆——————◆

The ceremonial gates, the ones meant to welcome rather than repulse, were a boy's own daydream, a rustic Tom Swiftian portal built of oversized Lincoln Logs. As Booter passed through them, a blue jay swept low over his shoulder, cackling furiously, and his welcome seemed complete.

He strode briskly, following the road into a forest so thoroughly primeval that some of it had been here when Genghis Khan began his march across Asia. Something indescribable always happened at this point, some soothing realignment of boundaries which contracted his world and made it manageable for the first time all year.

Sky and trees and river notwithstanding, the grove was not the great outdoors at all; it was a room away from things, a cavernous temple of brotherhood, locked to the rest of humanity. There was order here, and a palpable absence of anarchy. No wonder it made him so happy.

He whistled as he passed the post office, the grocery store, the barbershop, the museum, the telegraph office, the phone bank, the hospital, the fire station. Other members, already anonymous in comfortable old clothes, moved past him in jocular clumps, brandishing whiskey in plastic glasses, calling his name from time to time.

At the height of the encampment, over two thousand men would be assembled at the grove in one hundred twenty-six different camps. As Booter understood it, this made for a population density greater than that of Chinatown in San Francisco.

As he approached the Campfire Circle, he stopped to read the posters tacked to the trees—each a work of art, really—heralding gala nights and concerts, costume dramas, and Lakeside Talks. His own address was somewhat drably listed as: *Roger Manigault: Aluminum Honeycomb and the Future of the Strategic Nuclear Defense Initiative.*

Another shuttle bus—this one labeled "The Old Guard"—bumped past him as he skirted the lake. Henry McKittrick was seated in the back, red-faced and solemn in his sweaty seersuckers. Booter gave him a thumbs-up sign, but Henry merely nodded, obviously still sore about the contract with Consolidated.

He headed down the River Road toward Hillbillies, immersing himself in the sights and sounds of the frontier community coming to life beneath the giant trees. The very name of the camps triggered half a lifetime of memories: Dog House, Toyland, Pig 'n Whistle, Sons of Toil....

Someone was playing a piano—"These Foolish Things"—on the ridge to the left. To the right was a Dixieland band and a chorus practicing a classical number he didn't recognize. Their voices trailed heavenward, hovering like wood smoke in the slanting afternoon light.

◇————————◇

As night fell, he assembled with the others at the Owl Shrine for the Cremation of Care. The already drunken crowd fell silent as the lakeside organist began to play the dirge and the High Priest summoned his acolytes. Then the barge materialized, poled silently across the lake, bearing the palled figure of Care.

When the barge reached the shrine, two acolytes removed the pall, revealing the macabre effigy with its papier-mâché mask. The effigy was dutifully placed upon the pyre, but its incineration was halted, as always, by sinister, electronically enhanced laughter from the hillside.

All eyes turned toward the ridge as a puff of smoke and a flash of light revealed the presence of the ghostly white Tree of Care. From deep inside the tree thundered the voice of Care itself:

"Fools, fools, fools, when will ye learn that me ye cannot slay? Year after year you burn me in this Grove, lifting your silly shouts of triumph to the pitying stars. But when ye turn your feet again to the marketplace, am I not waiting for you as of old? Fools, fools, to dream you conquer Care!"

The High Priest answered:

"Year after year, within this happy Grove, our fellowship has damned thee for a space, and thy malevolence that would pursue us has lost its power beneath these friendly trees. So shall we burn thee once again this night, and in the flames that eat thine effigy we'll read the sign that, once again, midsummer sets us free."

Then, after lighting their torches at the gas-jet altar fire, the acolytes descended upon the pyre and set Care aflame, piercing the night with shouts of ecstasy. The band broke into "Hot Time in the Old Town Tonight."

Booter smiled, feeling the old magic, then withdrew into the darkness as fireworks burst in the trees above the lake. When he reached the phone bank, he was relieved to see that no one else was there. He placed a local call.

"Yello," said Wren Douglas.

"It's me," he said. "Just making sure you're comfortable."

"Sittin' pretty," she said.

"Good. I'll be up there tonight."

"No problem," she replied.

CZESLAW MILOSZ

from "SYMBOLIC MOUNTAINS AND FORESTS"

Upon publishing his first book at the age of twenty-five, Lithuanian-born Polish poet Czeslaw Milosz (b. 1911) established a firm reputation in Polish literary circles. Soon after publishing his second book in 1945, he defected to the West. Until 1980, when he won the Nobel Prize for literature, only underground editions of his work were published in Poland.

Milosz is now a professor emeritus in Slavic languages and literature at the University of California, Berkeley. This selection from "Symbolic Mountains and Forests" is from the collection of essays Visions from San Francisco Bay *(1969), in which Milosz examines life in contemporary California and his place in it.*

Thus, in general, the garden corresponds to heavenly intelligence and wisdom; for that reason, heaven is called the garden of God and paradise is called by man heavenly paradise. Trees, according to their type, correspond to the perception and cognition of the good and the true from which intelligence and wisdom derive. For that reason, the ancients, proficient in the knowledge of correspondences, performed their sacred rituals in groves. And thus trees so often replace Scripture, and the sky the church, and thus man is likened to a grapevine, an olive tree, a cedar and other trees, while good deeds are likened to fruits.

EMANUEL SWEDENBORG,
HEAVEN AND ITS WONDERS, AND HELL

How is it that nature seems to contain the shades of our feelings and passions, that its images can be serene, menacing, smiling, gloomy, benign, kind, mournful? I have read a good deal of Emanuel Swedenborg, the father of Symbolism in poetry. Like the majority of my contemporaries, I have, however, been deprived of faith in the pre-existence of material forms as ideas before they were clothed in flesh, or as the expression of certain spiritual states. For me an apple tree evokes many associations, because man has been fond of trees for ages and they have served his imagination in religion, poetry, and painting, not because the apple tree was destined for that use even before the creation of the world. The lion struck primitive hunters as a dangerous but splendid adversary, but probably no royal crown had been given him before human beings appeared in the lands where lions lived. A mountain peak has always been the proper place to contact the Divinity, but Sinai, Patmos, the monasteries built on the rocks, all corresponded to a need for rising above the confusion of daily endeavors, drawing nearer to the sky and making mortal men's short-lived troubles seem insignificant. Thus, before the liquid crust of the earth had begun to cool, mountains were not thought of as foundations for future temples or for opposed linguistic concepts such as baseness and loftiness.

Those are the reasonable explanations I offer myself, but experience, unschooled and stubborn, forces landscape obsessions and beast symbols upon me as if, within the forms perceived by the senses, there were a rich and hidden voice saying the same thing to everyone. Perhaps a memory older than our own lives, the memory of the species, circulates through us with our blood. That memory affirms our identity with others, and also makes us able to understand each other to some degree. All our metaphors revolve around sensations of above and below, darkness and light, greenery, fire, water; the same smile appears on every face at the sight of a bird, and the fear of touching a snake is common to us all.

There is nothing unusual in my rendering trees honor—people have been doing this since time immemorial, and the thrust of the trunk, from roots beneath the earth, through our middle dimension, to the sky, where the leaves sway, has always lent credence to the division of existence into three zones. Trees were writing their own Divine Comedy about the ascent from hell to the high spheres of heaven long before Dante wrote his. I wouldn't know how to dwell in a treeless country, and where I live now, the compass of my dreams always points north.

The redwood forest, the remains of a virgin sequoia forest. The interiors of certain Gothic cathedrals—Strasbourg, for example— replicate man's smallness and helplessness in his middle zone between hell and heaven, amid the columns of the primeval forests which still covered large areas of Europe when the cathedrals were built. But Europe never had trees like the redwoods, whose lifespans number over two thousand years. This forest is the idea of forest, a prototype drawn by God; no church columns attain that height, and never does a church's semi-darkness contrast so sharply with a ray slanting in from above the reach of sight. Small human figures are diminished not by the redwoods' trunks, too huge for comparisons, but by a lower level, in relation to ferns larger than a man and to the fallen, moss-covered logs which sprout new green shoots. To confirm their value as a forest symbol: the redwoods are such that the chunk of a felled tree does not die but regenerates itself in a multitude of swiftly growing sprigs....

Animals. The enigmatic quality of our relationship to the bear—fond affection mixed with fear, the ancient tribal ritual of apologizing after killing one, children's furry teddy bears. Our playful liking for raccoons, those thieves raiding forest campgrounds, cunning creatures able to open nearly any sort of food container with their paws. A sort of anxiety upon seeing caterpillars or worms swarming on a stump or a piece of meat, and the same cylindrical shapes, the same blind squirmings of sea lions on a block of basalt jutting out of the sea. Binoculars reveal the mighty bodies of the males amid their harems, their wrinkled muzzles open in roars of warning, they roll over each other, they battle, the young play, pushing each other off the surf-washed slabs into the boiling foam. In spite of myself, unable to satisfy myself with the statement that this simply is, I ask—what does this mean? Is it an allusion to the similarity of micro and macro movements, the uncertain attempts at spatial orientation common to microbes and worms and those sea lions, as well, whose way of life, after all, is the result of limbs unadapted to moving on land? Is this some signal informing us that more elements than the air of birds and men are inhabitable, since those warm-blooded relations of ours can feel at home in the dark ocean where life is cold? Is there some significance here I am unaware of? Or no significance at all?

THE HIGH EMBRACE

*William Everson (1912–1994) became a Dominican monk in
1951; as Brother Antoninus, he was a widely respected figure in
the Beat movement. In 1964 he took vows of priesthood,
renouncing them in 1969 just before his third marriage. During
his lifetime he achieved a national reputation as a poet, schol-
ar, and printer, publishing more than forty-five books. Like
Robinson Jeffers, whom he credited with inspiring him to write,
he focused on nature—the California landscape—in his poetry.*

They stand in the clearing of Kingfisher Flat,
Twin giants, *Sequoia sempervirens,* the ever-vernal,
And take in the arms of their upper branches
The last light crossing the bench-ridge west,
Sinking toward dusk.

     Standing between them
I look up the double-columned space to the soaring crown,
Where those red-ribbed branches clasp each other in a high
  embrace.
For hundreds of years they have stood here, serenely apart,

Drinking clear creek water through sequaceous pores,
Feeling the flake of mountains sift chalkstone gravel about their
    boles,
Watching giant grizzlies scoop gravid salmon on the spawning
    bars below,
And tawny cougars stalk for fawns in their leaf-dappled shade.
They heard the kingfisher chirr his erratic intemperate cry,
While over their tops the slow-wheeling condors circled the sun,
Drifting south to their immemorial roosting ledges in the Los
    Padres peaks.
And they felt the demon of fire lick its running tongue up their
    shaggy skin
And not flinched, scorched but unscarred in the long warfare,
The stress-tension shaping fuel to fire,
The life-flux of their kind.

       Tonight,
In the heat of the drought, we will forsake our bed,
Shutting the house-presence out of our thought,
Taking our respite in the open air. We will muse late,
And lay ourselves down by fir-bark embers,
Under the cape of the twin redwoods, swept back in time
A thousand years when this coast nurtured its kind—
The great beasts, the towering trees, the bird-flight migrations,
The shy coastal tribes. And in the sea-troughs of sleep
Our dreams will mirror the world above
Where stars swim over, and shadow the bloodstream's sibilance,
All through the foliage of the flesh, its fern-like fronds.

Up there above me the last light
Filters in as through stained glass windows,
Diffuse, glowing in the lofts of the upper branches,

Radiant and soft. And the mystery of worship
Descends on me, out of those far fenestrations.
And the God-awe, wake-wonder, envelops me,
Between the monumental straightness of columns
Bearing the sky, illuminate zone, twin towers
Conjoined above, clasped in the high embrace,
The soaring arch.

       And the face of my son
Dawns between the gigantic boles
As he runs to meet me. And I ask in my heart
The graciousness of God, that he may grow in their presence,
As the tan-oak grows, as the fir-tree and fern,
As the chipmunk and the jay shelter under their span.

And I invoke their mystery of survival,
That the lightning-shattering years,
And the raw surge of fire,
May skim but not scar him—
As they themselves are scathed but unscarred—
Through the skip years of his childhood
And the leap years of his youth.

Make over our heads, then, the high embrace,
Like a blessing, the numinous descent, faith-fall,
Out of the heights, the leaf-light canopy,
The lofts of God, induplicate
A gift regiven, the boon bestowed.

SAVING THE REMNANT

JOSEPH D. GRANT

from REDWOODS AND REMINISCENCES

As early as 1857, just a few years after A. T. Dowd happened upon the big trees of Calaveras County, James Russell Lowell published an article in The Crayon *calling for the protection of American trees, including the California redwoods. As technology grew more destructive, logging escalated, and so too did calls for conservation. By 1898, the Sierra Club, founded in 1892, was calling for parks that would preserve the coastal redwoods. In 1899, the newly formed Sempervirens Club purchased a grove of redwoods that had been scheduled to be cut down—the beginning of Big Basin State Park. In 1918 the Save the Redwoods League was formed. Since 1920 they have been purchasing redwood groves for parks and preserves.*

Joseph D. Grant (1858–1942), a wealthy and influential businessman and landowner, was also a founding member of the Save the Redwoods League. In his Redwoods and Reminiscences, *the passion of a conservationist who first came to the redwoods as a young man in the nineteenth century heralds the work of activists fifty years after his death.*

When I was seventeen years old, I traveled northward through the redwood belt, all the way to the Oregon line and a little beyond, in company with another youth and an experienced woodsman—a most interesting man, friend of my father, and by him commissioned to teach us forest craft. With eager attention we followed his instruction, learning how to still-hunt and to back-trail, and we were even initiated into camp cooking. As planned by my father, our older companion would continue with us awhile on our way and then would leave us for a space, returning as we took the trail again.

This unusual man, we learned, had three times captained covered wagon trains from the Missouri River to Sacramento, in the early days. Though inured to the rough ways of the frontier, he was an Oxford graduate—a remittance man, who had come to America that he might lead an outdoor life, to escape a taint of consumption in the family. With the pistol he was an unerring marksman, and never have I seen one so quick on the draw. In the course of the rough life which he had been obliged to lead, he had killed nine men and one woman—the woman being a camp follower who had stirred up a mutiny against him. "It was either their lives or mine," he apologized.

This lightning quickness in bringing his weapon into action was a lifesaving grace....He carried a pistol in front instead of in back of his hip as they do in the movies. It was always close at hand. "Never for a moment be without your pistol," was his urgent advice. On the march, all his game he shot with a pistol, unless in need of meat. The rifle, he averred, was too easy. Not only did he teach us to shoot, this *beau ideal* of a woodsman, but he showed us how to find our way through the wilderness by observing the trees. We followed trails where we could, though often we had to cut our path through dense undergrowth.

With all his woodcraft, our preceptor had never before been in the redwoods, and he said just before were to leave him, "Lads, we've been traveling a deal—let's have a day of rest. It is as important to rest as to go. I look upon these days that we have spent together as the most important days of my life, for here I have seen the most beautiful things that I have ever seen, and I've ranged all the world over. These giant trees may be cut down, many of them, and in after years you and your children will regret every stump, for as sure as you are living the people will wake up to the horror of it. If the government had brains, it would buy up all these forest lands and keep them, instead of selling what it has for $2.50 an acre."

In meditative mood, our master of woodcraft added, "Lads, there is no forest creature to be afraid of in these redwoods. You need not fear any of these animals you meet—we can tame all of them. The only truly wild animal is the mountain lion, and you have to hunt to find him. There are no poisonous insects and no rattlesnakes in this region. But these forests are dangerous, none the less. The only danger comes from the humans, for here, too, is a paradise 'where only man is vile.'

"You have noted that we have kept away from towns on our trip. Now, most of these places are the resort of the riffraff of the frontier—they are crowded with dangerous characters. You will recall that last time I left you I was away about a week. I went to a town over to eastward for supplies—Orleans Bar. I got my grub at the store; like all of them, it was a store with a saloon as its principal resource. As I was starting back, throwing the last rope in the diamond hitch, a villainous looking fellow, whom I had seen at the saloon, lounged up and asked, "Which way, pard?" "I'm going along the river," I responded, knowing full well that the man was planning to follow me, just as many such had in the past.

"I proceeded a few miles along the Klamath trail, then turned my horses over behind some rocks and back-trailed, waiting in a clump of fern. Sure enough, soon I heard voices, and along came the man who had questioned me and a companion, both armed with rifles. They were full of red liquor, and I heard them agreeing, as they rolled off their horses, that they would stop to take a little siesta in the redwoods shade. Waiting until they were sleeping the troubled sleep of the unjust, I approached and snaked their rifles from their sides, hiding them in a hole in a big redwood. Some day an axman is likely to discover a couple of rusty rifles in the trunk of a tree in that neck of the woods. I got both of their horses and you remember that I brought them along to camp, and turned them out as we left.

"Those men would have killed you for what you had in this camp—there is not a doubt in the world about it. Your father, Joe, is a usually cautious Scot, but I don't think much of his judgment if he lets you roam these redwoods alone."

Just as we were bidding him good-bye, we came out at a breath upon the ocean—from the midst of the dense forest to the vast open expanse fronting the Pacific, which mantled in foam the rock reefs below. It was a transition dramatic in its suddenness.

We had reached the sea just south of Crescent City, and the spot was marked indelibly in my memory. It was at just this point that Madison Grant and I, sixty years later, preserved the Grant Grove, as a gift to the State of California....

In those north woods I scraped acquaintance with the daredevil "timber toppers" and the stalwart axmen who could, two of them together, fell a tree in a few hours which had taken three thousand years to grow! Some shrank from such slaughter, even though they did it....

Even the dominant lumber barons harbored compunctions. Joseph Hergesheimer tells of meeting a bluff old lumberman who

Any fool can destroy trees. They cannot defend themselves or run away. And few destroyers of trees ever plant any; nor can planting avail much toward restoring our grand aboriginal giants. It took more than three thousand years to make some of the oldest of the sequoias, trees that are still standing in perfect strength and beauty, waving and singing in the mighty forests of the Sierra. Through all the eventful centuries since Christ's time, and long before that, God has cared for these trees, saved them from drought, disease, avalanches, and a thousand storms; but he cannot save them from sawmills and fools; this is left to the American people.

JOHN MUIR, *from* "SAVE THE REDWOODS"

admitted turning away every time his men brought a stately giant crashing to the earth. By God, he said, he didn't want to see it!

It was in those early days, too, that I first met the timber cruiser, the most tireless of all woodsmen. Every cruiser "has a high wheel"—I never saw a short-legged "brush monkey," nor a fat one, either. Lank and lean, "all whalebone and catgut" like the true frontiersman, the timber cruiser strikes in a beeline across country, with utter defiance to contours and gradients and at a terrific gait. I followed one once in the redwoods—then lay down and died on the way!

When I came to man's estate, I went on loving the redwoods. As a member of the Bohemian Club, that rare fellowship of artists and lovers of nature, I went year after year to our jolly camps on the

Russian River. There, in the Bohemian Grove, I could heave a sigh of security, for there, at least, was the forest protected....

In the early 1890s I traveled with a fellow Bohemian, Dr. George Chismore, from San Francisco into southern Oregon. We loafed along, as in the leisurely pastoral days, on horseback—traversing the length (more than three hundred miles) of the redwood belt north of San Francisco.

I thought I had seen some trees, but my first loves were Lilliputians compared to the Brobdingnagians which I now beheld! On our pilgrimage we wandered into the primeval redwood fastnesses of Dyerville Flat and Bull Creek Flat on the lower Eel River. There we blinked at sequoias towering straight up three hundred and fifty feet!

As we wandered and wondered, we saw sylvan grandeur that seemed to belong to a greater planet. A mystic half-light suffused the woods even at midday; at sunrise and sunset this became a

---

I feel most emphatically that we should not turn into shingles a tree which was old when the first Egyptian conqueror penetrated to the valley of the Euphrates, which it has taken so many thousands of years to build up, and which can be put to better use. That, you may say, is not looking at the matter from the practical standpoint. There is nothing more practical in the end than the preservation of beauty, than the preservation of anything that appeals to the higher emotions in mankind.

THEODORE ROOSEVELT, *from a speech ca. 1903*

---

rose-colored haze, the ambient air tinted by the russet-barked trunks, row upon row of colossal colonnades, in enchanting perspective.

Standing in the radiance of this filtered sunlight, slanting down in long shafts like angel paths in the primitives' pictures, it was impossible not to think of the forest as a cathedral or temple. Fluted columns rose on all sides in ionic simplicity and splendor, perfectly proportioned and without limbs for a hundred feet from the forest floor. Overhead, fan vaulting and an exquisite tracery of branches against a heaven of intense blue. More glorious to me than any Gothic fane, more inspiring to awe and devotion!...

As we wandered in Bull Creek Flat, penetrating jungles of man-high ferns, a sense of unreality, a spell of enchantment, came over me. We trod upon a prayer mat of mosses and mold, the accumulation of ages. Everywhere the air was sweet and cool, but heavy with the fragrance of rhododendrons, trilliums, oxalis, and other flowers of the woods. This primeval forest was a titan's garden. We felt as if we had traveled back through the centuries to behold the world as it was, in prehistoric luxuriance of foliage and bloom. Instead of deer and elk, we almost expected to see a grazing dinosaur or a pterodactyl flitting past us.

In this arcadia we camped, as did our remote ancestors—for the sequoias flourished in Britain and in most of northwestern Europe before the Age of Ice. Now, only here in California, where the continental ice cap divided and left a great area untouched, have they been preserved.

Changing temperatures, varying conditions of moisture, aggressive rivalry of other growths destroyed the sequoias. Here, as in their days of universal empire, they have made their last stand, heads among the stars, feet clasped to earth. In our kindly clime, in our sympathetic soil, where along and near our coast there is abundant moisture, the giants hold their own and defy the onslaught of all—save man!

JOHN MUIR

from THE YOSEMITE

Along with his poetic, sometimes ecstatic descriptions of the Sierra Nevada landscape and his ardent efforts in support of conservation, Muir's work is abundant in careful observation of nature and deeply pondered conclusions, such as the idea that Yosemite Valley was shaped by glaciers. The following selection, written in 1912, describes the relationship between sequoias and the water table.

It is constantly asserted in a vague way that the Sierra was vastly wetter than now, and that the increasing drought will of itself extinguish the sequoia, leaving its ground to other trees supposed capable of flourishing in a drier climate. But that the sequoia can and does grow on as dry ground as any of its present rivals is manifest in a thousand places. "Why, then," it will be asked, "are sequoias always found only in well-watered places?" Simply because a growth of sequoias creates those streams. The thirsty mountaineer knows well that in every sequoia grove he will find running water, but it is a mistake to suppose that the water is the cause of the grove being there; on the contrary, the grove is the cause of the water being there. Drain off the water and the trees will remain, but cut off the trees, and the streams will vanish. Never was cause more completely mistaken for effect than in the case of these related phenomena of sequoia woods and perennial streams.

When attention is called to the method of sequoia stream making, it will be apprehended at once. The roots of this immense tree fill the ground, forming a thick sponge that absorbs and holds back the rain and melting snow, only allowing it to ooze and flow gently. Indeed, every fallen leaf and rootlet, as well as long clasping root and prostrate trunk, may be regarded as a dam hoarding the bounty of storm clouds, and dispensing it as blessings all through the summer, instead of allowing it to go headlong in short-lived floods....

There is no absolute limit to the existence of any tree. Death is due to accidents, not, as that of animals, to the wearing out of organs. Only the leaves die of old age. Their fall is foretold in their structure; but the leaves are renewed every year, and so also are the essential organs—wood, roots, bark, buds. Most of the Sierra trees die of disease, insects, fungi, etc., but nothing hurts the big tree. I never saw one that was sick or showed the slightest sign of decay. Barring accidents, it seems to be immortal. It is a curious fact that all the very old sequoias had lost their heads by lightning strokes. "All things come to him who waits." But of all living things, sequoia is perhaps the only one able to wait long enough to make sure of being struck by lightning.

So far as I am able to see at present, only fire and the ax threaten the existence of these noblest of God's trees. In Nature's keeping they are safe but, through the agency of man, destruction is making rapid progress, while in the work of protection only a good beginning has been made. The Fresno Grove, the Tuolumne, Merced and Mariposa Groves are under the protection of the federal government in the Yosemite National Park. So are the General Grant and Sequoia National Parks; the latter, established twenty-one years ago, has an area of two hundred and forty square miles and is efficiently guarded by a troop of cavalry under the direction of the Secretary of the Interior. So also are the small General Grant National Park, established at the same time, with an area of four square miles, and the Mariposa Grove, about the same size, and the small Merced and Tuolumne groups. Perhaps more than half of all the big trees have been thoughtlessly sold and are now in the hands of speculators and mill men. It appears, therefore, that far the largest and most important section of protected big trees is in the great Sequoia National Park, now easily accessible by rail to Lemon Cove and thence by a good stage road into the giant forest of the Kaweah and thence by trail to other parts of the park; but large as it is, it should be made much larger. Its natural eastern boundary is the High Sierra, and the northern and southern boundaries are the Kings and Kern Rivers. Thus could be included the sublime scenery on the headwaters of these rivers and perhaps nine-tenths of all the big trees in existence. All private claims within these bounds should be gradually extinguished by purchase by the government. The big tree, leaving all its higher uses out of the count, is a tree of life to the dwellers of the plain dependent on irrigation, a never-failing spring, sending living waters to the lowland. For every grove cut down, a stream is dried up. Therefore all California is crying, "Save the trees of the fountains." Nor, judging by the signs of the times, is it likely that the cry will cease until the salvation of all that is left of *Sequoia gigantea* is made sure.

JOAN DUNNING

from FROM THE
REDWOOD FOREST

◇————————————————————————————◇

*Joan Dunning is a nature writer and artist in Arcata, Califor-
nia. In* From the Redwood Forest—Ancient Trees and
the Bottom Line: A Headwaters Journey *(1998), she reports,
with photographer Doug Thron, firsthand on the "liquidation
logging" practices of the late twentieth century and the passionate activists who are determined to stop the destruction of
ancient forests.*

◇————————————————————————————◇

When MAXXAM's resource manager, Tom Herman, presents a com-
puter-generated video of logging over the next ten years, showing
a progression of clear-cuts to regrowth to clear-cuts to regrowth,
the land panting in and out beneath what looks like bouts of
mange, he says with genuine glee, "Look! Here it comes again! The
orange PL [Pacific Lumber] pickup truck! Every time it comes on
the screen, something happens!" And, true to his word, the truck
zips across the screen and a clear-cut appears — tricky, cute, and
entertaining. But when someone in the audience asks the serious

question, "What about the mycorrhizal fungi?" the question is side-stepped with a joke, as if the concept of fungus were too esoteric to be taken seriously.

Therefore I thought there was something "new" about the concept of mycorrhizal fungi. I thought that word must not be quite "out" from the hallowed halls of science and that biologists should move along in communicating with industry about their important research. I was surprised, however, when I looked at an old botany textbook from 1964 in my personal library and found that it contains the word "mycorrhizae." "Mycorrhizae, literally meaning 'fungus root,'" it says, "are now recognized as organs of fundamental importance in the nutrition of the trees on which they occur."

I picked up a children's book from the same shelf, called *How Plants Work*, a very basic volume that tells only the barest essentials, but there it was again. "These organisms are important in the early stages of a tree's life because they help it to grow....They stimulate root growth and this helps the tree to make more food.... Mycorrhizae are important in forestry, especially in poor soils where conifers will grow well with help from these fungi." With the high amounts of rain that we receive in the Pacific Northwest, our soils, particularly those on hillsides, are consistently poor due to leaching. It is only the public's lack of schooling in natural history that allows MAXXAM to get away with minimizing this ancient key to soil health.

But how do the fungi interact with the trees?

If you were to dig up just one of the millions of roots of a single tree in Headwaters and follow it to its furthest tip, you would find that the tip looks slightly swollen and brownish. If you were to take that tip home and look more closely in good light, you would see that it appears furry. Under a microscope, you would see that this "furriness" is not due to hair, but to millions of fungal filaments. In cross section, you could see that these filaments grow not only outwards into the soil, but also inwards into the host root. Thus the fungus creates a connective layer between tree and soil, extending the roots' reach into the soil and simultaneously increasing the tree's capacity to absorb water and nutrients.

As you might well imagine, this layer is vitally important in the establishment of a seedling. Because a seedling has relatively few, blunt roots, a coating of these filaments vastly decreases the likelihood that the seedling will dry out. In addition, the coating is actually protective, providing a physical barrier that secretes both antibiotics and a gluelike substance that stabilizes the soil around the root and keeps passages open for air and water. In addition, the fungi break down the minerals in the soil, components that can be used by the trees. In a land where summers are rainless and a new seedling may suddenly find itself in parched conditions, its roots are protected by the fungi. Meanwhile, the fungi, which lack chlorophyll and are therefore incapable of photosynthesis, derive sugar from the roots of the seedling. In this harmless, symbiotic exchange, both prosper. It is hard for me, as a parent, not to warm up to these fungi that function so much like foster parents to the seedlings. I am reminded of how, when my children first started school, I hoped that someone would provide the same sort of transitional protection.

When an area is clear-cut and the soil heavily disturbed by bulldozers, however, the host tree species on which the mycorrhizal fungi depend are eliminated. Slash fires, which are a routine practice following clear-cutting, tend to burn hotter and closer to the ground than natural fires, scorching and killing the mycorrhizal spores in the process. Natural fires, in contrast, burn more coolly as they move higher off the ground through the canopy, leaving large logs and whole standing snags behind. Viable seeds and small animals hidden beneath the moisture-retaining logs usually survive natural fires as well.

In an area that is holistically logged through selective thinning, no clear-cutting and no slash burning occur. Most of the animals of the deep forest remain. Redwood stumps and young trees that have been suppressed by lack of light respond to the new openings in the canopy, yet most of the ecosystem remains naturally shaded. When Douglas fir seeds fall from the mature trees and sprout in the newly opened ground, the mycorrhizal fungi are still in place and readily recolonize by spores.

◆————————◆

I have come on a walk in the Arcata Community Forest with a man who is a mushroom specialist. This is a place that is walked by hundreds of people every week. Yet walking with this man in a place where I have walked countless times, I see the world turned upside down. Suddenly the important activity of the forest is below my feet. There is a wilderness there, however much its surface may be trodden daily, that is vast and mysterious. This man gently digs into the soil as if he fears he may be prying and exposes mycorrhizal filaments fanning out in such profusion that it seems as though he has come to the forest ahead of our visit to set up a tricky, exaggerated show of nature's abundance. He tells me a story: "A group of foresters went out in the woods. Some were American and some were Japanese. One Japanese man asked an American, 'Why do you look up when you go into a forest?' The American forester looked at the other American foresters. They were all peering into the treetops or examining the bark. He had to look down to see the Japanese foresters, who were on their hands and knees studying the soil."

He told me one fact that will forever change my concept of the forest. It is simply this: 51 percent of the biomass of an old-growth forest is fungal. More than half of the forest is not made up of branches and needles and the marketable trunks, but of mushrooms and their underground wanderings of filaments. When one walks on land that has been recently clear-cut, the dominant smell is not of sawdust, but of fungi.

from CALIFORNIA FAULT

In California Fault: Searching for the Spirit of State Along the San Andreas, *travel writer and novelist Thurston Clarke (b. 1946) explores the state of the California dream on a twofold path: the San Andreas Fault, and the route through California taken by his ancestor J. Goldsborough Bruff, whose journal of gold-rush era explorations was published as* Gold Rush *in 1944.*

I met Rondal Snodgrass, who has made it his business to save as many of Humboldt County's trees as he can, after Sunday mass at the Redwoods Monastery in the former mill town of Whitethorn, seven miles east as the crow flies from where the fault crosses Shelter Cove. A sculptor and a Hollywood set designer constructed the monastery's main building in the 1950s, and old-timers remembered the men tying bells around their livestock so the meadows could tinkle like wind chimes. After the sculptor married, the set designer joined an abbey and gave the Whitethorn property to an order of Cistercian nuns fleeing the Congo. A redwood trunk fills the high window behind what is now an altar, dwarfing a modest cross and making it possible for even a nature worshiper to feel comfortable here....

Snodgrass had a formal telephone voice, so I easily picked him out as the distinguished, straight-backed man with a gray mustache. His business card said RONDAL SNODGRASS, ENVIRONMENTALIST, EXECUTIVE DIRECTOR OF SANCTUARY FOREST. His strategy was to buy tracts of endangered old-growth redwood forest, then resell them to the state or a "conservation owner" who logged them according to principles of sustainable forestry. He was a modest environmental saint, preserving a few acres at a time. He lived on little, and admitted envying the rich counterculture types who grew dope. Their sudden embrace of the consumer society had disgusted their more principled neighbors, and he refused to save redwoods with drug money.

Driving with him through the Mattole Valley was like touring Virginia with a Civil War buff. Every road led to an old battlefield. We bumped to the end of a logging track, then stumbled through a stump-and-scrub wasteland where environmentalists had retreated before bulldozers after giving every tree a hug and naming it after a Greek god. We paused in a weedy field where rust ate at the peace signs and psychedelic rainbows of abandoned hippie cars. As a scrap dealer's flatbed truck lumbered down the road with a cargo of burned-out Valiants and Darts harvested from defunct communes upstream, he spread out a five-year-old aerial photograph of these once thickly wooded hills so I could compare them with the brutal clear-cut before us. He described the battle in the hushed voice of a soldier remembering a rout. Two weeks of sunrise prayer vigils, attempts to convert loggers, and sprawling in front of bulldozers had failed. The loggers called it a "rehabilitation cut," but it left the hills naked except for a line of trees parading the ridge like skeletons. "Exquisite hardwoods," he said in a dreamy voice, as if he could still see them. "The oak topping that knoll was exceptional. I begged a forester I knew to spare it as a personal favor, but it went down with the rest."

To reach the eighty acres of virgin forest Snodgrass wanted to save, we had to cross an abandoned marijuana farm, picking through collapsing sheds and garden hoses he thought would outlast the trees. The doper had been a troubled man who was arrested for killing a bear and jailed on drug charges before disappearing. His mother had recently hiked through this forest, nailing posters to trees carrying a blurry mug shot and beginning HAVE YOU SEEN....

A stark boundary separated the logged-out pot farm and the virgin forest Snodgrass hoped to buy. You stepped across it and left a faded landscape of stumps, scrubby trees, and hills threatening landslides for one of giant ferns, moss, and Douglas fir. Sounds became muffled and light softened, as if filtered through a stained-glass canopy. The squishy ground bounced back like a trampoline, and my glasses fogged. It was a mixed forest, with single redwoods towering over tan oak, madrone, and fir. Foresters had already been through, tying blue tape around the trunks of trees marked for harvest, spray-painting those to be spared with a red L for "Leave."

Snodgrass stopped opposite a blue-banded virgin redwood and whispered, "Oh no! Too close to the stream. I can't help myself. I see a tree like this and imagine how many people you'd need to hug it."

"Suppose you don't buy it in time?" I asked.

"I get queasy thinking about it."

Although I was raised on 1950s social-studies texts portraying loggers as Paul Bunyans and timber companies as planters of handsome tree farms, and although I live in a wood-paneled house in the Adirondacks where trees seem to grow as fast as weeds, and I recently cleared an acre of land to improve my view, this blue band made me slightly queasy, too.

The logging of old-growth redwoods was the most contentious issue in Humboldt and Mendocino counties, dividing communities and sometimes leading to protests and violence. For decades, environmental groups and the timber industry had been arguing over how much logging practices such as clear-cutting contributed to erosion, silted waterways, the destruction of the salmon industry, and floods like the one almost sweeping away Ferndale; over how many timber roads should be built, how close they should be to watersheds, how many trees should be left and how many taken, and how many years should elapse before a second-growth harvest.

Environmentalists believed clear-cuts were an indisputable atrocity; the industry countered that they produced the sunny conditions that encouraged stumps to sprout new trees. Environmentalists trumpeted a government study reporting that space photographs of the Pacific Northwest revealed a greater level of logging damage than in the Amazon; the timber industry denounced it as badly flawed. Environmentalists pointed to the thousand years needed to replace a three-hundred-foot redwood; the industry responded they were the fastest-growing conifers in the nation, sometimes soaring a hundred and fifty feet in their first fifty years. Environmentalists mourned the 90 percent of California's virgin forests lost since the gold rush; the industry said look at how many acres were preserved up in state and national parks. Environmentalists charged companies were closing north-coast sawmills because they had overcut inventory and moved their operations to lower-cost countries; the companies blamed logging restrictions meant to protect the spotted owl. But no one, as far as I could see, worried about losing part of California's seismic timetable.

In the end, where you stood on timber issues, particularly on the emotional issue of harvesting old-growth redwoods, was more a decision of the heart than the head. Either you were moved by the beauty of the tallest and oldest living things on earth, or you were not; appalled by the battlefield landscape of charred earth and stumps left by a clear-cut, or considered it an efficient technique leading to lower consumer prices. You believed every generation should preserve biological diversity for the next and that land had rights *sui generis,* or you were moved by timber workers abandoning communities where their families had lived for generations. You thought a tree farm's identically spaced and sized rows were an acceptable replacement for a redwood grove, or you saw a sterile plantation. You found redwood groves dank, monotonous, and claustrophobic, or places of mystery and wonder. You agreed with University of Oregon professor Ed Whitelaw that "clean air, forested mountains, and pristine beaches" had a dollar value because they attracted new enterprise, or with the chairman of a timber industry organization who called this "lunacy and fantasy economics." You thought, here is a tree that creates its own climate and was alive at Christ's birth, or thought, God has given us a miraculous building material with a clear, straight grain and wood that resists rotting for centuries.

I saw evidence of both reactions while heading down US 101, the "Redwood Highway" connecting Eureka to San Francisco. The hills flanking it in southern Humboldt County looked as exhausted as the towns responsible for them. Clear-cuts had left a patchwork of bald clearings and scrubby second growth. The muddy Eel River flowed back and forth underneath bridges, pinched by expanding banks of gravel and sending more silt downstream than the Mississippi. For most of its distance the highway was a brutal four-lane freeway. It had been built to accommodate lumber trucks in the mid-1960s, a time when California considered such roads so indisputably worthwhile that the Division of Highways (now Caltrans) had proposed naming one slicing through the coastal hills of suburban Contra Costa County the "John Muir Freeway."

Snodgrass's cheerful mixed forest had not prepared me for the thick redwood groves lining the thirty-three-mile-long "Avenue of Giants" in Humboldt Redwoods State Park. Although it was already a dark and drizzly March morning, the moment I entered the groves the temperature and light dropped so dramatically I turned on my heater and headlights.

I spent a day walking through the groves more because I felt I should than because I wanted to. I admired the trees, but their mass and humidity were smothering. I felt trapped in a somber, muffled Amazon without heat or parrots, and could understand the urge to open a sunny clearing. But when I flew over Humboldt County more than a year later, heading for another meeting...and a visit to Bruff's camp, I realized the groves I had seen were a red-wood Potemkin village, just a thin green snake wrapped around the highway, a viewshed for tourists. Elsewhere, logging roads penetrated remote hollows, rivers flowed brown and sluggish, and a chessboard of cuts and second growth stretched to the horizon. The eroded slopes reminded me of Haiti, or Pacific battlefields where marines had incinerated holdout Japanese with flamethrowers.

Those photographs of a 1950s family driving a wood-paneled station wagon through a hole in a giant redwood had been among my first California icons, but when I finally eased my Tempo through the 315-foot-high Chandelier tree at the Leggett Drive-Thru Tree Park to the accompaniment of Waylon Jennings blaring from a loudspeaker, I felt like a fool. My two dollars also bought the right to carve my initials into a log, and patronize a gift shop selling bathroom jokes carved into plaques that, because they are made of redwood, will survive centuries without rotting.

I sat watching in the drizzle as five cars navigated the Chandelier tree. Kids looked bored and wives sheepish, but the men insisted on circling it for a second go. One ordered his wife to videotape their Winnebago squeezing through the tunnel, and a man in a cowboy hat boasted, "I just drove that great big Cadillac through it!" They posed for photographs leaning against the tree, grinning in triumph, and pointing to a sign announcing its weight and height, like mountain climbers at a summit, or big-game hunters with a kill. I noticed the same poses and smiles on lumberjacks in the antique photographs in logging museums and gift shops. The men leaned on Bunyan-sized axes before fallen trees, painted their names on the end of a log, extended their arms to indicate its circumference, and sat in lines dangling their legs over a gargantuan stump. From the beginning, the impulse to turn a redwood into a freak had been irresistible. In 1853, five men spent twenty-five days cutting down a three-thousand-year-old sequoia before using its stump for a dance floor and its fallen trunk as a bowling alley, and a tree so huge it was called "Mother of the Forest" was felled intact and loaded on a flatcar for a tour of Eastern cities where gawkers decorated it with initials carved in intertwined hearts.

At the World Famous Tree House ("Tallest One-Room House in the World"), I stood in the middle of a gloomy, fire-blackened redwood trunk and stared hundreds of feet up into a yellow bulb that glowed like a gorgon's eye. It debauched into a gift shop with displays of rabbits' feet, cuckoo clocks, and more redwood slices decorated with vulgar jokes. Identical crap could be had at the Shrine Drive-Thru Tree, "a natural gap...once used by Indians for smoke signals"; Chimney Tree/Hobbiton USA, where redwood dioramas depicted scenes from *Lord of the Rings;* and the Tour-Thru Tree, where "a man-made cut through this 700-year-old redwood allows passage of most vehicles."

The nearby towns were as melancholy as their attractions. Weott was a huddle of the few clapboard houses to survive the great flood of 1964. Rio Dell's ramshackle main street would soon be consumed by fires caused by aftershocks of...the earthquake. Only Scotia, a company town with the largest redwood mill in the world, was thriving. Until 1985, it had belonged to the famously paternal Pacific Lumber Company, noted for, among other things, providing every worker's child with a college scholarship and serving only the best spirits in the company saloon in the belief that expensive brands were less likely to cause hangovers. A 1950 travel article said its hospital was as modern as any in California and its baseball park the equal of San Francisco's. The *Saturday Evening Post* called it "paradise without a waiting list."

Its enlightened owners, the Murphy family, had phased out brutal clear-cutting after the development of the diesel-powered tractor in favor of selective logging practices that left forests more intact. They balanced mill output against the ability of their forests to regenerate trees, and preserved extensive stands of virgin redwoods, holding twenty thousand acres in trust until the state or a private conservation group could purchase them. In the 1940s, A. S. Murphy noted in his diary that his grandfather had stood in the pinewoods of Maine, and his father in the forests of Michigan and Wisconsin. "Those other forests are gone," he wrote. "These towering redwoods are the Murphys' last timber holdings and I feel a responsibility to use them wisely."

This attitude resulted in Pacific Lumber having the largest private inventory of virgin redwood on earth, making it an asset-rich takeover target criticized as "sleepy" for not maximizing its profit. In 1985 it was acquired by MAXXAM, a revealingly named company controlled by a Houston investor named Charles Hurwitz. Michael Milken financed the takeover with junk bonds, while minority shareholders, including the young Murphy heirs, charged the company was "sold down the river" by senior executives and board members seduced by MAXXAM's stock-option and retirement plans. Warren Murphy warned that Humboldt County had lost "something money can't buy...a quality of life and a commitment to maintaining our natural resources."

Who, knowing this history, could resist examining Scotia for signs of decay? At first I noticed only the hallmarks of any company town: the dun-colored junior-officer bungalows and whiff of fear in the too tidy front yards. No one in the Scotia museum, on the street, or in the Ben Franklin store soon to be consumed by...the earthquake would discuss MAXXAM, and I received the hard stares and head shaking once greeting Westerners trying to initiate conversations on the sidewalks of Moscow or Tirana. The WE SUPPORT TIMBER signs in windows all came from the same printer, like the slogans and photographs of Kim Il Sung in Prongyang. A poster in the coffee shop declaring REDWOOD SUMMER COST YOU THE TAXPAYERS $252,000—$100,000 JUST FOR HAIRCUTS! referred to the expenses of a lawsuit brought against the county sheriff for shaving the heads of environmental protestors.

DANA GIOIA

PLANTING A SEQUOIA

◆————————————————————————◆

*Like "Becoming a Redwood" (page 3), "Planting a Sequoia"
is from Gioia's* The Gods of Winter.

◆————————————————————————◆

All afternoon my brothers and I have worked in the orchard,
Digging this hole, laying you into it, carefully packing the soil.
Rain blackened the horizon, but cold winds kept it over the
    Pacific,
And the sky above us stayed the dull gray
Of an old year coming to an end.

In Sicily a father plants a tree to celebrate his first son's birth—
An olive or a fig tree—a sign that the earth has one more life to
    bear.
I would have done the same, proudly laying new stock into my
    father's orchard,
A green sapling rising among the twisted apple boughs,
A promise of new fruit in other autumns.

But today we kneel in the cold planting you, our native giant,
Defying the practical custom of our fathers,
Wrapping in your roots a lock of hair, a piece of an infant's birth
    cord,

All that remains above earth of a first-born son,
A few stray atoms brought back to the elements.

We will give you what we can—our labor and our soil,
Water drawn from the earth when the skies fail,
Nights scented with the ocean fog, days softened by the circuit of
    bees.
We plant you in the corner of the grove, bathed in western light,
A slender shoot against the sunset.

And when our family is no more, all of his unborn brothers dead,
Every niece and nephew scattered, the house torn down,
His mother's beauty ashes in the air,
I want you to stand among strangers, all young and ephemeral to
    you,
Silently keeping the secret of your birth.

JOAN DUNNING

from FROM THE
REDWOOD FOREST

From the Redwood Forest combines detailed natural history (as in the selection on page 271) with eloquent personal observations and, as demonstrated here, a journalistic approach that does not balk at the complex.

Let me pause for a moment and recount some of the events surrounding the illegal logging of the ancient redwood–Douglas fir grove of Owl Creek, second largest grove in the Headwaters complex, and the court cases that resulted. The recent history of Owl Creek Grove is a good example of the forces at play, with only subtle variations, since MAXXAM took over Pacific Lumber in 1985.

Newcomers on the scene of forest politics often feel the way I did once when I attended a "steering committee" meeting of my children's elementary school. I left in despair after half an hour of what sounded like "The NYB depends on the HRF and the FSH can only be decided on the basis of the LQX." To save you from leafing around, as if you were trying to keep track of the characters in a rather sterile Russian novel, let me explain that a THP is a timber harvest plan; CDF is the California Department of Forestry, which is controlled by the California Board of Forestry, which is composed of twelve years' worth of Republican governors' appointees, the majority of whom are sympathetic to the timber industry; and PL is Pacific Lumber, a name which, in this part of the world, is used interchangeably with the name MAXXAM and generally considered to be synonymous, however cruel this may be in light of history. DFG is the California Department of Fish and Game, the state agency charged with looking out for the well-being of California's wild animals, specifically through the enforcement of the state Endangered Species Act. The U.S. Fish and Wildlife Service has a similar function, for animals listed as threatened or endangered nationwide. EPIC is the Environmental Protection Information Center, a citizen organization based sixty miles south of where I live, in the little town of Garberville, California. For twenty years the members of EPIC have used litigation to diligently protect fragments of the last ancient forests that remain on our continent.

On April 11, 1990, Pacific Lumber filed a Timber Harvest Plan to log 237 acres at the heart of Owl Creek Grove. Filing a THP is standard procedure prior to any logging operation. In the old days, THPs used to be only a couple of pages long, and they were virtually assured of automatic approval. In essence they simply said, "Here's what we're going to cut next," to which CDF would respond, in essence, "Why not?"

At the time of filing of the Owl Creek THP however, the marbled murrelet was just being considered as a "candidate" for protection as a rare, threatened, or endangered species on both a state and a federal level, and as a result, CDF denied Pacific Lumber's THP because PL had not provided adequate information on the marbled murrelet's status in the grove. PL, unaccustomed to being asked for details about the land it intended to log, simply refused to conduct any surveys.

On March 12, 1992, the marbled murrelet was officially listed as a California Endangered Species.

On March 13, the California Board of Forestry overruled CDF's denial of the Owl Creek THP and approved the plan due in large part to Pacific Lumber Company's lobbying of the board.

At this point, EPIC and the Sierra Club sued the Board of Forestry (EPIC *and Sierra Club* v. *Board of Forestry),* alleging that the THP would violate the California Endangered Species Act. They succeeded in convincing a Humboldt County judge to require the Board of Forestry to reconsider its approval of the plan. On March 16, the board again approved the plan, but this time on the condition that PL perform the requested marbled murrelet population surveys and "share" the results with the California Department of Fish and Game.

By June, sticking to the "letter" of the Board of Forestry's requirements, PL completed a hasty marbled murrelet survey. Company executives put the results in an envelope and mailed it. Before the letter actually reached its destination, however, Pacific Lumber commenced a surprise, all-out massacre of the grove. Unlike the usual procedure for logging virgin forest, Pacific Lumber scattered numerous timber fallers throughout the THP area with instructions to drop as many trees as possible. This massacre not only occurred on Sunday, a customary "day of rest" for PL, but on Father's Day.

After three days of illegal logging, which netted the company $1 million in ancient giants, PL was finally stopped by agency intervention. Heated discussions continued all summer and were finally suspended for the Thanksgiving holiday, just after the marbled murrelet had been officially listed as "threatened" on the federal level. On that Wednesday, just before the employees of the U.S. Fish and Wildlife Service and the California Department of Fish and Game went home to relax with their families, their agencies reemphasized that Pacific Lumber *was not to construe that during the discussions they had in any way been granted permission to harvest.*

Pacific Lumber chose not to heed the agencies' warning, however, and over the holiday, in spite of the Endangered Species Act's clear prohibition against injuring or killing listed species, they sent their loggers out to begin a second assault on Owl Creek Grove.

Chuck Powell, the man who took me with his son to see torrent salamanders, spent a few hours the day after Thanksgiving showing a visiting photographer the devastation left by the Father's Day cutting of Owl Creek Grove. They drove out the next ridge to the south of Owl Creek in Chuck's pickup and stopped, expecting to hear silence or perhaps the distant sound of Yager Creek from the valley below. Chuck couldn't believe his ears. He heard the sound of chain saws coming from the direction of the grove. PL was at it again! In just a half hour's time, he heard eight old-growth trees fall. He also noticed that, strangely, he did not hear the normal concurrent sound of bulldozers, and suspected numbly that the ancient trees were simply being dropped as rapidly as possible to fragment the grove so that murrelet occupation would be less likely in the future. Chuck and the photographer raced back to telephones to alert government officials and the public that a second massacre was under way.

EPIC's lawyer, Mark Harris, leapt into action, phoning the U.S. Department of Fish and Wildlife, CDF, DFG, and finally even the FBI to inform them of the illegal logging. To give you an idea of the government "apathy" that conveniently gives the timber industry a loose rein, Mark was greeted with a variety of responses, from "That's impossible. It simply isn't happening" to "Is this *really* such a big deal, Mark? It's only some trees, and what about jobs?" Even local judges would not take the suit against PL, so it was moved out of the area to the state Court of Appeals in Sacramento. EPIC finally obtained an emergency stay, and the logging was stopped after days of illegal cutting. Though EPIC sought to prevent PL from actually removing any downed trees, stating that such action would result in even more disturbance to the grove, Pacific Lumber claimed that the trees would rot. Though it takes centuries for a redwood to decay, Pacific Lumber was allowed to drag another million dollars' worth of lumber out of the forest. This is but one of countless instances of EPIC and other environmental organizations functioning, at private expense, in place of our government agencies, whose efforts have been sabotaged due to corporate influence.

EPIC at that point decided to file a lawsuit. The suit bore the no-nonsense name of *Marbled Murrelet and* EPIC v. *Pacific Lumber.* Just the name touches me. I think of the marbled murrelets that I have seen bobbing on the ocean, or those that I have watched speeding inland through the fog to a nest tree. I laugh inside to think of a marbled murrelet bringing a lawsuit. And I grow silent with joy because it won.

Mark Harris, at the time, was a fledgling environmental lawyer who launched himself into the case with the resolve of a marbled murrelet chick jumping from its home redwood into thin air. For political reasons, state and federal wildlife officials continued to refrain from taking legal action. Only EPIC, operating on a shoestring budget, stood up for the law of the land. The fact is, the Endangered Species Act clearly states that it is illegal to "take" an endangered species. EPIC contended that eliminating crucial breeding habitat, namely cutting down the very trees to which the birds return each spring to nest, constitutes a "take." In hindsight, now that EPIC has been victorious, this sounds ridiculously obvious, but at the time, prosecuting the case was beyond an act of faith. It simply had to be done.

Mark, a thirty-three-year-old surfer/attorney just three years into law practice, found himself pitted against one of California's oldest and most prestigious law firms, Pillsbury, Madison & Sutro, backed up by Ukiah's Rawles, Hinkle, Carter, Behnke & Oglesby, and led by Pillsbury partner Alston Kemp, Jr. Mark found himself sleeping nights on the floor of his office, sustained by EPIC staff who brought him food, did his laundry, and helped him process the massive amounts of paperwork being dumped on him by the opposition.

Meanwhile, in Colorado, attorney Macon Cowles, reading about Charles Hurwitz in his morning newspaper, turned to his wife, Regina, and said, "I'm going to sue this son of a bitch."

Cowles had just won a $24 million verdict on an environmental case in Colorado for which he had mortgaged his own house in order to prosecute. He was yet to learn that his role as one of the lead counsel on the *Exxon Valdez* case would help win a $1 billion settlement to clean up environmental damage in Prince William Sound, Alaska. Cowles got in touch with Mark and said that he wanted to see Owl Creek Grove before he agreed to sign on.

So Cowles came west to meet this young man and fly over Owl Creek Grove. From the air, the grove was an isolated fragment of luxurious forest surrounded by barren, clear-cut slopes and occasional areas of sparse second-growth trees. Cowles was instantly convinced. Before the case was over, he would spend more than $200,000 of his own money in this new gamble on the strength of our legal system. Visiting Philadelphia federal judge Louis C. Bechtle was not to let Cowles, Harris, the American people, and the marbled murrelet down. In fact, Cowles obtained a stuffed murrelet from DFG, which watched the proceedings in the San Francisco courtroom each day through its beady glass eyes and, conversely, was in plain view of the judge as the plaintiff in the case.

The Endangered Species Act is a line drawn in the sand. It is a statement of self-limitation. It is a tool, like a smoke alarm, set to warn us to ask, "Is there enough of an ecosystem left for *us?*" It is not something to dismantle, just as we do not dismantle our own smoke alarms, but something to heed.

As out-of-town attorneys and their assistants met fearful survey biologists in out-of-the-way cafes and hammered PL for its records, they began to get a sense of the repression and distortion that have become the norm in Humboldt County. An unflattering picture of PL began to emerge. They discovered that Pacific Lumber had concealed *seventy detections of murrelet presence* in Owl Creek. Judge Bechtle labeled PL's $2 million murrelet and spotted owl surveys as "highly suspect." Despite another $1 million that PL spent on legal defense, Bechtle commented that "EPIC has served the public interest by assisting the interpretation and implementation of the Endangered Species Act."

Judge Bechtle wrote in his final decision that "EPIC has proven, by a preponderance of the evidence, that marbled murrelets are nesting in THP-237....Moreover, Pacific Lumber's...marbled murrelet surveys were either designed to fail to detect murrelets, or they were administered with indifference." Judge Bechtle concluded that "a permanent injunction prohibiting Pacific Lumber's implementation of THP-237 is warranted."

The Owl Creek decision made history because it established the precedent that killing the *habitat* of an endangered species constitutes a "take" of the species itself and is therefore illegal. It was also the first time that the Endangered Species Act had been enforced *on private land.*

Pacific Lumber appealed this decision and the case went to the United States Supreme Court, where it was upheld in the spring of 1997.

Lest you have any doubts about PL's feelings about the little glass-eyed plaintiff in this case, in his decision Judge Bechtle observed, "At the end of the 1992 survey season [September], Pacific Lumber's Resource Manager, Thomas Herman, hosted a party at his home for Pacific Lumber's forestry staff, which included the company's marbled murrelet surveyors....At the party, there was a target of a marbled murrelet on a dartboard, at which the attendees were throwing darts."

JANE HIRSHFIELD

TREE

Jane Hirshfield (b. 1953), a longtime student of Zen Buddhism with a lifelong commitment to writing, was born in New York and now lives in Marin County. She is the author of five collections of poetry, including the recent Given Sugar, Given Salt, *as well as a book of essays on poetry,* Nine Gates. *She has also edited and co-translated two poetry anthologies,* The Ink Dark Moon *and* Women in Praise of the Sacred.

It is foolish
to let a young redwood
grow next to a house.

Even in this
one lifetime,
you will have to choose.

That great calm being,
this clutter of soup pots and books—

Already the first branch-tips brush at the window.
Softly, calmly, immensity taps at your life.

from THE LEGACY OF LUNA

Writer, poet, and activist Julia Butterfly Hill (b. 1974) climbed Luna, a thousand-year-old coast redwood, on December 10, 1997, and refused to come down. She was determined, as are the many other activists around the state who engage in similar acts of civil disobedience, to save the tree. By the time she came down more than two years later, having come to an agreement with MAXXAM that would save Luna, she had become an international symbol of determination and hope.

Tree-sitting is a last resort. When you see someone in a tree trying to protect it, you know that every level of our society has failed. The consumers have failed, the companies have failed, and the government has failed. Friends of the forests have gone to the courts, activists have tried to make consumers aware, but with no results. Corporations have neglected their responsibility as landowners, while the government has refused to enforce its laws. Everything has failed, so people go into the trees.

"I have no other way to stop what's happening" is basically what a tree-sitter is saying. "I have no other way to make people aware of what's at stake. I've followed the rules, but everything I've been told to do is failing. So it's my responsibility to give this one last shot, to put my body where my beliefs are."

◇————————◇

The moment the storm hit, I couldn't have climbed down if I had wanted to. To climb you have to be able to move, and my hands were frozen. Massive amounts of rain, sleet, and hail mixed together, and the winds blew so hard I might have been ripped off a branch.

The storm was every bit as strong as they said it would be. Actually, up here, it was even stronger. When a gust would come through, it would flip the platform up into the air, bucking me all over the place.

"Boy! Whoaaah! Ooh! Whoa!"

The gust rolled me all the way up to the hammock. Only the rope that cuts an angle underneath it prevented me from slipping through the gap in the platform.

"I'm really ready for this storm to chill out. I'm duly impressed," I decided. "I've bowed and cowered once again before the great almighty gods of wind and rain and storm. I've paid my respects—and my dues—and I'd appreciate it if they got the heck out of here."

My thoughts seemed to anger the storm spirits.

"Whoa! Whoa!" I cried, as the raging wind flung my platform, straining the ropes that attached it.

"This is getting really intense! Oh, my God! Oh, my God! Okay, never mind, I take it back. Whoaaah!"

The biggest gust threw me close to three feet. I grabbed onto the branch of Luna that comes through the middle of the platform, and I prayed.

"I want to be strong for you, Luna. I want to be strong for the forest. I don't want to die, because I want to help make a difference.

I want to be strong for the movement, but I can't even be strong for myself."

It seemed like it took all my will to stay alive. I was trying to hold onto life so hard that my teeth were clenched, my jaws were clenched, my muscles were clenched, my fists were clenched, everything in my body was clenched completely and totally tight.

I knew I was going to die.

The wind howled. It sounded like wild banshees, *rrahhh*, while the tarps added to the crazy cacophony of noise, *flap, flap, flap, bap, bap, flap, bap!* Had I remained tensed for the sixteen hours that the storm raged, I would have snapped. Instead, I grabbed onto Luna, hugging the branch that comes up through the platform, and prayed to her.

"I don't know what's happening here. I don't want to go down, because I made a pact with you. But I can't be strong now. I'm frightened out of my mind, Luna, I'm losing it. I'm going crazy!"

Maybe I was, maybe I wasn't, but in that moment I heard the voice of Luna speak to me.

"Julia, think of the trees in the storm."

And as I started to picture the trees in the storm, the answer began to dawn on me.

"The trees in the storm don't try to stand up straight and tall and erect. They allow themselves to bend and be blown with the wind. They understand the power of letting go," continued the voice. "Those trees and those branches that try too hard to stand up strong and straight are the ones that break. Now is not the time for you to be strong, Julia, or you, too, will break. Learn the power of the trees. Let it flow. Let it go. That is the way you are going to make it through this storm. And that is the way to make it through the storms of life."

I suddenly understood. So as I was getting chunked all over by the wind, tossed left and right, I just let it go. I let my muscles go. I let my jaw unlock. I let the wind blow and the craziness flow. I bent and flailed with it, just like the trees, which flail in the wind. I howled. I laughed. I whooped and cried and screamed and raged. I hollered and I jibbered and I jabbered. Whatever came through me, I just let it go.

"When my time comes, I'm going to die grinning," I yelled.

Everything around me was being ripped apart. My sanity felt like it was slipping through my fingers like a runaway rope. And I gave in.

"Fine. Take it. Take my life. Take my sanity. Take it all."

Once the storm ended, I realized that by letting go of all attachments, including my attachment to self, people no longer had any power over me. They could take my life if they felt the need, but I was no longer going to live my life out of fear, the way too many people do, jolted by our disconnected society. I was going to live my life guided from the higher source, the Creation source.

I couldn't have realized any of this without having been broken emotionally and spiritually and mentally and physically. I had to be pummeled by humankind. I had to be pummeled by Mother Nature. I had to be broken until I saw no hope, until I went crazy, until I finally let go. Only then could I be rebuilt; only then could I be filled back up with who I am meant to be. Only then could I become my higher self.

That's the message of the butterfly. I had come through darkness and storms and had been transformed. I was living proof of the power of metamorphosis.

JERRY MARTIEN

AT THE FOOT OF
THE MOUNTAIN

Jerry Martien (b. 1939), a carpenter in Arcata who also teaches English at Humboldt State University, has published several books of poetry including the recent (1999) Pieces in Place, *as well as* Shell Game, *a study of beads and money in North America.*

Only there—where the water
comes down against rock—
knees of rock, shinbone rock, squat
on heels, rock

set across the creek from my tent
where the water comes down
against this first steep coastal rising
only there—

where water last speaks to rock
the forest

against that rock
water
taking every sound to its numberless song

chain saw rising, whining out of a cut, falling
thump of a log, limbed & bucked & loaded
and where it spills over rocks as if another
truck pulling back up the ridge, empty

only there—
there was no hearing it
only water and the rock where it turns

the water singing
the forest cut down

and there only rock to hear it fall.

Upper Jacoby Creek

PERMISSIONS

Leydet, François, from *The Last Redwoods: Photographs and Story of a Vanishing Resource* by Philip Hyde and François Leydet. San Francisco: Sierra Club, 1969.

Lind, Anna, from "Women in Early Logging Camps" (*Journal of Forest History*, vol. 19, no. 3, July 1975).

London, Jack, from *The Valley of the Moon* (New York: Macmillan, 1913).

Markham, Edward, "A Mendocino Memory." In *Lincoln & Other Poems* (Garden City, N.Y.: Doubleday, Page & Co., 1917).

Martien, Jerry, "At the Foot of the Mountain." From *Pieces in Place* (Nobleboro, Maine: Blackberry Books, 1999). Printed by permission of the author.

Maupin, Armistead, from *Significant Others*. Copyright ©1987 by Armistead Maupin. Reprinted by permission of HarperCollins Publishers, Inc.

Milosz, Czeslaw. Excerpts from *Visions from San Francisco Bay* by Czeslaw Milosz, translated by Richard Lourie. English translation copyright ©1975, 1982 by Farrar, Straus and Giroux, Inc. Reprinted by permission of Farrar, Straus and Giroux, LLC.

Muir, John, from "Hunting the Big Redwoods," *Atlantic Monthly* v. 88 (Sept. 1901), reprinted in *Our National Parks* (Madison: University of Wisconsin Press, 1981).

Muir, John, in *The Life and Letters of John Muir* by William Frederic Badè (Boston & New York: Houghton Mifflin Co., 1923).

Muir, John, from "Save the Redwoods," *Sierra Club Bulletin*, vol. xi, no. 1, 1920.

Muir, John, from *The Yosemite* (New York: The Century Co., 1912).

Patterson, Vernon, from *Wise as a Goose* (Los Angeles: Lymanhouse, 1939).

Peixotto, Ernest, from *Romantic California* (New York: Charles Scribner's Sons, 1910).

Snyder, Gary, "The Circumambulation of Mt. Tamalpais." From *Mountains and Rivers Without End* by Gary Snyder. Copyright © 1996 by Gary Snyder. Reprinted by permission of Counterpoint Press, a member of Perseus Books, LLC.

Sterling, George, "Beneath the Redwoods." From *House of Orchids and Other Poems* (San Francisco: A. M. Robertson, 1911).

Stevenson, Robert Louis, from *The Silverado Squatters* (London: Chatto & Windus, 1883).

Taylor, Bayard, from *At Home and Abroad* (New York: G. P. Putnam's Sons, 1880, v. 2).

PERMISSIONS

Taylor, William, from *California Life Illustrated* (New York: Carlton & Porter, published for the author, 1858).

Thompson, Lucy, from *To the American Indian,* 1916 (reprint, with foreword by Peter E. Palmquist, introduction by Julian Lang, Berkeley: Heyday Books, 1991).

Van der Veer, Judy, from *November Grass,* 1940 (reprint, with foreword by Ursula K. Le Guin, Berkeley: Heyday Books, 2001).

Warburton, Austen, from *Indian Lore of the North California Coast* (with Joseph F. Endert; Santa Clara, Calif.: Pacific Pueblo Press, 1969). Reprinted by permission of the Estate of Austen D. Warburton.

Welch, Lew, "Redwood Haiku." Reprinted from *Ring of Bone* ©1979 by permission of Grey Fox Press.

Whitman, Walt, "Song of the Redwood-Tree," first published in *Harper's Magazine,* Feb. 1874, then in Two Rivulets (Camden, NJ: author's edition, 1876).

Wolfe, Tom. Excerpts from *The Electric Kool-Aid Acid Test* by Tom Wolfe. Copyright © 1968, renewed © 1996 by Tom Wolfe. Reprinted by permission of Farrar, Straus and Giroux, LLC.

Wood, L. K., from "Discovery of Humboldt Bay," in *Lure of Humboldt Bay Region: Early Discoveries, Explorations and Foundations Establishing the Bay Region,* Chad L. Hoopes editor (Dubuque: Kendall/Hunt Publishing Co., 1971.)